CRACKED IT!

George Reynolds

CRACKED IT!

THE AMAZING TRUE STORY OF A SAFE-BLOWER AND BARE-KNUCKLE FIGHTER WHO BECAME A MULTI-MILLIONAIRE SOCCER BOSS

JOHN BLAKE

Published by John Blake Publishing Ltd,
3, Bramber Court, 2 Bramber Road,
London W14 9PB, England

First published in hardback in 2003

ISBN 1 904034 69 1

British Library Cataloguing-in-Publication Data:

A catalogue record for this book is available from the British Library.

Design by ENVY

Printed in Great Britain by CPD (Wales)

3 5 7 9 10 8 6 4 2

Papers used by John Blake Publishing are natural, recyclable products made from
wood grown in sustainable forests. The manufacturing processes conform to the
environmental regulations of the country of origin.

Picture reproduced by kind permission of George Reynolds, Patrick Lavelle
and the *Sunderland Echo*.

Every attempt has been made to contact the relevant copyright-holders, but some
were unobtainable. We would be grateful if the appropriate people could contact us.

For the Besford Boys,
my wife Susan, my family and the
people of Sunderland.

Contents

Acknowledgements

Special thanks go to my biographer, Patrick Lavelle, and to my wife, Susan, for help with research.

Thanks are also due to Ian Robinson, Dave Powles, Richie Tennick, Stevie Molloy, Stuart Johnston, Ronnie Heslop, Davey Hall, Luke Raine, Kenny Mason, Davey Hopper, Joe Mather, Jimmy Conley, Geordie Lavelle, Danny Lavelle, Dempsey Green, Jimmy McEvoy, Mike Knighton, Paul Hamer, Nigel Overton, Nick Malenko, Royston Blythe and the many friends and characters in Sunderland who helped shape my life.

Preface

I have always been fascinated by the way events in our lives sculpt what we are; the way adversity or trauma can bring out facets of the character that might otherwise have lain dormant. Almost everyone who achieves greatness from humble beginnings has the kind of drive that the majority can't comprehend, and behind that driving ambition there is always a trigger.

My husband, George Reynolds, like many others, spent his boyhood during World War II in abject poverty and was sent to an institution at the age of eight. It was the events of his boyhood – in particular the events at the institution – that shaped his wonderful personality. He had the gift of being able to escape into his own fertile imagination and developed an outstanding talent as a natural storyteller. George, who has a hilarious outlook on life, can stand up and act out a story that has his audience mesmerised.

From an early age, having been branded illiterate, backward and mentally deficient, and having suffered appalling cruelty at the hands of his teachers, he had to learn how to fight. He fought his way out of poverty and fought his way into business, amassing a fortune of more than £120 million. His is a story of a man that overcame overwhelming odds to achieve success. It is a story that, I hope, can inspire others.

Susan Reynolds,
Spring 2003

CHAPTER 1

A Flying Visit

The grand, ancient, building imposed itself on the surrounding countryside, demanding to be seen. From a half mile up, it still looked austere, like some kind of institution. It gave the impression that it was the home of a fellow multimillionaire with a penchant for elegant architecture and a liking of vast, open, spaces. Even from this far up in the sky, looking down, there was still something very religious about the tenth-century building, something regimentalised, ghostly, monastic.

'Would you like to go down now, George?' Eric, the pilot, asked as my eight-seater Augusta 109 helicopter hovered, its blades cutting the air like a giant humming bird.

'Can we circle a while?' I asked. 'I just want to take the scene in. There's an awful lot of memories down there.'

The helicopter dipped and swung right and, as I looked out of the tinted window, the farms and orchards where, as a boy, I would chase rabbits and steal apples came into view.

'Have you heard that old saying?' I asked, as my personal assistant of many years, Ian Robinson, poured himself a drink from the mini bar.

'What saying was that, then, George?' he asked.

'They used to say, "Give me a boy until he is seven, and I'll show you the man."'

'But weren't you sent here at eight?' Ian asked.

'Yes, but it's the same principle,' I said.

The helicopter slowly circled and not too far distant I could see the Malvern Hills, below us Tiddesley Wood and, just south of that, the quaint market town of Pershore, where myself and hundreds of other boys would march in strict formation for our monthly treat: a visit to the picture house, The Plaza, in the High Street. Then Pershore was no bigger than a village, its streets lined with posh houses the likes of which I had never seen before. Some had three storeys with Georgian façades and Corinthian columns, others had Tudor frontages in stark black and white.

It all looked so different now. Many new homes, bungalows and two-storey houses, some within two or three acres, were dotted around the countryside; they must have sprung up during the 1960s as stressed executives in nearby Worcester and not-so-far-away Birmingham moved out of surburbia to their dream home, away from the hassle of city life.

'We've got to get back to Darlington by this afternoon,' said Ian. 'We can't have the official opening of the new stadium without you there to open it.'

'Don't worry, we'll make it back in good time,' I said. 'I've waited 66 years for this day to come, and I want to pack in everything I dreamed of doing. That includes spending some time here.'

The helicopter dipped left and I noticed the outline of a small wall on the perimeter of the site.

'There's the punishment wall, Ian,' I said, surprised that the 3-foot-high wall with an 8-inch, slightly pointed top had survived for almost 50 years.

Ian moved towards the window and looked.

'That's what you were ordered to stand on?' he asked.

'Sometimes for up to eight hours,' I said. 'You had to put your hands on your head and just stand there, staring into space. The pain in your calves was unbelievable.'

The helicopter hovered above the site, not moving forward and not moving back, as we surveyed the scene.

We'd left the site of the new £25 million stadium in Darlington, County Durham, at about 9.30am, and, after getting clearance from the air traffic controllers at Teesside Airport, near Middlesbrough, we'd made it to Worcestershire in less than an hour.

The helicopter had cost me £2 million, but the ease with which you could get from A to B quickly, with no hassle, made it worth every penny. The interior was plush: I've always been a bit of a perfectionist when it comes to the finishing touches. The eight seats were fitted out in leather, there was a deep, blue carpet, and the bar was always well stocked. I liked travelling by helicopter – I've always been a poor driver – but it was more for the convenience than the kudos of owning one.

'Would you like to go down now, George?' the pilot asked again, as I looked out of the window at the big Grade II listed building set within its 35 acres.

'Yes, let's go down, Eric,' I said. 'But we'll have to land in the field to the right of the site. There's someone there waiting for us.'

Slowly, and carefully, the chopper descended and landed on a field, creating a type of corn circle so perfectly formed the local paper might soon be printing a story that aliens had landed. I waited for the blades to stop turning before I climbed out of the 'copter. I was always fearful that if I alighted too quickly, the blades could do some damage.

The people we had arranged the visit with walked quickly towards the helicopter and when I stepped on the ground I was greeted by beaming smiles and strong and purposeful handshakes.

'Great to meet you, George,' said the man who Ian had spoken to on the telephone to arrange the trip. 'I've heard, and read, so much about you.'

After appearing on television more than 100 times, I was not surprised the man had heard of me. We walked towards the big house and the ghosts of my past came back to re-enlighten me. I looked to one corner of the site, where an army-style windowless but shuttered billet had once stood, but stood no more. And it reminded me of the worst winter Britain had ever seen, that of 1947, when the snow was so deep and the ice was so thick people died and children ran around with socks on their hands, because their parents couldn't afford woollen mittens.

And it reminded me of Jimmy Conley, breaking the ice with his bare hands in the deep trough filled with freezing water to get a wash; and of Joe Mather, on pissy-bed duty, who would be awoken at 3am to get the bed-wetters to the loo, but would be met by a wall of steam, and realise he was too late.

Our touring host led us up to the old masters' room, or the duty room, as it was known, and in a corner I could see the old vaulting horse – after almost 50 years a little the worse for wear, but still there nonetheless. And it reminded me of my old mate Davey Hopper, who, like many others, was slung over it, bare-arsed, and beaten with a type of cat-o'-nine-tails that left such deep welts in the buttocks he was probably scarred for life.

The wooden-handled leather strap would be dropped into a bucket and hiss when it touched the water, and the blood from a boy's bare backside would stain the water crimson-red.

Many, many boys were beaten mercilessly by Sisters or masters with sadistic streaks: Geordie Lavelle, Davey Hopper, Joe Mather, Jimmy Conley, Stevie Lavelle, Jimmy McEvoy, Dempsey Green – before us – and many others before, during, and after. This was a school for the bad lads: the boys considered too disruptive for mainstream schooling and out of parental control.

The ancient building, now converted into luxury apartments, was virtually deserted, apart from a few members of staff. Despite the modern conversion, there was still a familiar smell in the air: a mixture of food being cooked and floors being polished.

'This will be a great investment,' our host said, as we walked along one of the main corridors. 'These apartments have been designed by the best in the business and we're only an hour's drive from London.'

The man was obviously aware of my wealth, thus the invitation to a tour around my old approved school, but in truth I wasn't interested in buying an apartment, even though I could afford to buy several, in cash. The grounds were extensive, with several outbuildings and a main quadrangle inside the main block where myself and hundreds of other boys would be forced to stand to attention, our hobnailed boots highly polished, as one of the senior masters carried out an inspection.

Our host led us to the gardening area, behind a ten-foot-high serpentine wall that used to be covered in shards of broken glass to keep the boys in. I could see the row of five old pigsties: one had been home to Sylvia, a pig adopted by myself and a few other lads and saved from the slaughterhouse by us on many occasions.

Next to the sties we boys would have to boil up the swill and feed it to the pigs. We thought it was the norm to work eight hours a day; we thought it was the norm to polish floors, to demolish buildings and rebuild, to grow our own food, to cook our own food, to make our own beds, to clean our own dormitories, to be shepherded around like common criminals, unworthy of trust, unworthy of affection. We thought it was the norm to be beaten so badly we couldn't sit down properly for weeks.

We were all miles from home – some, hundreds of miles – in a place that was so different from what we were used to, and so isolated from other buildings, we might as well have been in a different country. The boys could be beaten without fear. Who would hear their screams as the leather strap came down on bare flesh? Who would hear their whimpering at night, as tears stained pillows, as pain shot through bodies? And who, in this oh-so-remote location, would hear them calling out for their mothers, after nightmares made them sit bolt upright in bed?

We continued our tour, and came upon the punishment wall.

'How long do you think you could stand on that wall, Ian?' I asked.

'I don't know,' he said. 'Maybe an hour or two.'

'Jump up and we'll find out,' I said.

Ian hopped on to the wall and stood straight, placing his hands on his head, while our host took me to have a look at the great house from the entrance. An impressive sight it was, too.

'Can I get down now, George?' shouted Ian.

'You've only been up there ten bloody minutes,' I shouted across the courtyard.

'I know,' said Ian, 'but my legs are bloody killing me.'

We walked back into the old house and our host led us along a narrow passageway, the entrance to which was a thick, wooden door, which looked virtually inpregnable. He turned a large key, slowly opened the heavy door, put his hand to the right and flicked a switch. The room was illuminated by a naked light bulb.

'This is the vault,' said the man, 'and here you'll find the records of all the boys who ever stayed here, including yourself, George.'

On the dusty wooden shelves stood box after box of old brown paper files, all in alphabetical order. There were literally thousands of them: all covered in dust and cobwebs and some of the paper, fragile with age, would crumble if touched.

'All these files are going off to Birmingham to the Archdiocesan archives,' our host said. 'They may be shredded.'

'That's not right,' I said. 'There's the history of thousands of boys spread across England in these boxes. Have they not got the right for others to know about what happened to them here?'

'That's not up to me,' the man said. 'The order has come down from above for them to go to Birmingham, and that's what will happen.'

As I picked up a file, the man gave me a knowing glance.

'I'm just off to make myself a nice cup of tea,' he said, 'would you both like one?'

'Not for us,' said Ian, 'but we'll join you shortly.'

The man walked out of the vault door, leaving it open, as Ian and I surveyed the mountain of paperwork lying on the shelves.

'Some of these lads will be dead now,' said Ian.

'Yes,' I said, 'but most will still be alive and in their sixties, even their seventies. I wonder what happened to them all?'

As we flicked our way through some of the records, I picked one from the shelves.

'John Thomas Straffen, born 1930, a pupil here from the age of ten,' I said.

'Who was he?' asked Ian.

'He grew up to be a child killer and he's now Britain's longest-serving prisoner. He murdered two girls in 1951, not so long after he had been in here. He was sent to Broadmoor, sentenced to death, but then reprieved. He escaped in 1952 and was convicted of killing another little lass. He's been in jail now for about 45 years, but protests his innocence.'

'Bloody hell,' said Ian. 'Was he in here when you were here?'

'Yes,' I said, 'but I can't say I remember him. Six years older than me. He was known as the Babes in the Woods killer.'

I flicked through more files, some more under S, R, Q, then O.

'Oh look what's here,' I said. 'William Orange. He was from Alnwick in Northumberland and was a great pal of mine. Really intelligent he was. His mother and father were professional people and William was educated at a private school. He always use to say to me, "It's not right what they're doing here, it's not right."'

'What happened to him, then?' Ian asked.

'I don't know, but I'd love to see him again. Oh, bloody hell,' I said, as I landed on another file. 'La Planche. Strange lad him, with a strange name. He used to eat live worms. And he could fight for fun. All he wanted to do every day was have a scrap with someone.'

I flicked my fingers across the tops of the files again, landing on Forbes, Bernard. Young Bernard was a half-caste and such a talented singer and dancer that I remembered him years later when watching Sammy Davies Junior on the television.

Time was getting on, so I rifled back to R, and pulled out my own file: Reynolds, George.

The file recorded my progress, or lack of it, through the school, charting that progress in what appeared to be fairly complicated and comprehensive charts.

'"Backward and mentally deficient." That's what it says here,' I said.

Ian looked shocked. 'Didn't they know you were dyslexic?' he asked.

'Never known of in those days,' I said. 'If you couldn't read and write properly you were just considered thick, or "backward and mentally deficient", as they put it.'

I turned another page in my file, lifted the page up to my face, and blew off a thick layer of dust, which caused me to cough.

'Fucking hell, Ian, look at this!' I said. 'I knew it, I fucking knew it!'

'Knew what?' asked Ian.

'This place here, it wasn't a school at all, it was a child slave labour camp.'

I slowly read out a passage from one of the letters in my file. 'Name of pupil, George Reynolds. We hereby guarantee the above named child will be purchased from you for the sum of £100 and we will from that point be responsible for the treatment, maintenance and training of the above whilst a pupil.'

'Who's it addressed to?' Ian asked.

'The Director of Education in Sunderland.'

'So you were purchased from the local education authority, just like that, the school gave them a hundred quid, and you were theirs to do with as they wished?'

'It's down here in black and white,' I said. 'If you tell people this they just stare at you in disbelief. They think you're a fantasist, or just a bloody liar.'

'Does it say anything else?' Ian asked.

'Just that they will be allowed to work the boy – that's me – for up to eight hours a day from the age of eight, and for 12 hours a day when he reaches the age of 12, with Saturday and Sunday set aside for education.'

'That's shocking, that,' Ian said. 'So, effectively, the school was allowed to buy boys from local authorities, and put them to work down here?'

'That's what they did. Unbelievable, isn't it?'

Our heads quickly turned to the vault door as we could hear the footsteps of our host rapidly approaching.

'Stuff them down your fucking trousers,' I said to Ian, handing him a bunch of papers from my file. Quickly I stuffed a bundle into the belt of my own trousers and placed my jacket strategically over to hide the documents.

'Well, George,' said our host. 'Have you seen everything you need to see?'

'Yes, I have, it's all fascinating stuff. But we've really got to make our way back now, a lot of business to sort out back up North.'

'Fine,' said our host. 'We'll see you out.'

Ian and I walked behind our host, out of the main school building, to the field where the pilot was waiting to whisk us back to Darlington. The fact that we appeared to have gained 2 stone each in the couple of hours we had spent at the school did not seem to concern our host too much.

As we approached the helicopter, and we were just about to board, five lads, aged about 14 or 15, came hurtling over the fence towards us.

'Here, mister, are you the Prime Minister?' asked one.

'You've got one hell of a big chopper,' said another, a big smile beaming across his face.

'Give us a ride in your helicopter, mister,' pleaded a third boy.

'Just give us a minute, lads,' I said, as I turned to Ian, asking him to get into the helicopter to hide the files.

We both quickly jumped inside.

'This must have brought a lot of painful memories back for you, George,' Ian said.

'It has that,' I said. 'I now have proof that I was sold into slavery, beatings, hunger, misery and fear, then branded illiterate, mentally deficient and backward.'

As we secreted the files under the mini bar, Ian looked out of the window. 'Bloody hell,' he said, 'there's another 50 lads running this way.'

We got back out of the 'copter, and the boys were visibly shaking with excitement, their eyes full of wonderment and curiosity.

'Settle down, lads,' I said. 'Now, come on. Settle down.'

'Who are you, mister?' asked one.

'It's him who owns Manchester United,' said another.

'Is that your helicopter? Are you in the Air Force? Have you got millions of pounds? What are you doing here?' The questions were coming thick and fast.

'Come on, lads,' I said. 'Sit yourselves down, and I'll answer any question you like.' I turned to the pilot, and asked him to cut the engine.

As the blades on the helicopter slowed, then stopped, and the boys stopped chatting, I could see I had their undivided attention. I sat on the step of the helicopter entry door.

'Right lads, let's be quiet. If you've got a question, just throw your hand in the air.' Twenty hands went up and I pointed to one young lad, with bright red hair and freckles, aged about 14. He reminded me of myself.

'You,' I said. 'What would you like to know?'

'What are you?' the lad asked.

'What are you?' I asked.

'Me? I'm a Besford Boy,' said the lad.

'That's funny that,' I said, 'because I'm a Besford Boy, too.'

'Are you crap!' said another lad, aged about 15 or 16. 'How can you be flying about in a helicopter if you're a Besford Boy?'

'I've done it, and so can you,' I said.

'I don't believe you,' said the mouthy young teenager.

'Gather round, lads,' I said. 'I'm going to tell you all my story.'

The boys sat closer together in the field, as the sun shone down on us, and I stood over them, ready to embark on a journey that would span 66 years, taking me from abject poverty in the backs streets of Sunderland to having all the riches any man could ever desire.

'Are you sitting comfortably?' I asked.

'Yes,' said the lads.

'Right,' I said. 'Then I'll begin …'

CHAPTER 2

The Bombs

The Explosion rocked the building so hard, it seemed like the bomb had dropped only next door and my mother Doris and Grandma Tennick were so gripped with fear they clung to each other for comfort.

'Are we going to die next?' I asked as we all sat on the floor of the cellar of the Albion pub on the Barbary Coast in Sunderland.

'For God's sake!' said Grandma Tennick. 'Will that boy stop saying such things?'

'George,' said my mother. 'Go and get us both a double brandy. You'll be the death of us, you will.'

I climbed the few steps up to the wooden cellar hatch and knocked on it, handing the barman two empty glasses. He handed then back after a minute, and I took the drinks to my mam and gran, sitting there ashen-faced and, by this time, slightly tipsy.

'Now sit yourself down, George, until we get the all-clear, and stop frightening your Grandma Tennick,' said my mother.

It was only a few minutes before the next bomb dropped, and this one seemed closer still.

'My God!' exclaimed my mother. 'They're getting closer. George, get us another double brandy.' Off I trudged up the cellar steps. This went on all night.

The Albion pub wasn't far from our house in Cooper Street, Roker, Sunderland, where I lived with my mother, Doris, and father, Dan – who was a deep-sea fisherman – and my older sister, Cathy.

The nearest the bombs had fallen to us was in Francis Street, Roker, in March 1941, killing a number of people. The next month a German parachute bomb was dropped on the town's old Victoria Hall, the scene of Sunderland's worst peacetime tragedy in the 1880s, when more than 180 children were killed, rushing out of the building. The children were all crushed to death in the stampede.

The bomb that dropped on the Victoria Hall caused substantial damage to the nearby Winter Gardens, in Mowbray Park, which was a massive conservatory full of exotic plants. Sunderland's own Crystal Palace had to be demolished as a result.

Gas masks, which we all had to wear, had been stockpiled at the town's Monkwearmouth Hospital since 1938, and Anderson shelters had been erected on many of the newly built estates in the town. Sheltering in the cellar of the pub was a bit more interesting and, of course, my mother and gran had easy access to the brandy to settle their nerves.

The town was born on shipbuilding, and was once described as the greatest shipbuilding town in the world. The thirty-nine ship repair and shipbuilding yards that lined the banks of the River Wear during and after World War II were testimony to the town's shipbuilding prowess. Towering cranes dominated the skyline and the yards provided work for thousands.

The area around Roker, where I lived, and Monkwearmouth had always been known as the Barbary Coast. The working men worked hard and drank hard and the women worked harder still, many bringing up families with ten children or more. My boyhood pal Davey Hall came from a family of eleven.

My mother worked hard to provide for us, as my dad was away at sea a lot of the time, but, despite her best efforts, what with the rationing and all that, I was forever hungry. It was the kind of hunger that gave you pains in your belly; the kind of hunger that meant you either stole or starved. I stole from the local bread van, which toured the streets of Roker. The freshly baked warm bread was absolutely delicious.

'Is there anything to eat?' I asked, as we all huddled in the cold pub cellar, waiting for the next bomb to drop.

'Haven't you just had your tea?' said my mother. 'And don't you know there's a bloody war on.'

War or not, I was hungry. But I just sat there, crouched in the corner, listening to my mother and gran gossiping away about her in number 36 and him in number 22.

A couple of cousins were coming around our house for dinner that Sunday, and my mother had already warned me and my sister Cathy to be on our best behaviour. Our cousins, and my aunt and uncle, were a bit posh, lived in a nice house in Fulwell and he owned his own car. Our mother had told us that there was little food in the house and what she had she would have to cook for the guests. When we were asked if we wanted any Sunday dinner we had to say no, we weren't hungry. I wasn't looking forward to that.

My uncle, my mother's brother, John Tennick, or Jos as he was known, ran a general dealer's shop in Roker and later a fishing tackle shop. Jos was the biggest fan of Sunderland

AFC and his fishing tackle shop in Dundas Street, near the Roker Park football ground, sold everything from scarves and rosettes to football programmes. The windows were always festooned with red and white banners and memorabilia, and it all obscured the fishing tackle he sold inside. He also arranged the coaches to take fans to away matches and made the drinks and sandwiches they would eat on the journey. Red and white barmy, Uncle Jos was – a great character.

As we waited for the all-clear, Jos would be going around the local bomb shelters, dishing sweets out to the youngsters. It took their minds off what was happening, I suppose.

At the Albion pub, my mother and gran and I finally heard the all-clear siren and we emerged from the cellar into the bar, rubbing our eyes as we got accustomed to the light. My gran kind of stumbled up the wooden steps, giggling, probably relieved that they had escaped the latest round of bombing, but sniggering more because she and my mother were more than slightly inebriated.

'Look at the state you're in,' the barman said.

'Give me another brandy to calm my nerves,' said Grandma Tennick.

The pair of them staggered, rather than walked, home that night, with myself holding both their hands. My mother was telling Grandma Tennick about a parcel that had just arrived in the post for our posh next-door neighbour, all the way from Australia. It contained a tin of real coffee: a luxury in those days of rationing.

The next morning, Davey Hall, who lived in nearby Gosforth Street, called round for me, and we, in turn, called on our other mates, Jimmy Dodds, Dicky Maguire, Billy Freckleton, Tony Megeson, and others, to pop down to our gang hut, which was underneath the Bungalow Cafe on the seafront corner at Roker.

'Don't forget to get back in time for your dinner,' my mother shouted, as I headed out of the door.

'I'll be back in time, mam,' I said.

We headed for the beach. 'Do you reject Satan?' I asked Davey, as we walked along Cooper Street.

'I reject Satan!' said Davey. 'Do you reject Satan?'

'I reject Satan!' I said, at which we both burst out laughing.

Rejecting Satan had been drummed in to us from the day we started St Benet's Roman Catholic Infant and Junior School in Monkwearmouth. It was all part of the Catechism, and we would sit quietly during assembly prayers while Sister Mary Claire or one of the other nuns recited the Catechism questions, to which we all duly answered, in repetitive monotone.

Davey, Billy, Dicky, Jimmy, John and I were quite an awesome force when we got together, despite the fact we were aged only 5 or 6.

The day was hot, the kind of day when you could have fried an egg on the pavement, and we all made our way to the Bungalow Cafe, quietly hiding under the building, which had small gaps in the floorboards so we could gape through and look up ladies' and girls' skirts.

'She isn't wearing any knickers,' said Davey, peering through a gap.

We all rushed to the scene, jostling for position.

'She's wearing trousers,' said Dicky. 'Have you got X-ray eyes, or what?'

We all started laughing and then headed out of the den to get hold of long sheets of corrugated steel, which were stored nearby, and which we used as sleds to fly down the steep, grassed embankment, down to the coast road next to the sands of Roker Beach.

The five of us stood at the top of the embankment, holding our sheets of steel, placed them on the grass, then sat on top of them.

'To Germany!' shouted Jimmy, and we all pushed ourselves off, gaining speed on the grass, and crashed into a pile, after reaching about 20 miles an hour.

We all knew we were heading for Germany, as there was a sign outside the Bungalow Cafe which said just that: 'To Germany.' It's still there to this day.

After we hit the beach, like a bunch of four-foot-tall commandoes, we noticed what appeared to be a mine, washed up on the sands. 'Look,' said Davey excitedly. 'It's a bomb.'

We ran over the pebbles, almost falling over each other, and reached the big object, which looked like nothing more than a massive iron football with a few spikes sticking out of it.

'That's not a bomb,' said Jimmy. 'It's just a piece of metal from the shipyards.'

Davey Hall pressed his ear to the object, and we all stared at him. 'Is it ticking?' I asked.

'No,' said Davey. 'I can't hear anything.'

'Mind out,' I said. 'I'll sharp find out if it's a bomb.'

I climbed on to the object and started jumping up and down.

'You're mad,' said Dicky. 'Are you trying to get us all killed?'

As I danced on the metal ball, in the distance I could see a man running towards us, waving his hands about. He seemed to be shouting, but I couldn't hear what he was saying. Davey and Dicky started pushing the ball, to see if they could move it.

'Get down!' shouted the man, when he got within range. 'Get down, you bloody idiot!'

The man was wearing a uniform and, as he got nearer, I could see his face was bright red and he was sweating like a pig.

'It's the coastguard,' said Billie. 'Let's leg it.'

I jumped from the object and we all ran back up the

embankment, puffing and gasping for breath, towards the Bungalow Cafe. We watched as more men joined the coastguard and they started erecting barbed wire around the metal ball, and then hammered danger signs into the sand.

'It must be a bomb, then,' said Davey. 'Why didn't it go off?'

Within a half-hour the beach was teeming with soldiers from the army and, as we continued watching what was happening, they carried out a controlled explosion. The bomb blasted and left a huge crater in the sand.

'We'd better not mention this to our parents,' said Dicky Maguire, as we headed for home. Then I remembered it was approaching dinnertime and we had special guests.

We said our goodbyes and as I entered the house the smell of roast beef and gravy hit my nostrils with such force my belly started rumbling. I walked into the room and there, sitting at the table, was my aunt and uncle from Fulwell and their two kids, all rigged out in their Sunday best. Our Cathy was sitting there, too, looking all prim and proper.

I walked into the kitchen where my mother was preparing dinner.

'Don't forget what I told you, George,' my mother said.

'When I ask you and Cathy if you want dinner, you say no, you're not hungry. Right?'

'Can't we have some, mam? I'm starving hungry,' I pleaded.

'There's only enough for our guests. Now, don't show me up, George. We don't want our guests to know we've got nowt.'

I sat in an armchair and my mother brought the dinner in on a huge tray. It smelt absolutely delicious. The plates were piled high with vegetables, potatoes, beef, Yorkshire pudding and covered in a rich, aromatic gravy.

'Here's dinner,' my mother said, placing the meals in front of our guests.

'Are you having some dinner, George?' she asked, as she turned to me.

'No thanks, mam. I'm not hungry,' I said, lying through my teeth.

'What about you, Cathy?' mother asked.

'Not for me, mam. I had a big breakfast,' said Cathy, her eyes as wide as saucers.

For the next 20 minutes, my tongue was drowning in a sea of saliva and there was so many rumblings from down below it sounded like my guts were playing The Last Night of the Proms. I could have mugged them two little posh cousins for that dinner. They left half of it anyway.

But then came dessert and, as mother brought in a huge dish full of pink blancmange and custard, I knew my sacrifice would be short-lived and worthwhile.

'Would you like some blancmange, George?' my mother asked.

'Yes please. I'd love some,' I said eagerly.

'Well, you're not getting any,' my mother said, 'because you wouldn't eat your dinner!'

Old Mrs Gracey, the posh woman from next door, walked into the room clutching the prized tin of coffee I had heard my mother talking about the night before. She'd always just let herself into our house, would Mrs Gracey, without knocking.

But it was well known that no one on the Barbary Coast locked their front doors. Neighbours came in and out all the time. That had nothing to do with the fact there were no thieves around, it was more to do with the fact no one had anything worth stealing.

Mrs Gracey, who always wore a fur coat and looked far too posh to live in Cooper Street, sat at the table and put the tin in front of her.

'Look what I've got,' she said. 'You'll never have tasted this before, George. And it has come all the way from Australia, from my cousin Charles.'

Mrs Gracey looked towards my mother. 'Put the kettle on Doris and I'll call in some of the neighbours,' she said. She walked towards me and pinched my cheek. 'We're going to have coffee,' she said. 'Real coffee. The first you've ever had.'

Within a few minutes the front room was packed with neighbours, all chatting merrily away, introducing themselves to my posh aunt and uncle and cousins from Fulwell, and my mother got out her best coffee pot and cups and saucers. She poured the coffee into the small cups and the adults, who had not tasted real coffee for years, slowly sipped, savouring the taste they had almost forgotten.

'It tastes a bit strange this,' said one of the neighbours, a woman who always forgot to take the rollers out of her hair and never remembered to put her false teeth in.

'That's because you've never had coffee for so long,' said old Mrs Gracey, sipping her drink with her little finger stuck in the air.

'It does taste a little bitter,' my mother said. 'But I'm still going to drink every drop.'

My mother, old Mrs Gracey and the rest of the women in the room talked about rationing, what people said you could get on the black market and how fortunate they were the other day when the back of the local coalman's flatbed wagon suddenly slipped open, sending lots of coal on to the cobbled street.

That happened a lot in Cooper Street, and as soon as the coal hit the deck everyone would be out in the street with their buckets and shovels. The poor coalman would be unaware what was going on, having moved on to do his rounds. It was always believed that someone deliberately loosened the locks on the back of the wagon when the coalman arrived, but it was never proven.

A week after our afternoon coffee, old Mrs Gracey received a letter from down under, informing her of the sudden death of her cousin and expressing the hope she had received her cousin's ashes and the request that they would be scattered somewhere in his home town of Sunderland. The letter writer explained the family in Australia were keen to avoid any form filling and, so, had sent the ashes by first-class air mail in a coffee tin.

Old Mrs Gracey, for some reason, had not received the explanatory note, but she had, as everyone in Cooper Street soon became aware, received the tin of coffee. Some neighbours complained of feeling unwell. It was a long time, rationing or not, before the Reynolds family drank coffee again.

CHAPTER 3

The Barbary Coast

A blanket of thick fog had descended quickly and without warning after we had rowed between the north and south piers at Roker, heading for Germany. The Luftwaffe had caused untold damage to the houses in Sunderland, and killed many people. Someone had to do something, and Jimmy Dodds, Dicky Maguire and myself, aged only seven but with brave hearts, were just the boys for the job.

But panic had set in as quickly as the fog had engulfed us and, three miles off the piers that symbolised home, we knew we were lost and didn't have a clue where we were going.

We had borrowed the rowing boat, which belonged to Jimmy's dad, from the beach at Roker and had set out with good intentions, but now we could hardly see each other, never mind the lighthouse, and the gung-ho boyish bravery we had displayed at the start of our adventure quickly evaporated, leaving us shivering with fear in the cold North Sea.

'Why don't we just row some more, until we hit land?' said Dicky, his voice trembling.

'Cos we don't know where the land is,' said Jimmy.

'We can't be that far from the beach,' I said.

We were lost and alone. Our childish prank was about to backfire and we could all end up drowned. I was frightened.

As we sat in the boat, tears welling up in our eyes, the lights from a ship came into view. As the ship neared, Jimmy was able to read the writing on the side. The ship was called *The Lady Charrington*.

'That's got be be heading for Roker,' I said and, as the ship passed us only about 30 feet away, Dicky and I grabbed the oars and started rowing with all our might. Our arms ached like hell as we tried to keep up with the ship and, though it gained on us, we then knew we were headed in the right direction. Jimmy, Dicky and I took it in turns to share the rowing, and we had never worked so hard in our lives.

After what seemed like an eternity, our energies zapped, the fog lifted and we could see dry land. But the *Lady Charrington* had not docked at Roker, as we had imagined, it had dropped anchor at Seaham Harbour, about seven miles south. We rowed into the harbour, docked near metal steps that would take us to land and a bus ride home, and moored the rowing boat by tying a thick rope to the metal steps.

We had some explaining to do, but that could wait until the morning.

Our little gang was always up to mischief: stealing cash meant for the families of shipwreck victims from a charity box made out of an old mine on the cliffs at Roker; nicking from the local shops; scavenging for driftwood on the beach, which we would sell door-to-door; and looking for pieces of shrapnel – and there was a lot of it – from the spent shells that blitzed our neighbourhoods.

The charity box was a tight squeeze, so one of the smaller

lads would be lifted into it and we'd hand him a kind of ice cream scoop, which he would load with copper, and then off we'd go to the fairground at Seaburn and have a great time, whizzing round the rides and filling our empty bellies with toffee apples and candy floss. I had no qualms about taking the cash from the charity box – we were all needy children, after all.

We'd spend most of our days in the gang hut under the cafe, setting out on daily adventures and picking winkles (or willicks as we called them) from the rocks on the beach, boiling them in sea water on a camp fire and eating them. Of course, once the willicks were out of the shells, they looked just like snots, and one of the lads – I'll spare his embarrassment by not naming him – picked his nose and ate it that much it was difficult to fathom whether he was eating a willick or a bogey.

It's strange to think that we ate all these willicks and never suffered bellyaches. It's even stranger to think that most of us lads learned how to swim in the heavily polluted waters of Sunderland's north dock, and never ailed a thing. The water was all the colours of the rainbow: it was full of oil, chemicals (some of them toxic), flotsam, jetsam and raw human shit. Yet we would run and jump from the water's edge, dive-bomb into the water and learn one of the first lessons in life: sink or try to swim. I, like the other lads, started off doing the doggy-paddle, but we earned our water wings later through trial and error, more by accident than design.

Under the cliffs at Roker, long underground tunnels ran from the cliff face right up through Roker and Monkwearmouth, one to St Andrew's Church and another, I believe, to St Peter's Church. Built in the seventh century, St Peter's is one of the oldest churches in England. There was also a tunnel running the full length of the north pier at Roker, where you could walk underneath the pier right to the lighthouse. As a boy these tunnels both fascinated and frightened me. Some locals claimed the tunnels were used by smugglers bringing in stolen cigarettes, bottles of spirits and other dodgy goods. Others said the tunnels were used by people fleeing religious persecution. We lads ventured into the tunnels at least twice a week and some would make it for at least a few yards, but others, like myself, would barely make it through the entrance before someone would shout, 'It's the witch!' or ' It's the bogeyman!' and we'd all flee, after scaring ourselves shitless.

I loved the sea: playing in it, staring at it, throwing smooth pebbles into it, seeing how many times I could get them to bounce on top of the water. My dad, when he wasn't at sea on the trawlers or serving on the minesweeper with the Royal Navy, had a pleasure boat called *The Windfall*, which he would pilot at Seaburn and Roker during the summer months, charging a shilling a ride.

There was so much to explore, so many adventures to be had, I'd spend more time on the beach or in the gang hut than I would at St Benet's School. It was little surprise that my mother would get regular visits from the school board man, wanting to know this and wanting to know that; and visits from the police asking why I'd stolen a bottle of vinegar from a shop in Brandling Street, or a packet of cigarettes which they had caught me smoking. The vinegar was for Davey Hall's mother, to make toffee cakes we'd sell door-to-door; the cigarettes were to trade for a loaf of bread to rid myself of hunger pangs. At the age of seven I was already learning two basic rules: steal or starve; sink or swim.

When I decided to go to school, Davey Hall and I would walk along the back lanes through Roker, munching our way through a slice of jam and bread each, or Cathy and I would share an orange, passing it between us all the way to school: it was breakfast on the hoof. Most of the teachers at St Benet's were nuns and, of course, with me being baptised a Roman Catholic at St Benet's RC Church, that was the school for me. Sister Mary Claire, Sister Clements and Sister Ninian are some of the nuns I remember. The male teachers included Mr Crowe, Mr Scales and Mr McCue.

One school visitor I always looked forward to seeing was the nit nurse, because my head was so lousy I knew I was guaranteed a lift home in the 'nit van' and the rest of the day off school. For my sister, Cathy, and for my mother, this was a huge embarrassment. 'What will the neighbours think?' my mother would ask. But the fact was most of the kids I knew had heads full of dickies (head lice) and most homes that I visited had their own small-tooth combs, to comb out the dickies on to newspaper.

There were many 'remedies' for dickies, but hardly any of them worked. One lad used to have turpentine poured on his head, and he was always told to stay away from his parents, who both smoked, or his head would turn into a fireball. Such was the shame of having dickies. I would get a lift home in the nit van and pretend I was a gangster, swinging from the van door and shooting at people walking down the street with my imaginary tommy gun.

School life, for me, was difficult. I had a short attention span, I got up to many mischievous tricks and I could not, however hard I tried, grasp the rudiments of reading, writing and arithmetic. The Sisters could write a word on the blackboard and repeat it, parrot-fashion, all day, but I would still be unable to read it. The teachers thought I was thick, or at least backward, but the fact was I was dyslexic: a condition that wouldn't be recognised for at least another 40 years.

Repeating things parrot-fashion was, obviously, a teaching method at St Benet's. Reinforcement, they would call it now. Everything from 'The cat sat on the mat' to the two-times table was repeated, drummed into us, over and over again. Religion was the worst, in the form of the Catechism. How many times did I have to say I rejected Satan before it would be believed?

My greatest desire at school was to get out of it. I craved adventure. Dolling off – playing truant – became one of my favourite pastimes.

We'd been dolling off when we took to the North Sea heading for Germany, and we were dolling off the next day when the rowing boat owner, Jimmy Dodds' dad, looked under the Bungalow Cafe where we were dreaming up our next adventure.

'Where's my fucking boat?' he asked angrily.

'Err. It's at Seaham Harbour,' I said sheepishly.

Mr Dodds scrambled into our den and grabbed myself and Jimmy by the scruffs of our necks. 'Come with me, you little gits!' he said. Mr Dodds put us in the back seat of his car, and drove us along to Seaham Harbour. Jimmy and I sat quietly, fearing the consequences of our actions the previous day.

'Does your mother know you're dolling off?' asked Mr Dodds. I didn't answer, but knew she would be told on our return to Roker.

At Seaham Harbour, Mr Dodds, his son Jimmy and I stood at the harbour edge. Jimmy looked like he was going to faint, Mr Dodds's face was red with anger, and I felt like legging it.

The water level in the small harbour could have been no more than three foot high and all the small boats and cobles were resting on the mud banks ... all bar one. Mr Dodds's rowing boat was hanging from the harbour wall from the thick rope we had tethered to the mooring. It was just dangling there, and the oars had fallen into the thick mud beneath.

'Are you fucking stupid?' asked Mr Dodds. 'Don't you know the fucking tide goes out?'

Mr Dodds could have given us both a good clip around the earhole, but even he saw the funny side of it. The boat wasn't damaged and he arranged with a couple of the dock-workers to have it brought back to Roker on the pilot cutter. He dropped us back at Roker and related the full story to my mother. She wasn't best pleased.

After being sent to my room without any tea, I slept like a log, and the next morning I was sent off to school with a flea in my ear, a piece of jam and bread and a pair of boots that my mother told me I should drop off at the Maguires' house for my pal Dicky. It was the kind of gesture that was commonplace in Roker: friends looking after one another in times of need. I delivered the boots, as asked, but I had no intention of going to school. There was so much more I wanted to do, such as climb the cranes down at the shipyards or, like today, grab a load of fish heads and try to catch some crabs.

Dicky was up for it, but Davey Hall and Jimmy Dodds decided to give it a miss.

A young lad who didn't knock about with us regularly, Geordie Stephens, joined us crabbing at the Folly Bank instead.

We walked from Roker to the fish quay, on the other side of the river in the town's East End, and picked up a box of fish heads. Each of us had a line and a hook and we knew the best place for crabbing at Folly Bank.

We lined the bank, dropped the lines into the water and waited for a bite. The crabs we would catch would be too small to eat, but it was all a bit of fun.

During the summer we would spend some nights under makeshift tents on Roker beach. The tents were made from tarpaulins we'd help ourselves to from Speedings, the sail-makers. We'd make a fire from driftwood and boil willicks and mussels, and watch the boats going through the piers to some far distant shore.

The days, when not at school or dolling off, were spent in the gang hut, and one day I had turned up in a brand new red velvet suit, ready to make my Holy Communion. The lads decided to get the corrugated steel sleds out, and I couldn't resist sliding down the grassed embankment. The inevitable happened: my trousers split, but one of the lads managed to obtain some white wool and a sewing needle and stitch it up. The only problem was he had stitched my pants to my shirt, and I was aching to go to the toilet. I ran all the way home, got a good telling off and then felt a great sense of relief when my backside hit the porcelain.

On the banks of the River Wear, Dicky Maguire and I had dropped our lines. Geordie had moved further up the bank, about 50 yards away. Eventually he drifted out of sight, telling us he'd have more luck further downstream. Dusk was setting in over the river and the constant hammering of the yards slowly petered out as the riveters, caulker burners, joiners and other shipyard workers made their way home for the night.

'This is boring,' said Dicky. 'There's nowt biting.'

'We'll give it some more time,' I said.

We gave it a little more time, but after catching only one small crab, and throwing it back into the river, Dicky and I decided to call it a day.

'What about Geordie?' Dicky asked. We both started shouting at the tops of our voices.

'Geordie! Geordie! We're going home!' we shouted, but there was no reply. 'Geordie! Geordie!' we shouted again, and our small voices echoed around the banks of the river, but still no reply. Geordie, like us, knew the docks like the back of his hand. Dicky and I made our way home.

Later that night there was a loud knock on the door in Cooper Street. I jumped out of bed and sat on the stairs, listening, as my mother opened the front door.

It was a police officer.

'Mrs Reynolds?' the officer asked.

'Yes. Oh, my God, what's happened?' she asked in a state of panic.

'You have a son called George?'

'Yes,' my mother said. 'What the hell has he been up to now?'

'George?' my mother shouted. 'George, come down here now.'

It transpired that young Geordie Stephens had not returned home. By this time it was approaching midnight.

'Honest, mam, we just left him at the Folly Bank. He went further up the river on his own,' I explained to my mother.

'You'd better be telling me the truth, George,' she said, looking into my eyes to determine whether or not I was lying. But I wasn't lying: young Geordie had gone further up river, away from me and Dicky.

The police officer left the house, and my mother gave me a grilling. I just repeated what had happened.

Young Geordie was missing for several days. His family and friends scoured the neighbourhoods, police put out a missing person appeal, but the hours turned into days, and still no sign of little Geordie.

A week or so later, young Geordie's body was found in the River Wear. He had drowned. His parents were inconsolable with grief and his death had a marked effect on the neighbourhood. It was a very sad time.

That tragedy marked the start of what were the unhappiest days of my childhood. A year or two after that, what with my mother being beside herself with my mischievous ways and my dad being away at sea, and with me showing little promise in the classes at St Benet's and dolling off, the people in the know within Sunderland's education department decided they would send me away; teach me a lesson in life.

At the age of eight, I was to spend the next eight years of

my life away from home, 'purchased' from the local education authority by a residential special school for the princely sum of £100.

CHAPTER 4

Sambourne

The winter of 1947 was the coldest ever recorded in Britain. The snow was up to six feet deep in places and, as those with cash kept the post-war home fires burning with coal, those without cash, many elderly, froze to death in their ramshackle homes. The icy grip had taken such a hold, services came to a standstill, and householders battened down the hatches to protect themselves from the next inevitable sub-zero white-out.

At St Joseph's Roman Catholic School in Sambourne, near Redditch, in Warwickshire, my body shivered so violently it was as if I was suffering some type of epileptic fit. It was three in the morning, and I hadn't managed to get any kip at all.

'Mather!' shouted the nun, from her room at the top of the billet. 'Mather!'

Joe Mather, a thin and softly-spoken lad from Plains Farm in Sunderland, jumped out of his bed and ran towards the bottom of the dormitory. 'I'm here, Sister!' he said. 'I'm here.'

'Get them up!' shouted the nun. 'Get them up, before they wet themselves so much they drown us all.'

Joe pulled back the blankets on the four beds, and so much steam rose from the covers you would think they'd been boiling a kettle.

'It's too late, Sister,' said Joe in an almost apologetic way. 'It's too late. They've gone and done it again.'

The dormitory was split into three levels, each with a step down to the next. The bottom level was for the bed-wetters. With them all sleeping in the same place, it was hoped they could be caught before the sheets were drenched in urine and Joe Mather, sent to Sambourne for stealing chocolate and cigarettes from the back of a van, was the lad who always seemed to be on pissy-bed duty.

'Get back to bed now, Mather,' the Sister said. 'The little lazy idiots can lie in their own stench until morning.'

I was a little envious of the bed-wetters, in one way, because at least their own piss would warm them up a little bit.

The six dormitories at Sambourne, away from the main eerie, gothic-looking main building, were windowless, and each of the beds had headboards facing the middle of the room, rather than out to the wall, as there was no wall, just wooden shutters. The wind would whistle through the shutters, and the drifting snow would land on our beds. We had two sheets and two blankets during the winter; one was a blanket of snow, as the shutters offered little or no protection from the outside world. It was bloody freezing.

The army-style billets had no running water, no electricity and no form of heating. The floors were wooden and so highly polished you could see your own reflection in them. We polished all the floors ourselves.

As Joe Mather drifted back off to sleep, I curled myself up into a ball and tried to force my eyes shut, but the icy wind whistled through the rafters and the cold bit into me with a vengeance. Rest would not come tonight.

In the near distance I heard an ear-piercing scream, then the voice of one of the Sisters, then the clatter of feet on wooden boards. The screams continued, but gradually became fainter: the Sister and a boy seemed to be moving away from the dormitories, possibly into the main building. It was obvious the boy was being slapped about the head. His screams were not the stuff of nightmares, they were screams of pain, screams of chastisement. I drifted off into a restless, disturbed sleep and wondered, in my childish fear, whether the screaming boy would ever be seen again. There was another little boy, with blond hair and blue eyes, who was often taken, against his will it appeared, to the priest's house over the field.

Dawn came and, as the sun cracked through the Warwickshire clouds, I could hear no birds singing, no cocks crowing; there was just an uncanny silence. I always found it strange that there appeared to be few, if any, birds flying around St Joseph's RC School at Sambourne, and never a butterfly in sight. And yet, here we were, in the heart of rural England, surrounded by nothing more than vast, open countryside, in an area so isolated we would rarely see another human being who was not associated with the school. We were so out of sight, so out of mind, we could have been on the moon.

'Time to get up, boys!' shouted the Sister, her heavy shoes making her steps reverberate around the dormitory. 'Get up, get the snow off your beds and get a good wash in this fresh morning air.'

One by one, we quickly jumped from our beds, the shutters went up and we shovelled the snow from the tops of our beds with our bare hands. We pulled on our shorts, put our feet into our hobnailed boots and, in an orderly fashion, walked up to a huge trough near the dormitory. The water had frozen over again.

'It's bloody freezing,' said Jimmy Conley, from Red House, Sunderland, who was sent to Sambourne for stealing a purse, which he denied. 'What are we supposed to do?' he asked. 'The ice is about an inch thick.'

Standing next to Jimmy, I slowly clenched my right fist and smashed it through the ice, grazing my knuckles in the process. William Orange joined us at the trough.

'It's not right what they're doing here, you know,' said William. 'It's just not right. It shouldn't be allowed, what they're doing to us.'

I remember William telling me his dad was a pilot in the Royal Air Force, but was killed when he came home on leave. William, from Alnwick, Northumberland, having had a decent education before circumstances dictated he came to Sambourne, was one of the very few lads at St Joseph's who could read and write.

'This is not right,' he said again. 'We should escape.'

Jimmy, William and I washed our faces in the freezing cold water, then went back into the dormitory to get properly dressed for the day, as the other lads took it in turns to wash from the trough.

As I shivered in the freezing dormitory, I longed for wash days in the back yard of Davey Hall's house in Gosforth Street, Roker, when his mother, Mary, would get the poss tub out (a large metal tub, about the size of a dustbin, that women used to wash clothes in, beating them with a poss stick) and thump the washing with such force, it created a tub full of hot, soapy water with the suds flowing over the sides. When the clothes washing was done, several of the younger Hall kids – and there were nine of them – would be stripped bare and would jump in the tub for a bath. And Mrs Hall didn't restrict herself to washing her own kids; there was many a time I would be in the back yard and she'd have me stripped down to my birthday suit for a quick dip in the foam-rich tub. The kids used to come out gleaming, the tide marks they had carried all week had vanished.

At Sambourne, our only contact with hot water and carbolic soap was in the main building where there was a shower, one wall of which held a series of shower heads. The boys were not asked to stand under one of the showers, they had to almost run through the lot, soaping themselves on the way. It was really more of a conveyor belt than a shower.

By the winter of 1947, I had been at Sambourne for almost three years, and the regimentalisation, the tedious daily routines, the brutality of the regime and the sense of order – very strict order – and control had made me, I know now, institutionalised. It had not taken the authorities very long. By the age of ten, I had become intrinsically linked to the system; a system where educational attainment and performance were measured in crude statistics and graphs invented by middle-class intellectuals who believed every young boy had a stable family life and was read bedtime stories every night. It was a system where everyone could be labelled or pigeonholed, categorised, branded, and the labels pinned to the boys for them to carry for the rest of their lives. It was a system where individuality was frowned upon, and mischievousness met with a swift punch or kick or a few lashes from a leather strap; where there was no such thing as personality, the human spirit or – apart from Mass, Benediction and Confession – the human soul. But the fact was, every boy at Sambourne had spirit, that intangible thread of human character that, weaved together, produces the very rich tapestry of life. And whatever they did to us at Sambourne, they could not break our spirit.

I travelled to Sambourne with Jimmy Conley, getting a train to Birmingham, then Redditch, then a bus ride to

Sambourne and a long, long walk. I cried all the way from Sunderland to Birmingham, and Jimmy Conley did, too. Our supervisors, a Mr Donaldson and a Mr Goodfellow, both linked to the education department based in John Street, Sunderland, accompanied us on our journey, but said little to us boys.

When we arrived at Sambourne we were stripped, showered deloused, and kitted out in green shorts, a green top and black hobnailed boots, which we were expected to polish every day. When I arrived, on 16 April 1945, I weighed 3st 8lbs, stood 4 foot 2 inches tall, and had the skin disease psoriasis all over my body. It's a condition that has stayed with me all my life, despite numerous efforts to get rid of it.

The teachers at Sambourne noted: 'Undersized boy with red curly hair and blue eyes. Nails look bitten. Receptions are slow. Affectionate and friendly. Easily led. Restless during sleep. Amenable but very undisciplined. One or two stealing incidents (packet of cigarettes from home).' Apart from the hair, eyes and reference to stealing, they could have been describing a dog. And that was it. I was labelled from day one.

There was one bit of kindness shown to me on my arrival, but it didn't come from any of the staff, it came from Geordie Lavelle, from Pennywell, Sunderland, who gave me his pillow and a packet of Spangles. I cuddled that pillow all night and cried myself to sleep. Geordie taught me another lesson, which stopped the bullies in their tracks. He said to me: 'The only way to stop it is to pick out the hardest one of the lot, and sort him out. Once you've sorted him out, the rest are easy going.'

I took Geordie's advice and when the big lad bully pushed me around again, I picked up a cricket bat and smashed him full in the face. His nose was broken and bloodied, his eyes were black and swollen. He never bothered me again, and nor did any of his pals.

But what did bother me was the nuns. They stormed into the dormitory, grabbed me by the neck and led me into a room where, up against a wall, stood several thick, long canes. One of the nuns grabbed a cane and ordered me to hold out my hand. I held it out but when the cane came swooping down, I anticipated the pain to come and pulled my hand away. Again she ordered me to hold out my hand and, again, I pulled it away just before the stroke struck. This incensed the nun and she hit me with the cane across my back. I struggled and kicked out, falling on to the hard floor and swearing at the nuns who crouched above me. They all hit out. One by one they brought the thick canes down on my body and the pain from each stroke ran through my bones like an electric shock. It was the worst beating I had endured, but it wouldn't be the last. I was so badly beaten they had to carry me out.

Geordie Lavelle had been sent to Sambourne for playing truant from school. His brothers Stevie and Danny also attended the school, probably for the same reason. Geordie was assigned as my 'partner' at Sambourne: an older pupil who would look after me. His bed was next to mine and we'd spend some time at nights lying awake talking about our heroes, such as boxer Cast Iron Casey from the East End of Sunderland – the man no one could knock out.

All we Sunderland lads were kept together. Davey Hopper, from Red House in the town, was detained because he had stolen a cricket bat from Monkwearmouth School; Jimmy McEvoy for truanting. But there was hundreds of lads from all over the country at Sambourne, all considered disruptive or underachievers, or 'retarded' in some way.

After our morning classes one day during a long, hot summer, the lads sat on the grass outside the dormitories. The shutters on the dormitories had been left open to let the warm air circulate. We picked blades of grass and talked, but

William Orange was particularly quiet. He looked subdued, depressed even.

Then, as quick as a flash, William jumped to his feet. 'Fuck it!' he said. 'Fuck this. I've had enough.' He ran towards the perimeter fence as quick as a whippet, and two nuns who witnessed his outburst quickly gave chase, their black uniforms flapping in the wind.

'Come back here, boy!' one of the nuns shouted. 'Come back here!'

We all got to our feet.

'Go on, William,' I shouted. 'Go on!'

'Go on William, run. Go on!' shouted another boy.

The nuns, gasping for breath, appeared to be gaining on William but he got to the fence and vaulted it like an Olympic athlete, his little legs giving it fifty to the dozen, and away he went, across the field, across the next, across the next, and then he disappeared from view. And for one moment, that moment, at Sambourne, I felt elated.

A week later, two men appeared at the entrance to the school, holding little William Orange by both hands. He looked as if he had been sleeping rough. His hair was unkempt, his skin as dirty as that of a young chimney sweep on a hard day and his clothes were covered in muck.

Then came another short, sharp lesson for us lads and that was that retribution would be swift and punishment barbaric. I had often thought some nuns and priests within the Roman Catholic Church had streaks of pure sadism, and it was proven to me that day.

William was frogmarched into the main building and every boy in the school was ordered to assemble in the main hall. We quietly walked into the hall in single file, unsure of what we were about to witness, but fearful that it would be something we would remember for the rest of our lives.

We sat on wooden forms lining every wall of the hall, and

waited. In the middle of the hall stood a highly polished, 12-foot-long oak table. There were at least 200 boys in that hall, but you could have heard a pin drop.

One of the Sisters walked in, her face looking stern and resolute, and at one end of the massive table she placed a metal bucket half filled with water. Many of the boys looked at each other, wondering what was coming next. Then, through the main hall door, William Orange appeared, with one nun firmly holding one arm, and another gripping the other, and two more walking behind. William was struggling. 'It's not right, this!' he shouted. 'It's not right.'

William was stripped bare, then forced face down on to the top of the table. His legs were tied together, and then the rope used was fed underneath the table and back along the top, and his hands tied. One of the nuns stood to his left side, holding his arm down, and another to his right.

Into the hall walked another of the Sisters, a stout woman who put the fear of God into the boys just by looking at them, and in her hand was a fearsome-looking leather strap, which looked more like a cat-o'-nine-tails. The wooden handle was about six inches long, and the 12-inch long piece of leather that came from it was split into strips. The Sister stood behind William. He forced his eyes tight shut, bit his teeth hard, and up went her right arm. Virtually every pair of eyes in the hall followed the strap as she lifted it and held it aloft.

Then, after the nun took a deep breath, she brought the strap down so hard on William's pale backside the loud crack bounced off every wall, and young William wailed like a banshee. Ten times the strap came down, one for each year of his life, each leaving a deep, red, bleeding welt on his bare white arse. His face was contorted in what must have been excruciating pain. The job done, the strap was dropped into the bucket of water. The water hissed.

William Orange could not sit down without pain for a week. The message the nuns wanted to deliver had been conveyed swiftly and effectively.

I knew then that I had never seen such raw, unrelenting cruelty. But more was to come, at Besford Court School.

CHAPTER 5

Besford

The master walked into the class, stood in front of the blackboard, laid his books on the desk in front of him and looked, in turn, at the face of every boy sitting there.

'I would like to tell you all something,' said Mr Martin, in his broad Scottish accent. 'There are no other masters here want any of you in their classes; they do not wish to teach you. You are all mischievous, you are all disruptive, you have no sense of decorum, you steal apples from the orchards, you steal sweets from the shops in Pershore. Not one of you can read or write. You are all insolent, surly, at times abusive; you swear, you pick fights, you all have the attention span of a gnat, and you're always up to some kind of villainy.

'In short, boys,' Mr Martin said. 'You are the utter dregs of humanity.'

We looked at each other, not knowing whether to laugh or look serious. But we all looked serious.

'However, despite your bad attitudes,' Mr Martin continued,

'despite your beastly behaviour, your rule-bending, your idleness and all the grief and damage you cause. Despite all that, I, Mr Martin, a master at Besford Court Roman Catholic School, love each and every one of you.'

Mr Martin again looked at every boy in the class, his eyes lingering just long enough to see if the point had registered.

In the harsh regime at Besford, his speech came like a bolt from the blue. But I, personally, had no doubt that Mr Martin, our teacher for several years, sincerely meant every word he uttered. He was the kindest teacher I met in my eight years at Sambourne and Besford, and he had a positive impact on the lives of scores of other Besford Boys because, when they left and returned, they showered Mr Martin with gifts.

Mr Martin taught me what he said were the ten golden rules to follow in life, and he recited them regularly in the classroom. They impressed me so much, I memorised them. One, look after the pennies and the pounds will look after themselves; two, never taken no for an answer; three, watch your friends, not your enemies (you know your enemies, you think you know your friends); four, never let your heart rule your head; five, never leave an enemy behind, as they will rise again; six ,business is just a game, it's knowing how to master the game that counts; seven, was never treat people as bad as the way you have been treated, it makes you worse than them; eight, when you shake hands on a deal, you stick to it; nine, never fight in-house and, if threatened from outside, close ranks; and ten, if, when you leave the school, you are better off than others, promise to help those worse off than yourself.

The head teacher was a Mr Kelly, and other masters included Allison, Clements, two called Hanratty, McKenna, Snowball, Willis and Fleming. Mr Snowball used to say: 'If I catch any of you lads smoking pasha, I'll kick yer arse, I'm telling yer.'

One of the masters, whose name I forget, was a violent

drunk, who would stagger into the dormitories after a heavy drinking session, lift his right leg and bring his boot down on the leg of one of the boys. We would lie in bed, shaking with fear, knowing that one of us would get the boot that night. One of the lads wrapped his legs in cardboard, but his boot still hurt.

Most of the masters were Irish, and they ruled with an iron fist: discipline and order were everything. For half of the day the boys would be taught basic education, reading, writing and arithmetic, and for the second half of the day we would be put to work with a supervisor. Joinery, bricklaying, painting and decorating, gardening, even shoe repairs; a lot of trades were covered and the skills we learned then we would use in later life.

The routine was always the same. A breakfast of porridge oats (I never once saw a rasher of bacon at Besford), one piece of dry bread (what the locals called 'chuffs') and one piece of buttered bread. Dinner was mainly vegetables.

First thing in the morning, all the boys would be lined up on parade and one of the masters would carry out an inspection. If your kit was out of order, or your boots dirty you would get a quick slap across the ear.

At night, we boys would sometimes listen to the wireless – boxing matches or the latest radio play – and at 9pm sharp it was lights out. Then, often for up to an hour, we would talk, quietly, about the school and about our hopes for the future.

'What do you want to be when you grow up?' Jimmy McEvoy would ask.

'I'm going to be a millionaire,' I'd say with confidence.

'You can't even spell millionaire,' said Jimmy.

Sleep would slowly come, but often we would be disturbed by the crying of one of the boys, particularly the new arrivals from Sambourne, or by the weight of the master's boot falling heavily on our legs.

Besford Court School, which opened in 1917, was inextricably linked with St Joseph's at Sambourne. Both were, I believe, run by the same Board of Trustees, even though they were separated by the Warwickshire and Worcestershire county border. It the 1920s the school was known as Besford Court Mental Welfare Hospital for Children.

It's history, however, went way back to the tenth century. The Besford uniform consisted of grey shorts, a grey shirt, a grey top and grey socks. The boys were split into four troops – red, white, blue and green – and you wore your troop colour on your socks. Every boy had a name, but all also had a number, which was sewn into the back of your shirt or jumper. Reynolds, George, was number 109, and I was a member, like my pal Davey Hopper, of the red troop.

Sports were well catered for at Besford – mainly football, cricket and boxing. I liked boxing, but was never very keen on football or cricket. Davey Hopper, Jimmy Conley, Joe Mather, Stevie Lavelle, another lad from Sunderland, Geordie Donnelly and Eddy Boddy were the mainstays of Besford's version of Sunderland AFC. Jimmy Conley and Jimmy McEvoy were also keen on cricket. The lads were good – so good, in fact, they often played cricket with the masters during the summer.

After our classes with Mr Martin, of the revelatory speech, we were marched off to the dining room for dinner. It was an orderly affair: we would each get our plates of vegetables and little or no meat, sit at the long tables and start to eat when ordered. There was no talking allowed and the masters would patrol the dining room ready to clout any boy that uttered so much as a whisper.

'This food is crap,' said Davey Hopper, sitting next to me.

'You'll have to keep your voice down, Davey,' I said.

'This food is crap,' Davey said again, as a master approached.

'Shut up,' said the master, as he slapped Davey across the

side of his face, leaving a handprint.

He continued walking the floor of the dining hall, looking over shoulders, keeping order.

'This food is crap,' said Davey.

'He's looking at you, Davey,' I said. 'He's on his way back.'

He stood over Davey again. 'What did you say, Hopper?' he asked.

'I said this food is crap,' said Davey.

The master grabbed Davey by the ear and slapped him so hard, it hurt me.

'Sit down and shut up!' ordered the master.

Davey stood up, lifted his plate, threw it on to the table and shouted: 'Fuck off! Fuck off! Fuck off!'

The master quickly walked towards the dining hall entrance. It was obvious he was going to fetch the strap. Davey picked up the huge boiling tea urn and ran after him. The boys in the hall were getting very excited.

Davey, who was always a big, strong lad, threw the boiling tea over the master. He squealed.

'I'm fucking off!' Davey shouted, as he turned to face the boys. 'Who's coming with me?'

Tommy McAllister and Geordie Wallace jumped to their feet, ran towards Davey and they legged it down the stairs, along the corridor, over the fence and across the fields.

With Davey Hopper on his toes, I would have to tend to the needs of our great friend Sylvia, our pet pig, on my tod. But Sylvia was easily pleased: a few sweet apples from the orchard and a bucket of swill, à la Reynolds, always kept her happy.

As some of the boys cleared the plates from the dining hall, others washed them in the kitchen and others worked on polishing the dining hall floor using big, heavy machines. It was always the same after dinner, cleaning up our own mess.

I brought the wheelbarrow round to the kitchen and filled

it with the leftovers, and then made my way to Sylvia, to the south of the site, through the gates on the serpentine wall to the boilerhouse and the row of four pigsties. Sylvia looked depressed, and she had every reason to be. She was in the sty where the fattest of the four pigs was made ready to meet its maker in that big pigsty in the sky. She was destined for the slaughterhouse and the breakfast table.

To the left of the sties was a row of trees, which had the reddest, sweetest apples I had ever tasted. After resting the wheelbarrow next to the boilerhouse, I plucked two of the biggest apples I could find and walked over to Sylvia.

'Hello, lass,' I said, and stuck one of the apples in Sylvia's snout. She gobbled it up greedily. 'You think you're on death row, don't you?' I said, as I stuck the second apple in her snout. 'But we're not having this lass,' I said. 'No way. You're staying here. George Reynolds is going to look after you.

'You're not going to market,' I said, patting Sylvia on her snout, 'that big fat pig next door is.'

The pigs were sent to slaughter after they were fattened up and, as one was taken away, the others would be moved up one sty. The pig destined for the butcher's hook was always the one in the sty right at the end of the left-hand side of the row.

With a little bit of coaxing and prodding, I managed to get Sylvia into the boilerhouse. Then, with a little more coaxing, prodding and kicking, I managed to get the fat pig next door to Sylvia esconced in her new home. The pig was a bit of a battler, but after a few boots in the snout its resistance was low.

'Get in there, you fat pig,' I said. 'You fat pig!'

With Sylvia in the relative safety of her new home, I got to work mixing and boiling the swill, then fed it to the pigs. Sylvia appeared to enjoy it, but I gave the lion's share to the pig I'd just moved to the sty next door, trying to fatten it up a little more.

I got hold of the wheelbarrow for another trip back to the kitchens and, as I walked away from the sties, I looked back at Sylvia. It might have been my fertile imagination, but I could have sworn that from pink ear to pink ear, she was wearing the broadest smile I had ever seen.

Some of the Besford Boys kept pigeons in huts on a patch of spare land near the market gardens where most of the school's produce was grown – the school was extremely self-sufficient – and I shared a pigeon cree with Davey Hopper. Geordie Lavelle also kept pigeons with his mate Cyril Sole.

During the holidays, for two weeks during the summer and two weeks at Christmas time, those lads who had parents were allowed home and those lads who were orphans would attend Besford's own summer camp at Rhyl in Wales. Davey Hopper and I once came back to Besford after a home visit and, at Birmingham Railway Station, we nicked two pigeons from baskets stacked up on a platform, just as we were changing trains. At Besford the birds' homing instincts kicked in and they winged their way back to their rightful owners.

Davey Hopper was still at large when the weekend arrived and with it our monthly treat, a visit to The Plaza picture house in Pershore. One troop a week was allowed the day in town, and this weekend it was red troop.

We set out on a Saturday morning for the four-and-a-half-mile walk into Pershore and all the boys were ordered to polish their boots. We were all showered after breakfast, and our uniforms had to look clean and tidy. To the outside world, and this was our only sight of the outside world, it was important to the masters that their boys looked respectable, disciplined and were kitted out well.

As we marched out of Besford Court in strict formation pairs, we turned left into Ladywood Road, left again into Salters Lane, over a bridge that crossed a beck, past Wright's Farm on the left, then a sharp right into Worcester Road, down the steep Allesborough Hill, then into Pershore, past Priest Lane, Lower Priest Lane and St Agatha's Court into the High Street. Priests, nuns, masters, church, Pershore Abbey, Mass, Benediction, Confession; religion was so much part of the scenery it had even crept into the street signs.

I liked the pure escapism of the picture house. Besford Court was something we all wanted to escape from. The Plaza in Pershore reminded me of The Cora in Roker, Sunderland, though it was cleaner. The Cora was known locally as the 'lop house' or Mr Tindle's Enterprise; we would joke that it was the kind of cinema so flea-ridden you could go in wearing a jumper and come out carrying a ball of wool. Davey Hall and I would go to The Cora carrying the entrance fee – four jam jars – otherwise you'd have to pay sixpence.

Our monthly visit to Pershore was something we Besford Boys always looked forward to, but the same couldn't be said for the locals; particularly the shopkeepers in the town, the owner of the cafe where we would go in and have a cup of tea, and the owners of the orchards that lined the route back home. We'd get back to Besford with our pockets bulging with apples, conkers, cigarettes and sweets, some of the latter bought with our one shilling pocket money, but most of it stolen.

Another treat was listening to the wireless in our dormitory on a Saturday night. We'd normally ask to listen to a boxing match, if there was one scheduled, or, if not, we'd tune into *Dick Barton, Special Agent*.

This weekend was an important one for me, I was told repeatedly by the masters, as I was making my debut as an altar boy in the chapel on Sunday. Several other Besford Boys were on the altar; those who had served for several years, the lads aged 15 or 16, were known as the Rovers. I was more than a little worried about my debut on the altar, as the Mass was said in Latin, and I had yet to even master the English language properly.

The morning arrived and I reported, as I was ordered, to the chapel, and there in the vestry was the priest, getting ready for Mass, and four Rovers, all dressed smartly in their black cassocks and a kind of white overshirt. One of the Rovers, Peter, handed me a cassock.

'I'm not wearing a dress,' I said quietly.

'It's not a dress, bonehead,' said Peter. 'It's a cassock and you'll have to wear it.'

Reluctantly, I placed the cassock over my head, followed by the white overshirt.

'Let's have a look at you, boy,' said Father O'Donnell, and I walked towards him. The bottom of the cassock trailed on the floor and the overshirt was about five sizes too big for me.

'You'll do,' said the priest.

We followed the priest from the vestry, two of the Rovers swinging a type of big silver metal ball with holes in it on a chain. Smoke, which I was later told was incense, spewed from the ball and left a vapour trail in the wake of the priest.

We altar boys each stood at the side of the priest, as he laid his vestments on the altar, lifted up his hands to the sky and addressed the congregation.

'In nomine Patris, et Filii, et Spiritus Sancti–ey', said the priest, half-talking, half-singing, and with an inflection in his voice that lifted at the end of the sentence.

'In nomine, nomine, nomine, no – mi – ney,' I said.

The priest looked at me with incredulity in his eyes, looked down his nose, shook his head from side to side and said: 'Tut, tut, tut.'

Some of the boys in the congregation put their hands across their mouths to stifle a laugh.

Peter the Rover dug his elbow in my ribs.

'You do not respond,' he whispered.

'We shall start again,' said Fr O'Donnell.

He looked down, looked up, threw his hands into the air

and paused for a moment.

'In nomine Patris, et Filii, et Spiritus Sancti – ey,' he said.

'In nomine, nomine, nomine, no – mi – ney,' I responded.

The boys in the congregation burst into laughter, and even Master Martin had a smirk on his face, but another master stormed to the front of the chapel, grabbed hold of me by the earlobe and led me back into the vestry. My punishment was spending the rest of the day on the dreaded punishment wall. My first day in the priesthood, and I'd already been defrocked.

'You, Reynolds, should be excommunicated. You're a devil, you are, a devil,' said the master, as he stood me on the three-foot-high wall, which had a pointed top, making it difficult to keep your balance.

As ordered, I placed my hands on my head and tried to stand straight. The pain in my calves after only 1 hour on the wall was almost unbearable.

Twelve noon arrived, and the boys were making their way to the dining hall. I was hungry. The master approached, his sadistic grin revealing the pleasure he was gaining from my plight.

'You really think you're funny, Reynolds, don't you?' he said. 'You'll not be laughing when you get down from that wall. Believe me.'

'Can I get down now, Sir?' I asked pitifully.

'No, you bloody well can't,' he said, loving every minute of it. 'Now stand up straight, stop slouching and keep your hands on your head.'

My right foot slipped slightly and I started shaking but, just as I was about to lose my balance completely, I managed to compose myself, standing straight again.

'Nearly went there, you little bastard, didn't you?' said the master. 'Think you can take the piss out of the priest? Think you can take the piss out of our Holy Mass? Don't you know what you've done, you ignorant little cunt?'

'I do, Sir. I do,' I said. 'I'll not do it again.'

'Too bloody right,' he said. 'You'll never be in chapel again. And by the time I'm finished with you, you'll be lucky to bloody walk straight.'

He turned to walk off. 'I'll be looking out of the duty room window,' he said. 'So don't think you can step down for a breather. I'll be down on you like a ton of bricks, you hear me?'

'I hear you, Sir,' I said. 'I hear you.'

Teatime arrived, and I was still standing on the wall. I had gone through the pain barrier that many times my legs were just numb and lifeless. It felt like I could not move my legs at all, or my arms. I had turned to stone. I was more hungry than ever and, as dusk was setting in, I was by now shivering with the cold.

The master who had ordered me to stand on the wall approached. He was picking meat from his yellow teeth with a toothpick. He stared into my eyes, and, even though his face was about two feet below mine, I could smell his vile, rancid breath. The man must have suffered from halitosis.

'You hungry, Reynolds?' he asked.

'I am, Sir,' I said.

'You cold, Reynolds?'

'I am, Sir.'

'Your legs hurting, Reynolds?'

'They are, Sir.'

'Have you learnt your lesson, Reynolds?'

'I have, Sir,' I said. 'I have. I'll never do it again, Sir. I give you my word. Can I get down now?'

'No, you can't, you little bastard. Now, stand up straight and keep your hands on your head. And don't forget,' he added, 'I'm watching you.'

He walked off again.

As I stood on the punishment wall and darkness fell, I

could hear noises emanating from Tiddesley Wood, and from rooms in the main school building, some familiar, some strange. A boy crying, the masters shouting, doors being slammed, the cold wind whistling through the trees, an animal foraging for food, a cackling crow, the hoot of an owl, something, or someone, rustling through the bushes. The only light, apart from that shining through gaps in the doors of the school, came from the full moon overhead.

It must have been almost midnight when the master approached again. This time he did not walk so confidently towards me; he staggered drunkenly. Again he put his face up close to mine, and the smell of his breath made me believe the gallon of beer he had just put inside himself must have still been fermenting.

'You learnt your lesson, Reynolds?' he asked.

'Yes,' I replied.

'Then get your fucking self to bed.'

He tottered towards his quarters, veering from left to right, and, slowly, I climbed down from the punishment wall and headed towards my dormitory.

I also staggered across the courtyard, wavering, unable to walk in a straight line. Pins and needles shot up my legs and around the rest of my body and when I hit my mattress I was out for the count. It was the deepest sleep of my boyhood.

The following morning a parcel had arrived for me from home and in it were cakes, chocolate, biscuits, crisps and pop. As I sat with my parcel on the bed, Davey Hopper appeared at the door, looking as if he had been pulled through a hedge backwards. As he walked towards his bed, I could see he was in pain. He lay face down on the mattress.

'It was the railway cops that caught us,' said Davey.

'Have you had the strap?' I asked.

'Aye,' said Davey. 'Over the vaulting horse and fifteen fucking strokes.'

I walked over to Davey's bed.

'Here you are, Davey,' I said. 'Have a chocolate bar.'

For the next year or two, the routine followed the same pattern, day in, day out. Morning classes, afternoon work, Mass, Confession, a monthly trip to Pershore, stealing apples, flying pigeons, working, working, working.

Eventually, despite my and Davey Hopper's best efforts, Sylvia was sent for slaughter. It was the only time I had cried over a pig.

There were many more beatings for the Besford Boys, and many more hours spent standing on the punishment wall. My mate Eddie Boddy was left to stand on the punishment wall at 3pm one day and forgotten about. It wasn't until 4amthe next day that one of the masters realised poor Eddie was still standing on the wall. William Orange received the worst beating I witnessed, after he set fire to the tuck shop. 'They will not beat me again!' he said defiantly. But the fact was, they did, every time he stepped out of line.

By the time I reached 16, I had spent eight years at Sambourne and Besford Court, all because I had stolen a packet of cigarettes, played truant from school once or twice and, mainly, because teachers at St Benet's School in Sunderland thought I wasn't applying myself well enough to studies. One thing I did not know, and they did not know, then, was that I suffer from dyslexia. Eight years of my early life, my most impressionable years, spent in an institution where brutality was the byword for discipline and care was never on the agenda.

In February 1945 – two months before I was sent to Sambourne – I had been certified 'mentally deficient' by the Board of Education in Sunderland. The form carrying the words was Form 306 M entitled: 'Form of Report on Child examined for Mental Deficiency.' The form also included the words: 'Attention wanders, very easily led. Educationally retarded for both reading and arithmetic.'

Eight years later, my report from Besford Court, when I reached 16, put my IQ at 75. I could now do sums like an average eight-year-old. And they considered this progress. My leaving report did state that I had good practical skills, but added: 'Has shown himself to be unstable in character and is not averse to petty theft.'

Now standing 5 foot 4 inches, and weighing 7st 6lbs, I walked to the stores at Besford Court and was issued with one suit, a mackintosh, one vest and one pair of underpants, one pullover, one shirt and one collar stud, a tie, a pair of socks, a pair of shoes, a handkerchief and a pair of pyjamas, which came to a grand total of fourteen pounds, one shilling, and eight and three-quarter pence.

As I stood outside Besford Court, with my small case, waiting for transport to the railway station, I reflected on the past eight years and wondered what the future had in store for me. Here I was, a teenager approaching manhood who had picked up some labels on the way: 'mentally deficient', 'educationally sub-normal', 'backward' and 'retarded' were all words found in my school reports.

Young George Reynolds, it appeared, had a hell of a lot going for him.

CHAPTER 6

Sailor Boy

The homecoming was a welcoming one. My mother and father met me at Sunderland's railway station, which had been refurbished after it was bombed during the war, and they had with them, in a pram, the newest arrival to the Reynolds clan: my younger brother Peter.

When I walked down cobbled Cooper Street, little appeared to have changed in my home town, and in the house I was warmly embraced by my sister Cathy. Grandma and Granddad Tennick, too, had closed their shop for the day to make sure they were there to greet me.

After the welcoming and the long chats about what I had been doing at Besford – I said nothing about the cruelty, I didn't want to upset my mother – the family conversation turned to what I would do next.

From my boyhood days at the beach and right through Besford Court School, I had always expressed a wish to go to sea. I suppose sea salt was in the Reynolds' blood, what with my dad being a merchant seaman, a master rigger and having spent the war on a minesweeper in the Royal Navy. Even when at home in Sunderland, he was never far from the sea, running *The Windfall*, or taking a coble out of the north dock to catch our fish supper.

In the Merchant Navy I would see some of the world, broaden my horizons, meet new people, meet new challenges, and earn a wage. It had been the longest conversation I had held with my mother and father, and grandparents; they all thought I had reached a critical stage in my life. I had approached a kind of crossroads where the decision I made now would determine where I was in the future. It was decided I would apply to the Mercantile Marine School at Mill Dam, South Shields, which was about eight miles along the coast road from my home in Roker.

The first problem I encountered was completing the application form. I still could not read or write; but I overcame that particular obstacle by asking one of my mates to complete it for me.

The training course at Mill Dam lasted almost four months and only about sixty trainees would be taken on at a time, and only forty or so could expect to pass out to join the Merchant Navy. I had a burning desire to be one of the successful trainees, but knew from day one I was badly handicapped by not being able to read or write. The coursework, I would discover, involved a lot of writing. With my forged application submitted, I decided I could only cross that bridge – and it was a big bridge – when I came to it, and I waited to hear if I had been accepted.

In the summer months, my thoughts turned to a life at sea and, on land, my thoughts turned to girls. After eight years in boys' schools many miles from home, where I had never even seen a girl's ankle, my knowledge of sex was limited and my practical experience more limited still.

In Sunderland's Roker Park – and that's the park as opposed to the football ground – my first close sexual encounter came with a girl who appeared to know what she was talking about. She asked if I had ever seen a girl's breasts. I said no. She asked if I had ever French kissed. I told her I had never been to France. Then she asked me if I could come, and I asked her where we were going. She walked off towards Roker Avenue and I never saw her again.

Success came in the form of a knee-trembler in a cave at Marsden Grotto, as hundreds of kittiwakes nested in the cliffs above. The Sunderland girl – and I'll spare her blushes by not mentioning her name – was a real looker and it was not her first time. We strolled along the sands at Marsden, holding hands, and from the deserted beach we made our way into the cave. As with most young lads about to do it for the first time, I was very eager to get on with the job, but she was more interested in kissing. My jaws were aching by the time she allowed me to hitch up her skirt and get down to the real business. It was all over in 45 seconds, and just as I was revving up for another go, the tide came rushing into the cave and the poor lass started panicking. 'We're going to drown,' she cried. 'We're going to bloody drown.'

The tide came in very fast. It was amazing how quickly the cave had flooded with seawater. Being the gentleman I am, I carried the lass on my shoulders out of the cave and on to the beach. We made our way up the cliff stairs, the water dripping from my clothes, and the lass jumped on a bus heading for Sunderland town centre. She didn't even say goodbye.

I didn't have to wait long for an answer from the Maritime Training College and it was the answer I had dearly hoped for. I had been accepted on to the course at Mill Dam.

It was a bright autumnal morning when I set off on my dad's old boneshaker of a bicycle to follow the old Economic bus on its route along the coast to South Shields. It was quite a long journey, eight miles or so, and by the time I got to the school at Mill Dam, I was panting and sweating, but by no means exhausted.

Then the studying started.

Up on the blackboard went the names of all the knots and splices, the international flags, the rudiments of morse code and semaphore, our timetable and what was expected of us. At that moment I was hoping to be swallowed up by a hole in the ground.

I took my exercise book and a pencil from my bag, opened the book on my desk and started to doodle. Smiley faces, sad faces, the cow jumping over the moon.

Captain Smith, one of the tutors, walked between the desks, looking over pupils' shoulders to check their work. I put my shoulder and arm well over my exercise book, blocking out any invasive eyes. For a full two weeks I bluffed my way through. Saying nothing in class, never answering a question, but memorising the pictures we were shown of flags and diagrams of knots and splices, and going over them over and over again, parrot-fashion – much like learning the Catechism ten years earlier.

'There's a lot of written work on this course, Dad,' I said, after my first day at Mill Dam.

The old sea dog could see I was worried. 'Then we'll have to do something about that,' he said, as he stubbed a Woodbine in the ashtray and jumped to his feet.

'Where are you going, Dad?' I asked.

'I'll not be long, son,' he said.

Half an hour later my father came back threw six six-foot-long ropes on the floor of the sitting room and moved his armchair to face mine.

He grabbed one of the ropes. 'Right, son,' he said. 'Watch this.'

As quick as a flash my father tied a knot.

'This is a fixed loop, or a fisherman's loop,' he said. 'The name comes from the fact that many fishermen couldn't read or write. They would send it home to their girlfriend as a marriage proposal, with the two knots a little bit separated, and if it came back with the knots together, the answer was yes.'

He placed the knotted rope on the floor. 'Just because you can't read or write,' he said, 'that doesn't mean the answer has to always be no. I can't read or write, son.'

I thought of one of Mr Martin's ten rules: Never take no for an answer.

A tug here, a loop there. 'This is a bowline,' said my father, showing me another loop. 'And this is a bone-on-the-bite. A bowline is stronger, so he will always get to the top.' His fingers moved again, and he threw the rope on to the floor. 'And that, son, is a reef knot.'

For six hours that first night, my father showed me how to tie most of the knots and splices I would need to know in the Merchant Navy: Turk's head, sheepshank, round hitch, clove hitch, round turn, monkey's fist ... the list went on and we finished at well past midnight. But there was a lot more to do, a hell of a lot more.

For the first week of my course at Mill Dam my father and I, and Granddad Tennick, sat in the front room of our house in Cooper Street, and I learned to tie every knot and splice I would be taught to tie at the school. We spent six hours every night, after tea, practising the knots.

During the second week, my father blindfolded me and, by the end of that 14 days, I was able, even blindfolded, to tie every knot to perfection and with such speed and accuracy it seemed I was a natural seaman. I had inherited, it appeared, one of the Reynolds family traits: that of digital dexterity. We were practical people, the Reynoldses; doers rather than talkers.

I was also becoming proficient in the alphabet, at last, but not the English alphabet; I was still mixing up my letters for that. The alphabet I was becoming more familiar with was that of the International Marine Signal Flags, and much of that was due to Granddad Tennick, who would write the letters on the back of the flags, so I could memorise them.

He would lift each flag, reveal the letter he had printed on the back and then turn it over and show me the colour of the flag.

'A,' I would say. My granddad revealed the flag on the other side. 'When stationary, diver below,' I answered. 'B? I'm taking on or discharging explosives. C, affirmative or yes. D, keep clear of me, I am manoeuvring with difficulty. E, I am altering my course to starboard. F, I am disabled, communicate with me. G, I require a pilot.' And this would go on for many hours, virtually every night, until every letter of every flag was so well imprinted on my memory I could reel them off, one by one, without hesitation. In much the same way, at home, I memorised the semaphore flag signalling system.

On the first day of my third week on the course I cycled the same route to Mill Dam, arriving at the school at 9am. I sat at my desk, pulled out a pencil, and, as the tutor started writing on the board, I started doodling. A smiley face, a sad face, the cow jumping over the moon.

Captain Smith was staring over my shoulder. 'Reynolds,' he whispered in my ear. 'You and I need to have a chat today. See me in my office, after classes.'

After school I cycled a little way along the coast road, as if heading for home, then doubled back to see Captain Smith. I didn't want my fellow trainees knowing my difficulties.

I politely knocked on Captain Smith's office door. 'Come in.'

I entered his office and believed it was inevitable that the Captain, a former Royal Navy Captain, would have to throw me off the course.

'You can't read or write, Reynolds, can you?' he said.

'I can't, Sir,' I replied.

'Then how the hell did you manage to fill in your application form?'

'I didn't, Sir,' I said. 'One of my mates did it for me.'

'So. This is a forgery,' he said, as he laid my application form on his desk.

'Yes, it is, Sir,' I said.

'Then can you give me one sound reason why I shouldn't kick you off this course, and inform the authorities?'

'I can, Sir,' I said.

'Then let's hear it, Reynolds. Fire away,' said the Captain.

'I've never had a chance in my life to prove myself, Sir,' I said. 'This is the first real chance I've had. It's my only ambition to go to sea. I really, really want to join the Merchant Navy.'

'I can see your point, Reynolds,' he said. 'But I really need more than good intentions. I'll be putting my own head on the block if I overlook this.'

'I'll make an excellent seaman,' I said. 'And what's more I can prove it.'

'And just how do you propose to do that?' asked the Captain. 'You can't even read or write.'

'I can do every knot and splice in the *Bosun's Manual* blindfolded,' I said.

'Right then,' said the Captain. 'Show me.'

I followed the Captain out of the office and into one of the main teaching halls. He pushed two long tables together, grabbed six ropes from a cupboard, laid them all out on the tables, two feet apart, and placed a seat in front of the tables.

He sat down and I stood behind the tables, looking out on my audience of one.

'Right, Reynolds,' he said. 'Monkey's fist.'

I picked up the rope, made three turns around my

fingers, put a turn in between two fingers, made another three turns around the first three, tightened the knot a little, made a space in one of the loops with my index finger, pulled a marble from my pocket and put it in the hole, checked the turns, then fully tightened the knot and laid the rope on the table. And all the time, I did not take my eyes off the Captain's.

'A monkey's fist, Sir,' I said.

'Sheepshank,' said the Captain.

Within seconds I had tied the knot and laid it on the table. 'Sheepshank, Sir,' I said.

'Reef knot,' said the Captain.

I grabbed a rope. 'Fisherman's knot.'

I grabbed another. 'Turk's head.'

I grabbed a fifth. 'Two half hitches.'

I grabbed the sixth.

Captain Smith stood up from his seat, and walked the full length of the two tables, picking up each rope and examining each knot in minute detail. 'Excellent,' he said. 'Excellent. That was an amazing display, Reynolds. How have you learned all that so quickly?'

'My dad's been helping me at home, Sir,' I said. 'He's a master rigger, you know.'

Captain Smith, a respectable, intelligent and articulate man, whom I came to respect immensely, risked his own credibility to some extent by giving me a chance in life; my first real opportunity to prove myself.

And when it came to the two days of theory tests and two days of practical, I'm pleased to say I did not let him down. I was the only trainee to make the grade and obtain my blue discharge book on practical alone, having achieved a pass rate of at least 98 per cent in practical and zero on theory.

At the results day – our own kind of graduation day – Captain Smith forgot the old English resolve and stiff upper lip for a moment and embraced me. 'I am so proud of you, George,' he said. 'So proud.'

I was about to embark on my first career, a life on the ocean waves, and Captain Smith was to put a word in for me to be assigned my first ship. I was to follow not only in my own father's footsteps, but those of his father, too, and his father's father before him.

There was time to kill before I would be assigned to my first ship, and I started looking for a job to do. I applied to Simmons Furniture Store in Sunderland for a job on the lorries delivering furniture, and Mr Simmons was impressed by my enthusiasm. What he wasn't impressed by was my illiteracy. It cost me the job.

I waited for my first ship, and the opportunity to prove myself.

CHAPTER 7

The Street-fighter

I smacked him so hard in the face, I dislocated the knuckle at the base of the small finger on my right hand.

'Go on, George, hit him again,' said Tony Megeson, one of about thirty men standing around the old open-air market site at the rear of Jacky White's in Sunderland.

I approached my opponent again, and landed him the best shot I had, pulling my right arm right back, my crêpe-bandage-covered fist smashing into the middle of his face. The man, from Doncaster, who was built like a brick shithouse, barely moved, his face hardly flickered.

'Go on, George,' said Tony again. 'You've got him worried.'

Yes, I thought, worried in case he bloody kills me.

The mountain of a man hit me once, so hard I thought I'd been hit by a runaway train from platform 1 at the town's central station. The second time he punched I thought I was surrounded and I fell to the floor, the chimes of the town hall clock in Fawcett Street striking midnight and slowly counting down my drift into semi-consciousness.

When I pulled round, Tony was handing a fiver to the Doncaster man's mate, and Bobby Knoxall, the town's finest stand-up comedian, who had been holding my coat, was handing over a tenner.

'There goes the sodding rent for the week,' said Tony.

'And there goes almost a week's bloody wages,' said Bobby Knoxall, who worked on the barrows in the market before he got his big break on stage.

The Doncaster street-fighter and his mate headed towards the town centre and, as quickly as they had arrived, the spectators dispersed, most out of pocket, heading for Polly's, not far from the town's Vaux Brewery: a pub where there was no such thing as last orders and the only entertainment was the drunken brawls at chucky-out time.

I'd got into bare-knuckle street-fighting by accident really, filling in one night when an opponent failed to show and £12 was up for grabs to anyone who would take on a veritable giant from Barnsley. It was the punches to his solar plexus that gave me the prize money; I could hardly reach his face. After that, every hard case from the north of England wanted to have a go and, for a spell, at least in the back streets of Sunderland, I reigned supreme.

The town hall clock in Fawcett Street was itself at the centre of one of Sunderland's most well-known annual sporting events: the New Year's Eve race. More than a few pounds would change hands as the racers – and some of them were very, very fast – would, at the first stroke of midnight, run along Fawcett Street to Mackies Corner, on its junction with High Street West, back along Station Street, and aim to make it back to the town hall clock before the last stroke of midnight and the first seconds of a New Year. Hundreds of people lined the streets to watch the race and it continued for years, until the powers-that-be – in their short-sighted wisdom – demolished the town hall, built a new Civic Centre that resembled Alcatraz and lost, yes *lost*, the old town hall clock. It was found several years later, languishing in someone's back garden.

Street-fighting, watching the New Year's Eve race, pubbing, nightclubbing, thieving, scamming and breaking into shops were some of the main activities I enjoyed while on shore leave from the Merchant Navy, and one of my most hapless crimes was carried out at Mackies Corner.

A big jeweller's at Mackies Corner was the most popular in the town and when the store was closed people could still look at the trays of beautiful gold and silver rings, dazzling gems, sparkling gold chains and bracelets and the most elegant wristwatches available in the large shop window. It was always lit up, but, at night, covered with heavy locked metal grilles to ensure the window shoppers looked but did not touch.

'That tray 49's got a hell of a lot of signet rings on it. Look how heavy they are,' I said to one of the lads, as we passed the jeweller's window.

'Number 16 looks good,' he said. 'Them bracelets must be at least nine carrots.'

'It's carat,' I said. 'Not carrots.'

Myself and two of the lads – I'll not name them because we were never caught – managed to hot-wire an old Ford Zephyr – they were enormous cars Zephyrs – and hatched a plan which, we were sure, would give us riches beyond our wildest dreams, or at least enough for a few decent nights out on the town. We had identified all the trays we were after in the jeweller's window.

We stole a massive, six-foot-long, thick chain from one of the shipyards, modified the Zephyr's boot and welded the heavy chain, which had a huge hook on one end, to the back axle of the motor.

In the early hours of the morning, we pulled up at Mackies Corner, well tooled-up and fully prepared, both mentally and physically, for our audacious smash-and-grab. When we reached the corner of High Street West, me and an accomplice jumped out of the back of the Zephyr, the driver reversed to within a foot of the jeweller's window and we opened the boot, pulled out the hook and chain, and attached the hook, firmly, to the metal grille, behind which our trays shone into the night.

'Put your foot down!' I shouted to the driver, and as he stamped on the accelerator he slowly slipped his foot from the brake, and the Zephyr's front tyres went into wheelspin overdrive. The smell of burning rubber hit the night air, the Zephyr shot across High Street West doing 0 to 60 in about six seconds, the grille and the chain took the strain ... and pulled the back off the Zephyr which fell on to the road with a clank.

'Leg it!' shouted my masked accomplice, and I ran up to the car.

'We can't get away in that,' I said.

'I bet I can,' said the driver. 'Watch me.'

He put his foot down again, the front tyres went into wheelspin, and he sped off towards the bottom of High Street West, with more sparks coming off the rear of the Zephyr than you'd see from a welder's torch, and making so much noise the uniform duty inspector on nightshift at Gill Bridge Police Station would surely have his sleep disturbed.

As the unmistakable 'ding, ding, ding' of the Old Bill's bells cut the early morning mist, myself and my other mate legged it across Wearmouth Bridge. My shore leave was coming to an end, and soon I'd be many hundreds of miles away from Sunderland, frigging in the rigging.

After leaving the sea training school at Mill Dam, I'd seen a lot of the world in the last three or four years: Germany, the Suez Canal, the Panama Canal, Australia, Venezuela. I'd been around the world twice within nine months, first as a deckhand and then on a big tanker called the *Avonfield*.

I had moved up from deckhand to become the youngest petty officer – at the age of 21 – to set sail out of the River Tyne. That sailing was to Hamburg and I had thirty-three men under me, and they all took the piss, until they realised how well I could do the job.

My first ship, *The Broadhurst*, ran to Shoreham and it was while on shore leave from her in Poole, Dorset, that my skills as a sailor and swimmer were really put to the test, when a young lad on a bicycle fell into the drink in the harbour.

A few mates and I had stopped off for a pint or two and a bite of lunch in a pub called the Jolly Sailor before heading outside towards the jetty to see if we could chat up any local talent. I saw the young lad fall into the drink and dived in to save him. As the lad panicked, he was about to go under for the third time and I managed to grab a lifebelt that one of my mates had thrown into the water, put it around his head and back paddle towards the wall of the jetty. One of my mates threw me another rope and, as quick as a flash, I tied a bone and bite knot, which acts as a kind of seat, and the petrified young lad was winched to safety. I was left in the drink to fend for myself, and managed to clamber to the metal steps at the side.

A reporter and photographer arrived from a local paper and I was hailed a hero. I was just happy I was able to use some of the skills I had learned at the Maritime Training School to do some good.

From *The Broadhurst* I moved on, gaining my steering certificate, which enabled me to steer a 38,000-tonne tanker through the Suez Canal, and an 18,000-tonne tanker through the Panama. I could read the gyro-compass and the nautical compass and could even tell the Captain where we were just by looking at the stars.

I was proud of my achievements at sea, and thankful that I

had seen so much of the world, but, when on shore leave, I always craved the kind of excitement that can only be offered to someone free to roam dry land, not tied to the deck of a ship or the confines of a small cabin.

As the mid- to late Fifties kicked in, when ladies' skirt lengths went up, when everyone seemed to have a job and plenty of cash in their pockets, and we were all being told we'd never had it so good, I seemed to have drifted from my old mates Davey Hall, Billy Freckleton, Jimmy Dodds, Dicky Maguire and the rest from the old Bungalow Cafe gang days.

Davey, and some of the rest, were Teddy Boys, and they'd walk along the promenade at Seaburn and Roker, their bright Edwardian drape coats flowing in the sea breeze, but the breeze having no impact on their heavily-greased, heavily-coiffured quiffs, thick with Brylcreem, and their drainpipe trousers strangling their ankles.

Me, I was more of an early Mod than a rocker, preferring sharp, dark suits – from London's Savile Row if I could get them – crisp, clean, white shirts, thinly-knotted ties and very sharp, highly-polished winklepickers.

As Davey and his new mates posed on the promenade, I would be walking through the town centre, drop into Louis Milk Bar in Crowtree Road for a shake or pop into the Park Inn in Park Lane for a swift half.

Nightclubs sprang up across town: Club 11 in Villiers Street, the La Strada, Weatheralls and, down at the seafront in Roker, the Ro Ko-Ko, which attracted some top-name acts at the time.

It was at this time that I came across the first copper – and he was the first of many – who took it upon himself to see that Petty Officer George Reynolds, of his parish, would be put behind bars for his many misdemeanours – providing he could be caught. The copper's name was Detective Inspector Graham Bimingham Knott. Where he got his middle name from, I don't know, but the lads and myself assumed he had been conceived in the West Midlands city.

My first run-in with Det Insp Knott was over some minor, petty offence of criminal damage, which I denied, which revolved around a grass monkey.

My cabin mate in the Merchant Navy was well into exotic pets, and claimed to have all the outlets where they could be sold, if we could smuggle them into the country. He once tried to smuggle an eight-foot-long snake, but it caused such pandemonium on board it had to be killed and thrown overboard. He successfully smuggled canary birds and a chimpanzee the size of a gorilla.

We picked up a grass monkey each and mine proved to be a bit of a handful. My mother adored the monkey, but it was so mischievous we had to get rid of it. First, I sold it for £10 to a pal, who brought it back because it was always trying to mate with his cat. Then I sold it to a donkey owner at Seaburn beach, and it would sit on the head of the donkey as children were taken on rides across the sand. Very popular, it proved to be.

The incident involving the monkey which landed me in the cells happened in Cooper Street, when it broke free from its chain on the front wall outside the house, picked up a ball-bearing and hopped along the street, smashing up a lot of windows as it went.

At the station I followed the drill: taking off my belt, tie and winklepicker shoes, then placing them outside the cell door. I didn't sleep well, and the next morning Det Insp Knott decided to release me without charge, but as I put my shoes, tie and belt back on he ordered me to back into the cell, leaving the door open, and told me to scrub the floor on my hands and knees. I decided to do as ordered; there could have been consequences if I didn't.

For up to two hours, on my bended knees, I scrubbed the floor clean and, when I had finished and stood up, the toes on my Italian-designer-type sharp winklepickers were the curliest I had ever seen. By this time knackered, and rather humiliated, I left the station and made my way to Louis Milk Bar. As I walked along Crowtree Road, young children walking with their parents were pointing down at my shoes and giggling.

In Louis I ordered a coffee and spotted Tony Megeson sitting at a table. I went over to sit next to him.

'How are you doing, Tony?' I asked.

'I'm fine, Ali Baba,' he said. 'Where's the forty thieves?'

Tony said it loud enough for the rest of the people in the cafe to hear, so I left my coffee and headed home. I had been the subject of ridicule because of my shoes. Perhaps Det Insp Graham Knott had set out for that to happen. If he did, he had gone up in my estimation, and keeping one step ahead of him – wearing curly winklepickers or not – was a task I decided to set myself in my life of crime ahead.

It was at this time, too, that I met and married my first wife, Emily, a good Sunderland lass. We had our first child, Catherine, and settled into a nice flat in Cooper Street, not far from my mother's old house, and my parents were obviously hoping that I would settle down to married life, keep my nose clean and try to find a decent job.

But now that I was out of the Merchant Navy, I was finding it difficult acclimatising to life on Civvy Street. Few employers wanted to take on someone whose only track record was at sea, and who could not read or write.

But I knew I had the ability to do business and I had a head full of ideas. I decided to branch out into self-employment with the help of my uncle, George McDonald, a wheeler-dealer from Dock Street East who was also full of money-making ideas but who always lacked the capital to invest.

We put our ideas in motion and invested my capital, heading for the market places across the north-east where we knew shoppers had an eye for a bargain.

CHAPTER 8

Not Even Five Bob

The quayside market at Newcastle was heaving with people, as George McDonald and I set out our stall next to the gleaming barrow which had spoke wheels so bright and shiny you would think they had just been painted silver.

On the tabletop George placed a porcelain basin and a large jug, as I set out, neatly, row upon row of little brown envelopes containing the product that we knew would amaze shoppers and earn us both a handsome wage.

'Ladies and gentlemen!' I shouted. 'Please gather round.'

'Here, for the first time today, we have an incredible new product, so amazing that we have been offered huge sums of money by a well-known pharmaceutical company to sell them the patent.'

A small crowd gathered and listened.

'But we have turned down their offer,' I said, 'because we wanted to bring this fantastic new product direct to the people.'

'Get on with it!' shouted a man in the crowd.

Slowly, I picked up one of the little brown envelopes and picked out a small cube, the size of a sugar cube.

'This, ladies and gentlemen,' I said, 'is the wonder cube, and it will revolutionise wash days in a way you will find hard to believe.'

George poured water from the jug into a glass. I spotted a pretty young girl in the crowd and handed her the glass.

'Water,' I said. 'Nothing but cold, clear water.'

The girl sipped the water from the glass and nodded her head in acknowledgement.

'Now, Sir,' I said, pointing to a well-dressed, middle-aged man in the crowd, wearing a tweed jacket with a white handkerchief protruding from his top pocket.

'That is a clean handkerchief, isn't it, Sir?' I asked, as I pulled it from his pocket and handed him a pound note. 'And there is a pound for your trouble,' I said.

With a theatrical flourish I dropped the handkerchief on to the cobbled street and stamped on it, twisting it into the ground.

'Madam,' I said, pointing to a young woman with child in tow. 'What are the worst stains to remove?'

'I don't know,' she said. 'Probably grease or oil.'

'Grease or oil. You've got it in one, Madam,' I said.

I took hold of the now grubby handkerchief and ran it around the hub and spokes of the wheelbarrow, lifted it up by two corners and showed it to the crowd, which by now had grown to about fifty people.

'Observe,' I said, placing the cube into the porcelain dish as George poured the clear, cold water from the jug over it. I dropped the handkerchief into the water, rubbed two ends of the handkerchief vigorously together and the water suddenly came to a thick white head of soapy foam.

I slowly pulled the handkerchief from the water, unravelled it fully and displayed the brilliant white square piece of cloth to the open-mouthed crowd.

'Eeeh!' said a woman. 'That's bloody marvellous, that is.'

'Now,' I said, 'have you ever seen anything look so white and clean?'

I picked up one of the small envelopes. 'In these packets,' I said, 'there are four wonder cubes. And are we asking for ten bob a packet? No, we're not. Are we asking for eight shilling a packet? No, Madam, we're not. That's right, Madam, we're not asking for even five bob. Not even five bob a packet. All we want is half a crown for a packet of four. Do we have any buyers?'

Scores of hands shot into the air.

The wonder cube had started life as a massive box of soda soap in a ship's chandlers in Newcastle which George and I had spotted one day. We only went into the shop to get out of the rain. The five-foot-long box of soda soap, used to clean the decks on ships, was weeping and the chandler was only too happy to flog it to us for ten quid. It had been in the shop for years and he couldn't get rid of it.

Back at George's house in Dock Street East we used a chipping machine to cut the soda soap down into narrow strips and cut it down again into small cubes. We borrowed the spoked wheelbarrow and cleaned it until it shone like a mirror, and then added the finishing touch: soft green soap – a little like Swarfega, in use today – into the hubs and spokes on the barrow's gleaming wheels. The scam worked a treat, and George and I covered many markets in the north-east: Sunderland, Seaham, South Shields, Stockton, the lot.

Our next scam involved a job lot of hundreds of shirts and, as in each of our enterprises, it was me who had to stump up the £50 to put it into operation. The shirts were all seconds because they were all the same collar size, but we were able to shift them with a little cunning and a stamp that went from a 14inch collar right up to about 20 inches.

We'd visit all the markets in our van and George would start his spiel, persuading shoppers they had the opportunity for a real bargain, and the crowds would gather. I'd sit in the back of the van with the stamp and as soon as he shouted at the collar length – bang, bang. Job done.

It was approaching Christmas and the shirts were popular with shoppers, particularly the miners' wives at the markets in and around the colliery villages such as Seaham and Murton, and further afield. The shirts could have been ideal Christmas presents, but they weren't. The backs were longer than the fronts, or vice versa, the arms too short or too long, and the collar too tight to fasten or too loose. My uncle George and I were making quite a lot of money.

The best money could always be made at the big events that attracted thousands of people, and two of the biggest annual events in the north-east were the Durham Miners' Gala and the seafront illuminations at Sunderland. For the Gala we managed to obtain a very old, box-type, pinhole, instamatic-style camera and hundreds of old rolls of film, so old they were in danger of self-combusting. The punters complained that in their portraits they looked like nothing more than negatives, but we urged them to give it time. The film would develop by the time they arrived home, we told them, knowing that, by that time, we would be home ourselves with their money. For the seafront illuminations we made meat pies in George's kitchen and sold them along the seafront. They started off as three-quarters mince and a quarter barley, then half mince and half barley, then a quarter mince and three-quarters barley and, finally, virtually all barley. We didn't last long in the pie business.

Another money-making enterprise involved 2,000 cartons of golden crunchy peanuts which would pop out of the box when the front was pressed. We sold these along with packets of Mayfair toffees, and the customers were keen to snap them up. The peanuts looked mouthwatering, but were really putrefied and when the box was open they gave off such a rancid smell it was nauseating. The punters, forever in search of a bargain, still bought them.

My daytime ducking-and-diving gave way to night-time bobbing and weaving in a small coble I rowed out from the north dock at Roker to just beyond the pier where I would meet up with a ship bringing its cargo into Sunderland. The ships, mainly Polish, would be loaded with cartons of Chesterfield or Lucky Strike cigarettes, watches and all sorts of other consumer goods for which there was a ready-made market. I stored the cartons of cigarettes in the chimney breast at the flat in Cooper Street, wedging them in tightly with lengths of wood. We had electric heating in the flat, so I wasn't to know that my wife Emily would light the open fire. Hundreds of cigarettes went up in smoke and the smoking population on the Barbary Coast got their biggest free nicotine fix just by walking along the seafront and inhaling the sea air.

My daytime and night-time activities had not gone unnoticed by the local constabulary and the men from the Customs and Excise Department, but, thankfully, I was always one step ahead of the law. Even the most innocent of remarks, however, can land you in trouble and, on one of the many visits to my home by Detective Inspector Knott and his colleagues, an innocent remark from my baby daughter, Catherine, who was just learning to speak, landed me in hot water.

In the flat I stored the smuggled watches in loaves of bread, pulling the soft bread from the middle of a crusty loaf, stuffing the watches inside and sticking the crust back on. Det Insp Knott and his colleagues turned the flat over one night and could not find a thing, until little Catherine, in all her innocence, remarked: 'Tick tocks, in the bread. Tick tocks, in the bread.' I was up before the local beak before you could say 'Accurist', and fined.

My wife Emily, like most wives, just wanted a quiet life. The visits to our flat by the police and my best endeavours at the markets and night-time smuggling was not the life she had envisaged when we were married. She did not relish the thought of being married to the last pirate on the Barbary Coast, with all the uncertainty that such a relationship entailed.

I went in search of gainful, legitimate employment and saw a chap called Billy Wright, who managed to get me a job at the local Vaux Brewery, delivering booze around the pubs on a dray wagon. I liked the work and believe I could have hacked it full time if I hadn't been spotted by two local police officers humping crates of beer into the Park Inn. Word soon got back to my employers about my criminal activities and I was instantly dismissed.

The only real skill I had, for which I had trained hard, was rigging, so I joined the sailor gang touring the thirty-nine shipyards and ship repair yards lining the River Wear, working at J.L. Thompsons, Austin and Pickersgills, Bartrams, Shorts, Doxfords.

When a ship was launched in Sunderland it was the kind of event that attracted hundreds of people to the banks of the River Wear – people who were proud of the hard labour and skills that went in to building ships. A member of the royal family or some local bigwig dignitary would crack the bottle of champagne against the ship's hull – as the band struck up – to launch the vessel and a great cheer would emanate from the massive crowd. It was always a very proud moment for the town, the launch of a ship.

I attended several launches and one sticks in my mind, from when I was a member of the sailor gang, standing on a platform near the ship's hull. It sticks in my mind because the bottle hurled against the ship veered to the left and struck me on the head, leaving me concussed and with a bump the size of a duck egg. That might sound far-fetched, but it happened.

At Austin and Pickersgills yard, I had the pleasure of working on one of the first – if not the first – private yachts built on the River Wear. If I remember rightly it was called *The Rhondo* and was built for the Onassis family.

On its first sea trials the luxurious yacht's forecastle was too far out of the water, so pig iron had to be installed in the front to keep its nose down. I helped load the pig iron and carved my initials, GR, on the back of the porthole-type door which was bolted to the back of a panel. A big picture was placed over the porthole.

When my mates and I walked home from the Rink nightclub, across Wearmouth Bridge, I would often look down at the yacht in its moorings and, like most people earning a crust on the daily work treadmill, dream of owning such a yacht myself. It was a magnificent vessel, rivet-built rather than welded, and, in the midst of the dirt and grease of the shipyards, it shone like a beacon.

Working nine to five and earning an honest wage gave me the respectability and normality that Emily so craved, but the lure of ill-gotten gains and the thrill of the chase were never far from my mind. I drifted back into crime, and it cost me my marriage. I couldn't blame Emily for that. I couldn't expect her to live with the uncertainty of not knowing where I was and what I was up to, and the inevitability that I would end up behind bars while she was expected to cope alone.

Not long after the break-up of our marriage came my first taste of porridge: six months for larceny. It was a crime I did not commit, but it was expedient to put my hands up and do the time as it gave me the perfect alibi for a more audacious and profitable crime that I did carry out, which earned me £6,000. Admitting the larceny meant I could not have been in the area at the time of the bigger crime. I would do the time, then plan a better future.

For the bigger crime – details of which would be foolish to divulge – I stood to get sent down for six years. For the larceny it would be a maximum of six months. It all made perfect sense. I had fallen in love with a beautiful girl who was a window dresser for the upmarket Books Fashions store in Sunderland, and just before my appearance at court and the inevitable jail sentence I met up with her in the Bizz Bar in the town's Crowtree Road. She was dressed in a smart, fashionable, two-piece pinstriped suit and her raven-black hair was swept up in a sculpted beehive style. She looked a million dollars.

As she sat opposite me, sipping her coffee, I pulled out six grand in a big envelope from my inside pocket and told her I had to go away. She burst into tears. I asked her to keep hold of the cash and told her that, when I came out after six months, we could buy a brand new Ford Zephyr and a nice little Bungalow in Roker. There was no comforting her, the poor lass was heartbroken.

'Will you wait for me?' I asked.

'Of course I'll wait for you,' she said, wiping away her mascara-stained tears. 'I love you.'

We said our painful goodbyes and I walked along to the court, savouring my last few moments of freedom.

During my first six-month stint at Her Majesty's Pleasure, in Durham Prison, the lass visited me twice in the first two weeks, and the love letters, in which she poured out her heart, kept coming thick and fast. 'I will love you until the desert turns to ice and the camels come skating home,' she wrote. It was gratifying to think that this beautiful, vivacious girl, with the model figure and sultry looks, would be waiting for me on the outside. But the visits, and the letters, became less frequent.

I was not a model prisoner and, being so young and it being my first time inside, I ended up on the chokey block, in solitary confinement, restricted to bread and water, for comparing the prison Governor to the men who served in the Nazi SS. All the Governor wanted was an apology, but my stubbornness kicked in, and I refused to apologise. Hindsight is a wonderful thing and I know now that I was wrong, but at that age I thought I was invincible and could take anything the prison authorites threw at me.

I did survive the chokey block. I thought they intended to break me and I was adamant I would not give in. I served a total of 21 days in solitary confinement, with a day's break after each three days to go on normal diet. I tried every desperate measure I could to make my time in solitary more bearable, from imagining my bread tasted like chicken – surprisingly I was able to convince myself it did – to befriending a mouse who popped into the cell from time to time.

And all the time, in my naivety, I mistook bravado for courage, demonstrating to the prison warders that they could throw whatever they wanted at me, but they wouldn't break me. Perhaps they didn't want to break me at all, they just wanted me to apologise to the Governor. When my 21 days were up they could hold me no more and, although I had lost weight and looked pale, I saw it, in my young eyes, as a personal victory. Now, I know, it was nothing more than a pyrrhic victory, equal to defeat.

The six months, with no time off for good behaviour, passed remarkably quickly and, when I arrived back in Sunderland, I made my way to Books Fashion Store, stood outside the window, and there she was, dressing a mannequin in the latest designer outfit.

I tapped on the window and smiled. 'I'll see you in the Bizz Bar in ten minutes,' I mouthed.

Over a cup of coffee the lass broke down in tears.

'I'm in love,' she said.

'I know you are, sweetheart,' I said. 'We both love each other.'

'No,' she said. 'What I mean is, I'm in love with someone else. He's a footballer.'

The penny, a very bad penny, dropped.

'Where's my money?' I asked, and she told me there was only a few hundred pounds left. After dropping the bombshell she got up to leave the cafe and for a moment I imagined she would run back into my arms and beg for forgiveness. She didn't. She just left the cafe.

For the rest of the afternoon I drowned my sorrows in the Park Inn and at about 5pm I walked along to Fawcett Street to catch a bus home. It was pissing down with rain. As I stood waiting for the bus, a brand new red Ford Zephyr passed with a fit-looking bloke at the wheel and the lass in the passenger seat waved. It was the lass from Books Fashions.

After a bout of depression which lasted all of two hours, I picked myself up.

I spent the next few weeks looking for jobs, legitimate and illegitimate, and managed to secure a good job at the town's Wearmouth Colliery as an assistant to a shot firer. The job gave me access to something which would enable me to carve out an explosive new career ... dynamite.

CHAPTER 9

The Safe-Cracker

Vincent Francis Luvaglio, a swarthy, black-haired conman of Italian extraction, was headed north on the A1 and his big shiny American Cadillac was turning a few heads on the motorway. Luvaglio had been involved with the Kray twins in London, installing the latest money-making 'entertainment' machines, one-armed bandits, which took sixpences or 'tanners'. Many of the machines were American imports, but were easily converted from taking dimes.

Luvaglio was heading north to new territory. He had effectively been given the nod by the Krays to start out on his own in the north, somewhere like Scotland, but was to maintain a link with the London side of the business.

As he shifted gear after taking a roundabout on the A1 near Doncaster, he noticed three young girls in the back seat of a fifty-two-seater coach, admiring his motor. They were good-looking girls, he thought, and one in particular stood out from the rest, a dark-haired beauty with the type of inviting come-on eyes that said, 'Try me'. Looking out of the rear window of the coach, the girls waved and Luvaglio, maintaining as cool a persona as possible, lifted his sunglasses to look, placed them back on his nose and waved back. Then he put his foot down to overtake, and looked at the coach destination board. 'Sutherland,' he said to himself. 'That'll do me.'

He slowed down, so the coach would overtake, and decided to follow it north to its destination. Sutherland, which he knew was somewhere in Scotland, was as good a place as any to lay his hat, he thought. As the Cadillac clocked up the miles, the girls in the rear of the coach still looked, waved and smiled, and Luvaglio waved and smiled back.

At Scotch Corner the coach pulled into a service station, and Luvaglio followed. Within 15 minutes the dark-eyed girl had been wooed and shagged, and was sitting in the front passenger seat of his Cadillac. They followed the coach – it still had the girl's case on board – and Luvaglio learned he had misread its destination. It wasn't headed for Sutherland, the girl told him, it was destined for her home town of Sunderland. 'Never heard of it,' Luvaglio said.

Luvaglio, who later changed his name to Landa, managed to get ensconced with the girl in a flat in Sunderland, and during their first two weeks together they visited the Gilley Law Working Men's Club in the town.

'Where's the bandits?' Luvaglio asked his young girlfriend.

'What's bandits?' she asked.

All Luvaglio could see then was pound signs. He may have entered Sunderland, but to him he had come across the promised land. It was the start of the gaming wars, which would see him build up a multi-million-pound gambling empire.

At this time, a future business associate of Luvaglio's, Dennis Stafford, who was born in the East End of London in 1933, was making British criminal history by becoming the first prisoner on special watch to escape from Dartmoor Jail. He later served time with John McVicar, the first man credited with escaping from the tough Durham Prison. But in the McVicar case, the history books had got it wrong.

Safe-blower Ronnie Heslop, of Page Bank, County Durham, was doing time in Durham Prison for blowing a couple of safes. He'd been sentenced to three years and, at the age of 26, Ronnie, who, like me, learned how to deal with explosives in the mines – Brancepeth Colliery, among others – had managed to dig an eight-inch-wide hole in his cell wall using nothing more than a spoon. There was a cavity between his cell wall, which was two-foot thick, and an outer wall, also two-foot thick, and when he chipped away at the outer wall with his trusty spoon, his second eight-inch hole was slightly out of sync with the first. His cellmate was hoping to escape with him, but was too fat to squeeze through the holes. Somehow, Ronnie managed it. Bending his obviously pliable body this way and that, he squeezed himself through the two small holes, scaled the prison wall and headed home to Page Bank.

He became known as Ronnie 'Rubber Bones' Heslop.

After a few days, Rubber Bones was caught by the police, hiding under the floorboards of a neighbour's home in Page Bank. Someone had grassed him up. On top of his three years, he was given nine months for the escape and spent much of it in solitary. Frankie Fraser was in Durham at the time, and he and Ronnie would often be the only prisoners on special watch, walking the exercise yard.

Ronnie had a few years on me handling explosives, but my work as an assistant shot firer at Wearmouth Colliery, watching the shot firer work, helping him, handing him the explosives and, occasionally, blasting the coalface myself, gave me the experience, the expertise and the know-how to be confident handling dynamite and explosives such as Ajax and

Unigel. It was nice of the National Coal Board to help me train for a new, and what would turn out to be lucrative, career.

One of my heroes was Eddie Chapman, a first-rate safe-blower who was a double-agent during World War II. He came from Sunderland, too.

My first safe jobs were small affairs: an office here, a north-eastern Co-op there. I was gradually feeling my way through, getting used to handling explosives, finding out the best sources for the material and deciding who, if anyone, I should work with. I did one or two jobs with George 'Blower' Shotton from Newcastle; he was quite an expert in the field.

One of the Co-op jobs, in a County Durham town, turned out to be a bit of a Robin Hood affair. Me and a pal had gone out to screw a post office, which was also a general dealer's, but when we jemmied the door and got inside, there was sweet fuck all on the shelves. The post-office-cum-shop was run by a woman who had, apparently, just lost her husband. It was just before Christmas. Feeling really sorry for this woman, my pal and I screwed a Co-op store instead, and many of the goods we thieved we took over to the post office and stacked the woman's shelves. I can only imagine what her reaction would have been the following morning. Perhaps she thought Christmas had come early.

A big job approached and a pal and I cased the target; a big office block in the centre of Newcastle which, we had heard, had three large safes, and within each was a large brown envelope containing wads of cash. The information had come our way through someone on the inside. It was just the right type of job for us; we liked screwing the big companies, rather than the little corner shops. The big companies robbed us all, anyway; but rather than a crowbar, detonators and a stick of gelignite, they used pens and paper.

We got into the big office no problem, and I laid my little

tool kit on the floor. Detonators, explosives, wire, a screwdriver, pliers and a little pen-shaped torch. Any safe, of course, can be opened with explosives, but I always found the trick was to use just enough explosive to open the safe, and not attract too much attention. All prepared, my pal and I sat back, well away from the safe, and I tripped the detonator switch. The tumblers purred like a kitten, it was real poetry in motion, and then I knew there was artistry in these fingers; a little like the artistry through dexterity I had displayed when tying the knots at the sea training school in South Shields. The other two safes opened just as easily.

My pal and I decided to head for our hideout, but he was so untrusting he insisted we did not open the big brown envelopes until we got there.

As I drove south, he kept the parcels tightly clutched to his chest.

'There must be £500 in each of these,' he said, as we crossed the Tyne Bridge. 'That's £750 each. Not a bad night's work.'

I joined the A1, and we passed the big service station at Birtley. 'There must be a grand in each of these,' my pal said. 'That's one-and-a-half grand each.'

We reached the County Durham border, the Land of the Prince Bishops, and I kept my speed at a steady 70mph. I didn't want to attract any attention from the patrol cops.

'There must be at least five grand in each of these,' my pal said. 'That's seven-and-a-half each.'

'Shut the fuck up!' I said. 'We'll soon find out how much is in them. You're getting on my fucking nerves.'

We arrived at our destination and, in the old shed on an allotment site, we started a small fire on a stove and sat and opened the envelopes one by one.

'Fucking hell. What's this?' my pal said. 'There's no fucking money in this one.' He pulled out a number of photographs, pornographic photographs, which appeared to show a man in a suit, his trousers down around his ankles, shagging a woman doggy style over a photocopying machine. 'The dirty sod,' my pal said.

'Here, we've been bloody robbed,' he said.

'No,' I said. 'They've been robbed.'

The other two envelopes did contain some cash, but not as much as we had hoped.

'I'm going to blackmail this sod,' my pal said.

'You're not,' I said, and I grabbed the photos and threw them on to the fire.

There were many other safe jobs, all across the country, not just in my home territory, and there was one job in particular where I got the biggest shock of my life, and it wasn't when the safe had blown.

I had travelled to the outskirts of Sunderland with two others to do a safe at a big factory. We were well tooled up and we all scaled a 20-foot-high security fence. We landed safely on the other side in a field, and the two lads urged me to move forward. It was very dark, and the light from the full moon was intermittently blacked out by thick, rain-filled clouds sweeping across it. We slowly moved forward, unable to see anything in front of us or behind.

Suddenly, there was a strange noise, like a low, deep, growl, and we could see the silhouette of an animal in front of us, but couldn't make out exactly what it was.

'It's a cow,' said one of the lads.

'It couldn't be a cow,' I said. 'It's got a head on it twice the size of a pit pony.'

'It's got to be a bull,' said the other lad. 'Go and give it a kick, and it'll scarper.'

'No way,' I said. 'Hand me the torch.'

He handed me the torch and there, right in front of me, stood a huge lion. I froze.

'Don't move,' said one of the lads, who had managed to

flee and, with our other partner in crime, had climbed the fence to safety.

'Don't move,' he added. 'If you move it will go for you.'

But I did move, as fast as my legs could take me, and scaled the fence within seconds, jumping the 20 foot drop on the other side.

'You weren't much cop,' I said to the lads.

We walked a few yards down the road, and I shone the torch on a sign above us. 'Lambton Lion Park', it read. The factory we were after, we discovered, was further down the road, but after the shock of the lion park, we decided to call it a night.

There were many other safe jobs, some for which I was given time and others for which I was never convicted, such as a job in Scotland that earned me and a pal £12,000, and another when a cat sat on top of the safe and wouldn't budge. It sharp shifted when the dynamite ignited and went hurtling around the walls and ceiling. Thankfully it was shocked but uninjured

It was inevitable that, sooner or later, I would be caught on a job. It happened when someone had broken into an explosives shed at a colliery site in County Durham, thieving detonators and explosives. I appeared in court charged with handling the explosive. I denied the offence, but was convicted and sentenced to six months in prison.

I was sent, again, to Durham Jail.

CHAPTER 10

The Prisoner

The cell door opened and – clutching his blanket, a mug, his shaving gear and a toothbrush – in walked Ronnie 'Rubber Bones' Heslop. I had heard a lot about him, but it was the first time we had met. Ronnie, just off special watch and into the last six months of his sentence, was to serve out the rest of his time with me and a lad who stood about 6 feet 4 in his stockinged feet. We called him Big Stu.

Big Stu was a worrier, and he couldn't take his mind off what his missus might be doing on the outside. He would worry even more if he didn't receive a letter every day, and today he hadn't received a letter.

As we settled down for the night – Ronnie taking the bunk to the left of me, Big Stu on his bunk above me – we talked about the various courses available which would help us wile away the time.

'There's all kinds we could do,' said Ronnie. 'There's a course on electrical engineering, another on motor mechanics, there's even one on current affairs. Personally, I wouldn't mind trying my hand at pottery, I could make our lass a nice set of Toby jugs.'

'You're a bit handy with clay then, are yer?' I asked Ronnie.

'Aye,' he said. 'But I can't say I've ever had a go on the potter's wheel. I just used to make little models out of clay with my hands. You know, little farm animal figures and that for the bairns, like. They used to call it Old McDonald's Farm. Even made them a little tractor, I did, all from clay, like.'

'What about you, Stu. Do you fancy owt?' Ronnie asked.

'I couldn't give a flying fuck,' said Stu.

'Ignore him,' I said. 'He's got a monk on, 'cos their lass hasn't sent him a letter today.'

'Have you got kids?' Ronnie asked Stu.

'Aye. I've got three,' he replied.

'Why, man, you don't want to worry about your lass. She's got her bloody hands full there,' said Ronnie. 'What with feeding the bairns, making their meals, doing the washing and ironing, dropping them off at school, picking them up from school, putting them in the bath. She'll have no time for herself, poor lass.'

Big Stu fell silent, reading the print off yesterday's *Daily Mirror*. Ronnie and I stared at the walls.

'It always puts my mind at rest if I get a letter,' said Stu. 'It's not that I don't trust her. It's just, well, you know, it's nice to know she's thinking about me, like.'

'Do you really think she's got the time to sit down and compose a letter for you every day?' asked Ronnie. 'Why, man, the lass'll be run off her feet. She'll have enough on her plate without worrying about you.'

'I fancy that pottery lark,' I said. 'I reckon I could make a vase, one of them big milk jugs, or something like that.' I looked at the clock. 'Half past six,' I said. 'They'll all be getting ready to go down the club now; putting their make-up on in the mirror and that.'

Big Stu and Ronnie fell silent again. Seven o'clock arrived.

'They'll be in the club now,' I said. 'Ordering their first drinks, setting out the table with cheese, crisps, pickled onions and pickled eggs.'

Big Stu and Ronnie didn't say a word. Ten o'clock arrived.

'They'll all be well oiled now,' I said. 'Up on the dance floor, doing the jive, the lasses flashing their knickers.'

'You'd better shut the fuck up, Reynolds,' said Big Stu.

We all fell silent for a while.

'It's chucky-out time now,' I said. 'They'll all be going to their homes or someone else's for a quick leg-over. She'll be licking his bollocks and feeding him grapes.'

'That's it, you fucking bastard!' shouted Big Stu, and he jumped from his bunk, grabbed me by the throat and pulled me out of my bunk, pinning me to the wall. 'I'll fucking kill yer. I'll fucking kill yer!'

'Hit him with the fucking piss-pot! Hit him with the fucking piss-pot!' I shouted, but Rubber Bones was protecting himself, curled up in a ball on his bunk.

Quickly, I managed to squeeze myself under my bunk, but Big Stu pulled my mattress from the bed, put his hands through the springs and tried to strangle me.

Ronnie hit the alarm bell and the screws came racing in, putting the boot in. It was a good half hour before order was restored, and that wasn't until Big Stu was moved to another cell.

'Fucking hell,' said Ronnie. 'Did you have to wind him up that much? I hope she sends him a bloody letter tomorrow.'

Ronnie and I soon got another cellmate – it was always three to a cell in those days – and it wasn't long before we started the pottery classes. Ronnie turned out to be a bit of a dab hand on the potter's wheel. There was about four potter's wheels in the class, and I wasn't very good at using it, so I was put in charge of the oven, or kiln, and when the prisoner had finished his piece of work, he would hand it to me, under the close eyes of a prison warder, and I'd set the oven to the right temperature and time, put the piece of clay in, shut the door and fire it.

Ronnie had an awful habit, which used to annoy me, of humming, in tedious monotone, Bach's 'Air on the G String', while he pressed the pedals on the wheel and sculpted his piece of clay. I suppose it helped his concentration, but it didn't half get my back up.

He'd get his piece of clay, sit at the wheel, pour a little water over the clay, then as soon as his feet started moving on the pedals, he'd be away: 'Bom, bom, bom, bom; bom, bom, bom, bom; de, de, de, de, de, de, de, de, diddle, de; de-dee.' I only knew the tune myself because of the cigar advert on the telly.

The first piece he brought to me for firing was a Dick Turpin Toby Jug. I put it in the oven, it came out well formed, and for the rest of the class Ronnie sat at a table with a small brush, patiently painting it in the finest of detail. As we walked back to our cell, he held it out in front of him, beaming like a Cheshire cat. He'd done a remarkable job. I suppose I was a bit envious.

Before the next pottery class got under way, I'd discovered that if a small piece of asbestos happened to find its way into the oven it would knack it. I decided to intervene in Ronnie's next project: a Toby Jug of Barnacle Bill. I pulled a small piece of asbestos from the lagging around the pipes in the toilet and secreted it away in the turn-ups of my prison-issue strides.

The next class started, and Ronnie, looking very pleased with himself, got hold of a piece of clay, sat at the potter's wheel and started pedalling, watering the clay and moulding it into shape: 'Bom, bom, bom, bom; bom, bom, bom, bom; de, de, de, de, de, de, de, de, diddle-de; de, dee.' He was getting right on my nerves. After crafting the Toby Jug into shape, using a small tool to shape the eyes, nose and mouth, he carried it over to me sitting at the oven, looking smug and pleased with himself, and I placed it in the kiln, set it to the right time and sat a few yards away.

'What are you sitting there for?' Ronnie asked.

'Just getting a different perspective on the room,' I said. 'Besides, it gets bloody hot beside that oven, you know.'

The minutes ticked away and as Ronnie worked a little more, painting more detail on his Dick Turpin Toby Jug, and the other prisoners busied themselves on the potter's wheels, the room was rocked by an almighty explosion. The oven door flew open and Ronnie's Barnacle Bill flew around the room in hundreds of tiny pieces. 'That's Reynolds' doing, that!' screamed Ronnie. 'He's fucked my Toby Jug!' Ronnie looked absolutely apoplectic, his face red with rage and his eyes welling up with tears.

'Bom, bom, bom, bom; bom, bom, bom, bom,' I hummed sarcastically. 'De, de, de, de, de, de, de, de, diddle-de, de dee.'

Ronnie ran towards me like a raging bull, and I legged it out of the craft room as fast as the racers tried to beat the midnight chimes of the town hall clock in Sunderland on New Year's Eve. It was the last pottery class Ronnie and I attended.

Back in our cell, after I had given Ronnie two days to calm down, we discussed what other courses we might like to do.

'I'm not doing any other fucking courses with you,' said Ronnie.

'There's a canny one here,' I said. 'Current affairs.'

'Sod that,' said Ronnie.

'How about motor mechanics?'

'Sod that. Do you think they'll let you near another piece of machinery?'

I suppose old Rubber Bones had a point.

It was approaching Christmas, the worst time of the year

for prisoners, and myself, Ronnie and our new cellmate, whose name I forget, were dreaming up other ways to fill our time. Ronnie used to sketch a lot, he was a bit of an artist was Ronnie, and our other cellmate spent a lot of time reading, newspapers, books, magazines, anything he could get his hands on.

As we sat on our bunks, and the Salvation Army sang Christmas carols outside the prison gates, I said: 'Ronnie, I've made up a poem.'

'Go on then,' he said. 'Let's hear it.'

'The Downfall of a Prisoner,' I said. 'I was walking in the park one day; in the very merry month of May, when I was taken by surprise, by a pair of copper's eyes, walking in the park one day.

'Oh judge, oh judge, I have come to confess; I did leave that safe in a hell of a mess. Those bloody old gemmies just cannot be trusted, I put it in the lock and the fucking thing busted.

'The judge said, "Sit down, boy, and wipe away your tears; for I'm giving you a term, a term of three years. Three years in that prison is a mighty long time, but you have no option, you must do the time."

'There's bars on the windows, and a bell on the door, and there's a spring mattress attached to the floor. Now, I'm here myself, and I'm able to tell; there's no place on earth like the Strangeways Hotel ... Reynolds, Shakespeare and company.

'Did you like that one Ronnie?' I asked.

'Very funny,' he said.

'I've got another one. Do you want to hear it?'

'Do I have to?'

'You'll like this one,' I said.

'Why, go on then,' said Ronnie.

'The Prisoner's Best Friend,' I said.

'Night after night, for months on end, my mattress has been my closest friend. My mattress and I are cosy and pally;

it's the hills on my side, and I sleep in the valley. Where it is thick, I am so thin, it really reveals the shape that I'm in. I'll miss my mattress when I am gone. It's the only thing in Durham Jail, I made an impression on ... Reynolds, Shakespeare and company.

'Did you like that one, Ronnie?' I asked.

'Very funny,' he said, as he turned over in his bunk. 'Now let's get some kip.'

As I was approaching the middle of my six-month sentence, I was assigned to an outside working party pulling up sleepers from an old railway line near Finchale Abbey, which is just on the outskirts of Sunderland. I was away from the main block in the jail housed in an army-style billet within the prison grounds, but still under lock and key, nonetheless.

In a remarkable coincidence, and just because there was another inmate called Heslop whom Ronnie was confused with by the prison warders, old Rubber Bones joined me in the billet, and on the outside working party. It was the cushiest six weeks Ronnie Heslop spent in jail, because every Wednesday night he would escape, scale the wall and get home for a quick leg-over with the missus and bacon and eggs for breakfast. He would return at about 4am.

Ronnie and I managed to remove a grille from the toilet window in the billet, sawing through it with a guitar string. Every Wednesday night, after midnight, he would tug on a piece of thread attached to my big toe, which meant he was about to get on his toes. I'd go to the toilet, replace the grille and stick the sawn-off nuts back on using that old sticky condensed milk. On one of his night's back home, old Rubber Bones hot-wired a car near the prison gates ... he wasn't to know it was the Deputy Governor's!

It all stopped when he broke back into the jail and fell on a prison warder's head while he patrolled the inside of the perimeter wall. When he had been on the outside, he screwed a north-eastern Co-op store and, apparently, his fingerprints were found all over the shop.

But that particular crime never did make the newspapers, or the record books. It was too much of an embarrassment to the authorities.

One other huge embarrassment for the prison authorities involved an apparently dim-witted prisoner called Marshy and the handles from aluminium piss-pots. Marshy, an inoffensive chap who cleaned the prison landings, was a sandwich short of a picnic, according to some of the other lags, but what he had, and used to great effect, was a photographic memory.

Marshy memorised the minute details of a prison key held by one of the warders and managed to make a duplicate that worked, from a handle he cut from an aluminium piss-pot. Word soon spread and those in the know were into store cupboards nicking sugar, jam, tea, milk and anything else they could get their hands on to trade for tobacco. I earned myself several ounces of baccy in exchange for the stolen goods.

Inevitably, the prison governor got to know what was going on and there was a huge inquiry. Every lock in the jail had to be changed. Marshy, it appeared, had coughed in exchange for scores of Senior Service cigarettes, which made him cough even more. The authorities continued making aluminium piss-pots, but started perforating the handles.

Whilst in Durham on my second stretch I got myself a job as a landing cleaner, but I could have chosen a better landing. I cleaned for E wing, where all the lifers and notorious hardmen were incarcerated. Dishing out the food to their cells, and keeping to the regulation helpings, proved a daunting task, but, with more than a little cunning, I managed to get in their good books by posting out 'stiffs' – uncensored letters – to the outside world. It earned me massive brownie points and kept me on the landing, rather than being thrown over it, as had happened to E wing landing cleaners in the past.

When I left Durham Jail for the second time, somehow I just knew it was not the last I would see of old Rubber Bones Heslop. We did a few jobs together, including one near High Force in Teesdale where we were surrounded by cops and had to jump from a cliff top into the river below like Butch Cassidy and the Sundance Kid.

The screws didn't think it was the last they'd see of me either. 'You'll be back,' said one of the warders, as I walked out into Old Elvet, the street outside Durham Prison.

CHAPTER 11

The Bandits

A tanner in the slot, pull the handle and plink, plink, plink; the bandit either paid out or it didn't. It was a simple operation for the punters in working men's clubs across the north-east of England, but despite the simplicity of it all, the punters would stand there, a fistful of tanners, and they were mesmerised. They would spend hours on them, pushing sixpences in, pulling the handle, trying to recoup their losses, hoping for the jackpot. Invariably the jackpot never dropped, as most, if not all, the one-armed bandits were fixed.

The bandits, or fruit machines, were all imported from America and converted from dimes to tanners. Once the tanner was inserted there was one of three routes it could take into the machine: either it went into the jackpot, into the tube which carried the float or into a metal box, which fitted snugly into the back of the machine. The metal box, which could hold between £70 and £100, was pure profit.

Mechanics doctored the machines by cutting up little bits

of brass into squares, drilling holes in the corners on each side, coupling them with washers, then attaching them to cogs on the arms inside the machines. Two of the icons would regularly fall into place, but the third, which would trigger a jackpot, invariably didn't. It would often come tantalisingly close, but would quickly drop below the winning line. So close to winning, the punter would think, I must have another go.

The metal boxes, at the base in the rear of the machine, fitted perfectly into one of those open-from-the-top metal toolboxes. So, when it was time to collect, the mechanic, or a collector, would simply have to open the back of the bandit and replace the metal box full of tanners with an empty box from the bottom of his toolbox. Simplicity in itself, and very, very profitable. There were other methods of doctoring the machines and scamming the gullible public, but the metal box switch-over was one of the most popular.

The Gaming Act 1963 had relaxed the gaming rules, and many entrepreneurs, among them Vincent Francis Luvaglio, knew better than most what vast profits could be made. The hundreds, or more like thousands, of working men's clubs in the north-east were an untapped reservoir of easy profits. The one-armed bandits, many believed, were just a licence to print money.

In the early days, two companies dominated the vast market: Cam Automatics, which was based in Seaham Harbour and run by Frank Hoy and Bob Murray; and Social Club Services Ltd, which was based in Olive Street, Sunderland, and run and operated by Vince Luvaglio. I was a collector for Vince, and I was also his left cuff – not exactly his bodyguard, but someone who would be there to protect him if there was any argy-bargy and, more often than not, there was. His right cuff was a chap called George Jones: a fit, very smartly-dressed and softly-spoken young man, who was basically a chick-magnet. George's quiet approach to life was often mistaken for weakness, but that would be to the cost of those under that dangerous misapprehension.

One night George and I were in a Newcastle nightclub, waiting for closing time to do a bit of business, when five young lads, all tanked up, approached us and one told George he was sitting in his seat.

'I do apologise,' said George, in his own inimitable and gentlemanly style. 'Can I get each of you a drink?'

George went to the bar, bought five pints, and brought them over to the young lads' table.

'I'm so sorry for taking your seat,' he said, as he placed the beers on the mats.

'Are you a fucking puff?' one of the lads asked aggressively. And the verbal abuse continued as George walked back towards me. He appeared to shrug it off.

I walked over to the lads, bent down to speak to the ringleader and said, 'Take my advice. Do not upset that man.'

'Fuck you,' said the ringleader loudly. 'Here!' he shouted across the bar. 'Get us another pint, you puff.'

I bent down to speak to the loudmouth again. 'The man is not a puff,' I said, 'and please take it from me, you must not upset him. Do you hear me? Do not upset him.'

'Fuck you,' the loudmouth said again, and continued to hurl insults across the bar, as I walked back over to George. George looked neither angry nor intimidated, in fact he looked quite cool. He took a cut-throat razor from his pocket, casually walked across to the lads' table, swiftly opened the razor with a flick of his wrist and, in one fell stroke, sliced off the top of the loudmouth's left ear.

'You're fucking mad, you are!' screamed the loudmouth, clutching his ear, trying to stem the flow of blood. You could almost smell his fear as he and his mates quickly made for the exit. George Jones had no trouble from those lads again.

At the Olive Street offices of Social Club Services Ltd, I would often bump into some of Vince's other collectors or other staff. Dennis Stafford, who had a history as a playboy and had done a few stretches inside, as well as escaping from Dartmoor, was often in the office, dealing directly with Vince. Vince's brother, Michael Luvaglio, a quiet man who wouldn't harm a fly, was also part of the set-up. One of the main collectors was Angus Stuart Sibbet, a giant of a man, with a beard and glasses, who always wore smart suits and, whenever I was there, seemed to have little to say. He and Vince would sometimes have words about takings from the bandits. I got the impression there was a little animosity there. Their relationship reminded me of one of the ten golden rules of my old master at Besford, Mr Martin: Keep your friends close, but your enemies closer still.

The bandits business was very closely linked to the entertainment business, through the booking of acts for the clubs, and even the fitting out of some of the clubs. What they were trying to offer was a full package. It wasn't unknown for some of the club singers to act as collectors for Vince. John Gaffney, 'The Gaffer', as he was known, who went under the stage name Johnny Dawn, collected from the machines occasionally, as did club comedian Al Collins and singer Raymond Hill.

There was a funny story told to me about a night Al Collins had finished his act at a club down on Teesside, and had collected from the machines. He was driving back up the A19 heading for Sunderland, when his motor hit an obstacle in the road, overturned and sent him crashing into a field. When the ambulance staff arrived Al was lying in the field badly injured and covered from head to toe ... in sixpences.

Social Club Services Ltd was expanding rapidly and Vince had moved another salesman/collector into an office in Albert Road, Middlesbrough, by the name of Davey Snowball, from

Sacriston, County Durham, who used to be the secretary at The Big Club in Sacriston.

Social Club Services had managed to get hundreds of clubs on its books; often the easiest way was to offer a club steward or secretary a backhander. Twenty quid was a week's wages in those days, so the offer of easy money to get Vince's machines into the clubs was a temptation many, and I mean many, club officials and committee men found hard to resist.

Virtually every one was on the take; some of the collectors were lining their own pockets with more tanners than they should, club committee men had never had it so good, and even the punters were trying to get in on the act by attempting to screw the machines. There was a few bandits put in a bingo hall in Easington Lane way and they had to be screwed to the wall, because the punters were regularly shaking the machines to get something for nothing.

In one of the clubs someone was shoving their arm up the front of one of the machines, helping themselves to a fistful of tanners, so a committee man decided to place razor blades inside the front of the bandit. A couple of days later, another committee man was walking round the club ... with his fingers all bandaged up.

Vince's salesmen were all earning about £15 a week basic, but where they really made up their wages was through commission. It paid for them to get as many of Vince's bandits into the clubs as possible. Of course, the commission side of the business also paid very well indeed for Vincent Luvaglio.

Vince, like Dennis Stafford, was always a smart dresser. He would fly to London to have his suits tailor made in Savile Row or Carnaby Street. Flying to London and back, in those days, was virtually unheard of, but it was Vince's chosen method of travel.

I would also travel to London on business for Vince, but driving rather than flying, picking up cash from the London end of the mushrooming bandit business at the Florida Club in Bayswater. I always used to collect a few thousand pounds and the men I dealt with were some of the biggest bruisers I'd even seen. They were all brawn, no brains, with big, flat, broken noses and cauliflower ears or a face full of scars. Vince still had bandits in several clubs in London and collecting the cash from down south was one of my main tasks.

I also collected cash from the bandits in the north-east, and would take bags full of tanners into Vince's office in Derwent Street. One of the bandits I collected from was a Jennings machine, which had an Indian brave's head on the front. More tanners fell into the front cover of the machine than they did into the jackpot, tube or metal box. We had to replace this machine, and it took four of us to remove it from the club on piano wheels, it was that full of cash.

One of Vince's big pals at the time, who got heavily involved in the bandits business, was Ray Thubron, a former miner from Silksworth, Sunderland. Before he met Vince he was driving around in a battered, old Austin Wolsley, but afterwards he had one of the best motors on the market.

One of Ray's greatest passions was greyhound racing, and Vince also liked a big flutter on the flapping tracks and the more regulated tracks dotted around the north-east. Vince and Ray became good pals, and spent many a night at the dog track, such as the track – now a greyhound stadium – in Newcastle Road, Boldon, on the outskirts of Sunderland.

Like the bandits, it was well known that some of the greyhound races were well fixed; there was a lot of cash to be earned if you were a greyhound owner who knew the ropes and the scams. One of the scams was feeding a half pound of butter to the dog, which would turn its insides sour and slow it down on the track. Another was placing a piece of chewing gum on each of the dog's big ball paws to slow it down, but that one was a bit of a giveaway. Some owners used to stick a ten-inch-long reed up the greyhound's arse, which would slow it down on the bends, and probably cause it a lot of discomfort.

Owners wanted their dogs to lose races, so their handicaps would go up, giving them better prices at the betting booths.

Ray Thubron used to travel to Ireland to buy some of the fastest greyhounds that could be found and there were at least two he shared with Vince. One was called Tiny Tim and the other LAT, which stood for Landa and Thubron – as by that time Vincent Luvaglio was using a different surname. The pair would visit the dog tracks, dressed in their flash suits and fedora hats, looking every inch like Chicago gangsters from the Twenties.

I attended the Newcastle Road track with Vince and Ray one night, when one of the dogs in the starting line-up was Tiny Tim. It looked nothing like the dog that I'd see Vince with earlier in the week. The dog he was calling Tiny Tim then was all white; the one in the starting line-up today was black from head to tail.

Vince had placed £100 on a straight win for Tiny Tim and Ray had put up £50. As clouds drifted over the track, we stood on the terrace, the bunny whizzed passed, and the doors went up on the traps.

'They're off,' said Vince, getting all excited. 'Go on, lad, go on.'

'Go on, lad,' said Ray. 'Go on, go on!'

The dogs took the first bend and Tiny Tim was about two yards in front. With its odds at 10–1 (because Tiny Tim was never heard of and thus had a big handicap) Vince stood to make a cool grand and Ray £500.

'Go on, lad!' said Vince. 'Go on!'

As the dogs took the second bend, the heavens opened and a torrent of rain came crashing down on to the track. Tiny Tim, it appeared, was changing colour.

'What the fuck's up with number six?' said one of the punters.

Tiny Tim raced ahead and, at the third bend, as the torrential rain washed more black dye from its coat, it had a white face, a white body, a white arse, black legs and a black tail. By the time it whizzed past the finishing line it was way ahead of the rest of the pack and had almost caught the bunny. The only thing black on its body now was the tip of its tail.

Vince looked at Ray; Ray looked at Vince and Vince looked up at the race board. 'Fuck it,' said Vince. 'There's a steward's inquiry.' The white Tiny Tim was a well-known winning dog, and this would be reflected in the odds of it winning the race. Dyed black, it became an unknown entity, would attract more favourable odds, and win the owners more cash.

My work with Vince Landa took me to some interesting places. The best tables at the best nightclubs in the north-east; on regular trips to the Florida Club in Bayswater, where I met the Kray twins once or twice; to the best restaurants, in the flashiest cars, and meeting some very interesting, and some very strange, characters that occupied that shadowy and sinister place known as the north-east underworld.

Vince Landa introduced me into a brave new world, full of glamour and colour, where money was to be made and scores could be settled by 'having a word' in the right ear. Being seen on the north-east club scene in the company of the right people carried a lot of weight.

We got together quite regulary and ended up in some bizarre situations, not least with a Sunderland funeral director, Tommy Downey, using my big black Mercedes as a hearse more than once.

One thing about Landa, and to some extent Dennis Stafford, had always intrigued me. Why did it appear, at least to me, that both of these men, feared as they were in the north-east to varying degrees, appeared to fear me? It's a question that's never been answered.

CHAPTER 12

The Alibi

A thin blanket of snow had fallen overnight as miners in the pit village of South Hetton, near Sunderland, were making their way home after another hard shift at the coalface. Tom Leak, who lived in the village, had got out of the pit baths early and was heading towards his home in Phalp Street, when he came across a very unusual sight: a green Mark X Jaguar parked underneath Pesspool Bridge, its sidelights burning and one of its headlights damaged. He looked inside the car and there, slumped on the back seat, was the body of Angus Stuart Sibbet.

The collector for Social Club Services Ltd, of Sunderland, had been shot three times: once in a forearm, once in his stomach and once in the lower part of his chest. The third bullet had ripped through his left shoulder. There was no doubt that the flamboyant businessman, a married man with a daughter, a £6,500 house in Dunston, Gateshead, and two mistresses – two sisters from Sunderland – had been shot dead.

It was a strange series of events. It transpired that Angus, for whatever reason, probably to check over a one-armed bandit, had been called to the Shiney Row Working Men's Club on the outskirts of Sunderland. But what happened between the time he was seen in the club, some time before midnight, and the time he was found dead in the Jaguar car at 5.15am the next morning was open to conjecture, rumour and a lot of speculation.

A miner, James Golden, was cycling home in South Hetton at about 11.50pm and reported seeing a green Mark X Jaguar and a red E-type Jaguar passing him on the road. At 12.20am, Nora Burnhope, of Moor Farm, South Hetton, said she heard two gunshots. At 12.30am, another miner, Tom Feather, passed a green Mark X Jaguar and said an arm, with a white band across the wrist, came out of the Jag driver's window and ushered him to pass. Between 12.55am and 5am, miners Reuben Conroy, Tommy Purves, Stan Simpson, Watking Pickering, Edward Wallace and a hawker, all reported passing and seeing the green Mark X Jag, undamaged and with no corpse inside. Police said Angus Sibbet was shot dead and his body placed on the rear seat of the Jaguar at 11.50pm.

At about 7am there was one hell of a knock on the door of my flat in Cooper Street – it was only across the road from the family home in Roker – and I was confronted by two police officers who asked me to accompany them to Gill Bridge Police Station to help them with enquiries. At about the same time, coppers were knocking on the door of Davey Snowball, in Sacriston, County Durham, and on the doors of many other associates of Vince Landa, including Dennis Stafford and Vince's brother Michael Luvaglio, asking them much the same thing.

At Gill Bridge Police Station, I was put in a cell, not for too long, and then taken into the interrogation room. A team of about six detectives, none of whom I had seen before, sat behind a row of desks. One of the tecs had a foot on a chair, and he kicked it in my direction. It slid across the tiled floor, and I sat down. These tecs were all big lads; they must have been drafted in from Newcastle or elsewhere.

'George Reynolds?' asked one of the cops.

'That's me, George Reynolds,' I said.

'Right, George,' he said. 'Where were you between 9 o'clock last night and 7 o'clock this morning?'

'I'm telling you fuck all,' I said.

Another detective piped up. 'Look, George,' he said. 'We're investigating a serious crime, a murder. We're not trying to catch you out or anything like that, we just want to know where you were between 9 o'clock last night and 7 o'clock this morning. Nothing sinister about it, we just want to know your whereabouts.'

I was obviously getting the tough cop, soft cop routine.

'I know there's nothing sinister about it,' I said. 'I know you're just doing your job. But I'm still telling you fuck all.'

The first tec stared at me with the kind of stare that he knew, and I knew, was a stare that showed he meant business.

'I'm going to ask you one more time, Reynolds,' he said. 'Now, you can do yourself a favour here, and do us a favour? All we need to do is eliminate you from our enquiries, and, at the moment, you're doing us no favours and you're doing yourself no favours by playing the big-time gangster. Do you understand what I'm saying?'

'I do,' I said.

'Right then, George,' he said. 'I'll ask you one more time. Where were you between 9 o'clock last night and 7 o'clock this morning?'

'I'm telling you fuck all,' I said.

The big tough cop got up from the desk, took his coat from the back of his seat, put it on and straightened his tie.

'Fair enough then, George,' he said. 'You've got no alibi, so I'm going to charge you with murder.'

'Whoah, whoah! Hang on. Fucking hang on!' I said. 'You can't do that. It was fuck all to do with me.'

The big tec took off his jacket, placed it over the back of his seat, loosened his tie, moved a notepad under his nose, picked up a pen and said: 'Right. Let's start again.'

'Now, George. Where were you between 9 o'clock last night and 7 o'clock this morning?'

'I left the house at about eight,' I said. 'I went down to the Palatine, where I met a lass called Brenda. Nice lass, she was, and we got talking. She was wearing a red, blouson-type jacket and drinking a cherry brandy. Then I went to the Burton House where I met my mate Stan – and all this can be checked – and I bought him a pint of best and a pint of lager for myself. The landlord there, Sammy, he'll remember me. Then I went up to the Park Inn, and I bumped into Terry, another mate of mine, outside Louis Milk Bar, and he joined me for a pint in the Park Inn. I went over to Polly's for last orders, and there I bumped into Billy, who used to work with me down the pit, and when last orders was over, I got a taxi over to the Ro Ko-Ko in Roker.'

'Slow down, slow down,' said the cop taking the statement.

'Tommy what's-his-name was the driver, he always seems to pick me up. At the Ro Ko-Ko, where I said hello to the doorman, who knows me, I had one or two more pints and I got talking to this lass called Lisa, she was the singer in the turn that was on. Nice lass, she was, and had a voice like an angel. At about 2 o'clock I walked home with my mate Jimmy, and said goodnight to him at my door. Then I got into bed with our lass, and the next thing I remember is being knocked up at about seven this morning, and being brought here.'

'All right, all right,' said the tough cop. 'We get the picture. You're free to go.'

Davey Snowball , from Sacriston, it appeared, was having more difficulty than myself convincing detectives he had an alibi. The night before he was at a nightclub in Middlesbrough, acting as a kind of unofficial bouncer. The bubbly Scottish singer Lulu was performing; she was just about reaching the peak of her popularity on the club scene. A fight had broken out on the dance floor, and Davey waded in to sort the troublemakers out. During the melee, one of the troublemakers suffered a bloody nose, and blood ended up on Davey's crisp, neatly ironed, white dress shirt. Davey had got back home to Sacriston at about three in the morning and crashed out on the sofa, and when he was knocked up by the Old Bill, only four hours later, he answered the door still fully dressed and with bloodstains on his shirt. He had quite a lot of explaining to do.

Two men who had more to explain than most to the cops were Dennis Stafford and Vince Landa's brother Michael Luvaglio. They were arrested and taken to Peterlee Police Station for questioning, were charged and the following day appeared before magistrates in Peterlee charged with the murder of Angus Sibbet. They both denied the killing.

The newspapers were full of details about the murder. There were reports of gang warfare, racketeering and links with London gangsters, and MP Gordon Bagier declared: 'The mafia is now in this country.'

After a few months, the murder case opened in Newcastle amid tight security. The crux of the prosecution case rested on the police evidence that there had been a collision between the green Mark X Jaguar, owned by Vince Landa's firm Social Club Services Ltd, and used that night by Angus Sibbet, and a red E-type Jaguar, which had been used by Dennis Stafford.

Stafford and Michael Luvaglio had been in The Bird Cage nightclub in Newcastle at the time of the killing, they said. Police said the E-type could have made it from the nightclub to South Hetton and back within the time, still giving Stafford and Michael Luvaglio time to carry out the dirty deed.

During the high-profile case, several of the witnesses who reported seeing the Mark X Jag between the time police said Sibbet was murdered and the time his body was found on the back seat of the car were not called to give evidence. Many of these witnesses claimed to have seen the car undamaged and no corpse on the rear seat.

Dennis Stafford and Michael Luvaglio, much to their surprise, were convicted of murder. They protested their innocence throughout their 12-year sentences, but appeal after appeal failed. During the time of the arrest and later trial, one man was conspicuous by his absence: Vincent Landa, Michael Luvaglio's brother.

Many supporters of the convicted men have, throughout the years, claimed they were the victims of a huge miscarriage of justice, though no one has been able to come up with fresh evidence to shed new light on just who killed Angus Stuart Sibbet.

There is a very small circle of people, close to many of the parties involved, who know exactly what happened that winter night in January in the pit village of South Hetton, and of the circumstances leading up to it. And I am one of them. All I will say here is there was a huge miscarriage of justice in the so-called one-armed-bandit murder case; one of the most notorious murders ever carried out in the north-east, and on which the cult film *Get Carter* was very loosely based.

One of the men jailed for the crime was certainly innocent. The second was, possibly, innocent too.

CHAPTER 13

The Showdown

The town, it appeared, wasn't big enough for the both of us: that's myself and Detective Inspector Graham Birmingham Knott. So when two police officers hammered at the door of my flat in Cooper Street and suggested, in the way only police officers can suggest, that it would be in my best interests to leave Sunderland, I had a lot to consider.

Det Insp Knott had been unable to pin anything of any real substance on me, though I had been active, a few burglaries here, a few safes there, a few scams, dodgy dealing, ducking and diving, bobbing and weaving, clinching deals. I had even broken into the vestry at St Mary's Church in the town centre, stolen a priest's garments and posed as Father Michael O'Flaherty in the town's court to give one of my associates a very glowing character reference. I almost got away with it, but for some reason, the case against me did not proceed. Perhaps it was on some kind of legal or ecclesiastical technicality.

There had been another parting of the ways: my mother and father had separated and my mother had gone to live in a town called Shildon in County Durham, not far from Bishop Auckland. Shildon was only about 30 miles or so from Sunderland, but it might as well have been near London for all that I knew about the place. All I knew was that the town was linked in some way to the railways.

I still had a lot of friends in Sunderland and knew its streets and back lanes, particularly on the Barbary Coast, like the back of my hand. I had spent a lot of time, money and effort turning my flat into a little palace, with the best furnishings in every room and fish tanks built into the wall; it was like Buckingham Palace in Coronation Street. One my greatest friends, whom I had only recently met, was Tommy Robson, who lived in Melvyn Gardens, not far from Cooper Street, behind the Roker Park football ground. Tommy worked at the technical college and he had a lock-up workshop in Gladstone Street, where he had a small lathe and dabbled in turning bad antiques into good antiques. His wife ran a tobacconist's in Hendon. I passed quite a bit of business Tommy's way. He was moving into antiques in a big way. He was a great bloke.

The cops had given me only 24 hours to get out of town. It was a bit like the showdown at the OK Corral, when the sheriff confronts the gunslinger. The cops had put it to me in such a persuasive way that I felt I really had no choice. I packed my battered old Ford Consul – which had two bald tyres – with a few belongings, gave the flat keys to the landlord, jumped in the motor and headed south. I had 38 shillings in my pocket, the wrap that contained the tools of my trade, and a few meagre possessions in the boot of the car. Despite all my criminal chicanery, I had made nothing from my life of crime; in fact I was on the bones of my arse.

My mother had opened a shop in Shildon called the Cat's Nest, a general dealer's, and kindly gave me a room above the shop where I could stay until something better came along. She gave me the name of a local garage where I could get the bald tyres replaced on the Ford Consul.

After a good 40 minutes drive from Sunderland, I arrived in Shildon and thought I had entered a ghost town. It was so quiet. Had it been the Midwest, tumbleweed would have been rolling along the main road in a cloud of fine sand dust.

I was soon to discover that the town of Shildon was very much steeped in the history of the railways. It was famed for the first regular building of railway locomotives and the first railway to carry passengers. Indeed George Stephenson's first steam train set out from Shildon on 27 September 1825. The town was home to that great railway pioneer Timothy Hackworth, and the town's wagonworks, affectionately known as the Shildon Shops, provided employment for the town.

After unpacking my few belongings, I got back in the car and drove to Freddie Davidson's garage, knowing I didn't have enough cash to buy two new tyres, but hoping I could strike a deal.

'Hello, Freddie,' I said. 'You don't know me.'

'That's right,' said Freddie. 'I don't know you.'

'If you put me two new tyres on the motor, so I can get to London and back, when I return I'll pay you double the price.'

Freddie looked at me, weighing me up. 'And what happens if you don't come back?' he asked.

'Then you can visit me in Wandsworth with a bottle of Lucozade,' I said.

Freddie laughed. Then he changed the two tyres on my motor.

I got in touch with my old cellmate Ronnie Heslop, and we headed for the capital; our target, a large Chubb safe in a plush office block, which, we were told, held a substantial sum of cash. The information wasn't given out freely, of course, it was always on the basis of a 10 per cent cut.

After the job, another safe-cracking success, Ronnie Rubber Bones headed back to Page Bank in County Durham and, as I had just been effectively driven out of my home town for pastures new in Shildon, I decided to stay out of circulation for a while, chancing my arm in the capital, using my nice little safe earner to rent a room.

My short stay turned into more than 12 months, and during that time I drifted from job to job. First I was a silver service waiter in a small restaurant known as Nan's Pantry, in a side street just off Kensington High Street. I didn't even know how to lay a table, the boss found out, and I was relegated to washing up in the kitchen, but even that did not last. I got a job as a scaffolder, working on hotels, and was so hungry one day I nicked the dinner from a table inside the hotel when a window was open, and ate it on the scaffold. The diner had only popped to the loo and came back to find his meat and two veg had disappeared. For a few weeks – despite the fact I had always thought tinkling the ivories meant brushing your teeth – I got a job as a piano salesman. Surprisingly, that job worked out well. I was making more cash than the regular salesmen.

But the bright lights of London could not hold me in their gaze for too long; it was a place I didn't belong. After 12 months had elapsed I decided it was time to head back north and try something new. I had been away long enough for the local constabulary to realise I was out of the picture.

I headed back to Shildon and immediately called in to Freddie Davidson's Central Garage, and handed him £100 for the two tyres he had fitted on my old motor.

'I'd given up hope of ever seeing you again,' said Freddie. 'Thought maybe you'd ended up in Wandsworth, as you predicted.'

Freddie became a good friend of mine. I had not long been in Shildon when someone took Freddie's safe. I managed to get it back for him, and every penny that it contained.

Word of my safe-blowing expertise, and links with criminals, soon circulated in the town and beyond, particularly in Darlington, from where I was contacted by the boss of a big transport firm, Allison's Transport, after thieves had physically stolen his safe from his offices. The boss, George Allison, wasn't too concerned about the cash in the safe, there wasn't that much, but he was concerned about all the firm's documentation that had gone missing.

He approached me and said he had already had a word with the police who had told him George Reynolds would not be behind the crime as 'he's too lazy to lift a safe'. The businessman offered me a £1000 reward if I could put the word out and get the safe back, its contents intact.

As lady luck would have it, I was contacted the same day by the two lads who had nicked the safe; they were having problems opening it.

'Can you help us open it?' one of the lads said.

'I can,' I said. 'But I've got to tell you there's fuck all in the safe apart from papers, which are no good to you or me.'

I explained to the lads that the owner of the safe was a friend of mine, and the papers inside it were crucial for him to run his business effectively. I told the lads that if they fetched the safe to me, I would give them £100, which was more cash than was in the safe. After a little bit of haggling, we agreed on £200 and the lads brought the safe from where they had hidden it, behind a portable building at Eldon Drift, to a place we had earlier pinpointed.

I arranged for the safe to be put outside the front door of the transport firm's office in Darlington. Then I called the transport boss.

'Your safe is outside your front door,' I said.

'Bloody hell. That was quick,' said George Allison. 'I can't thank you enough, George. I'll be round with the grand first thing in the morning.'

'There's no need for that,' I said. 'I don't want your reward. I just want you to remember that I've done you a favour. And I don't want you to go to the police, otherwise I will definitely not be a happy bunny.'

'I'll remember this as long as I live,' said the transport boss. 'If you need anything in the future, and you think I might be able to help, just give me a call.'

We left it at that, and I knew that the seeds of friendship I had sown then would, like with so many other people, later blossom and the rewards would come. Man cannot live on bread alone, and the bread I was making, the proceeds from my life of crime, was insufficient for my daily needs. I needed something else, something legitimate, to earn a daily crust. So, I started out in the ice cream business. It turned out to be a cut-throat business.

CHAPTER 14

The Ice Cream Man

The first rule of business, I was learning, was knowing your market place, and one of the best market places in Shildon for selling ice cream was the Jubilee estate; a large estate full of council-owned housing occupied by hundreds of families, where children would jump to the sound of an ice cream van's chimes, and parents would be pressurised into dipping their hands in their pockets and shelling out for an ice cream cone.

Another rule of business, even semi-legitimate business, was knowing your opposition, and my opposition in Shildon was a Mr Whippy van. I say my business was semi-legitimate because I was far from going straight, in fact my gelignite for safe-blowing was kept in the bottom of the ice cream van's freezer. It needed to be kept cold so it didn't weep.

I sized up the opposition. Mr Whippy would start off on a morning and always take the same route, never veering from it. You could almost set your clock by seeing his van in a certain street. If he was at the bottom end of Jubilee Road, you could guarantee it was 11.20am; if he was at the top end, it would be 12.40pm. I had two options to maximise sales: either I would do the exact opposite of Mr Whippy, starting on what would be the end of his route, and ending up meeting him somewhere in the middle, or – and this appeared the more sensible thing to do – starting off on the same route, but 20 minutes earlier.

And so it was that ice cream wars arrived in Shildon, for when Mr Whippy sussed I was on his route 20 minutes before him, and he was following me but attracting no business, he upped the ante by starting 20 minutes earlier still. I would do the same and, when the competition really hotted up, you could buy an ice cream in Shildon half an hour after you had finished breakfast.

The problem there, of course, was that some people, those unemployed or nightshift workers, for example, would still be in bed, and they would not want their slumber interrupted by the repetitive, ear-piercingly loud chimes of the ice cream man. It all came to a head one day when I arrived in a certain street on the Jubilee estate and a man came running out of his house, stripped to the waist and wearing slippers, waving his arms around, gearing himself up, it appeared, for a fight.

'Do you have to play those chimes so bloody loudly?' he asked, rubbing the sleep out of his eyes. He explained he was a nightshift worker, so I apologised and told him I wouldn't play the chimes at all in future when I arrived in that section of the street. I had set out before Mr Whippy, so I backed up on the route to alert Mr Whippy to what could be a problem.

I parked the van up, got out and walked to Mr Whippy's counter.

'What the hell do you want?' he asked.

'Just putting a bit of business your way,' I said. 'There's a fella down the road, always gets a 99 cornet and a tray of ice cream for his dog, but I've run out of chocolate flakes. Can you see to him?'

'All right,' said Mr Whippy. 'I'll sort him out.'

'Oh, and there's one other thing,' I said. 'This fella's a bit hard of hearing, so when you get there you'll have to turn your chimes up a little bit.'

'OK,' said Mr Whippy.

I parked my van up the road, not far from where the chap lived, far enough away to be out of sight, but still able to witness the sale. Mr Whippy moved up the road and his 'Greensleeves' chimes were deafening. The nightshift worker bounded out of his home, taking giant leaps down the road, got hold of Mr Whippy by the overall collar and tried to pull him through the serving hatch. Mr Whippy ended up half way out and half way in. The nightshift worker then got into the back of the van, got hold of one of the deep trays of ice cream and started smearing it all over the van windows and Mr Whippy's face. Wafers were flying all over the place. The nightshift worker finally squirted monkey's blood all over Mr Whippy's head. I was creased up with laughter. The worker went back in his house and two little girls arrived at Mr Whippy's van, saw the bright red monkey's blood dripping from the end of his nose and ran back home screaming, 'Mr Whippy's dead! Mr Whippy's dead!'

I headed down the A1 to try to pick up some business in another village, when I noticed I was being followed by a police patrol car, its lights flashing. I slowed down, believing it was headed to some major incident in Newton Aycliffe or Darlington. There was nothing wrong with my van that I was aware of, and the incident in Shildon had nothing to do with me. As I slowed down, the patrol car slowed too, and I started to panic, knowing there was gelignite still in the bottom of the freezer, underneath the raspberry ripple and Neapolitan ice cream. I slowed again, the patrol car slowed again and then flashed its headlights, indicating for me to pull over to the hard shoulder. Shit, I thought, if they search the van, I've had it.

An officer got out of the passenger seat, slowly walked towards the van and his face looked serious. My heart started beating a little faster, and I was perspiring. He arrived at the hatch.

'Two 99s,' he said.

'Cer, cer, certainly, officer,' I said, stammering a little. 'Certainly. Would you like monkey's blood?'

The officer put his hand in his pocket and pulled out a little loose change.

'Never mind that,' I said. 'These are on the house.'

The officer got back in the vehicle, handed a 99 to the driver, and the patrol car headed south.

After my shift, I popped into a favourite pub of mine, the Wear Valley, in Bishop Auckland, just for a swift half. I've never been a big drinker. But I enjoyed cigarettes – I was smoking almost 100 a day, started off the day with one match and would not have to strike another – and the occasional cigar. I bumped into a good friend of my mother's, Marjorie, who was from nearby Coundon. Marjorie was a trained operatic soprano who did cabaret spots in the north-east working men's clubs under the stage name of Sonia Field.

Sonia was in the company of a very tall, and very heavy, Irishman, who she introduced to me as her husband, Steve Molloy. Steve and I hit it off straight away; he had some fascinating tales to tell, though his Irish brogue was so heavy I sometimes found it difficult understanding just what he was saying. But, I suppose, he was having the same difficulty with my broad Mackem accent.

I was meeting some new, and very interesting, people in County Durham, and I could see there could be new business opportunities for me; it was just a question of steering my enthusiasm in the right direction.

But legitimate business, such as selling ice cream, was not giving me anywhere near the returns I could acquire through crime; nor was it giving me the kind of excitement I craved. The challenge of the unopened safe, the lure of easy money for a few minutes' work, the thrill of the chase and the adrenalin rush from being able to blow a safe to reveal the hidden treasures that lay within were thoughts never far from my mind.

One little scam that involved explosives, detonators, but, in this case, no safe was a job at a trout farm in County Durham with my old mate Ronnie Heslop. There was a lot of money to be made selling fresh trout to local restaurants. It was just a question of catching the fish.

Very early one morning, at about 6am, Ronnie and I travelled to the trout farm, and Ronnie was telling me how you could catch trout by tickling them under the chin, under the water.

'Fuck that,' I said. 'Have you never seen flying fish? All we need is to put some explosives in the river and detonate them. That will starve the fish of oxygen, and they'll fly out of the river, or at least come to the surface.'

It seemed so easy, in theory.

Ronnie laid the wires and the explosives while I sorted out the detonators and, after we had fully prepared ourselves, we sat on our haunches on the river bank, ready for the trout to come to us.

'Blow it,' said Ronnie, and I slowly depressed the detonator plunger, expecting a muffled type of explosion underneath the water. There was a bloody huge explosion as a small bridge to the right of us collapsed some of the bricks flying into the air.

'You've blown the bloody bridge, you daft get!' I said.

The huge explosion was bound to have been heard, so we legged it, sharp.

It was inevitable, as sure as night follows day, that I would soon find the attraction of a big safe job too tempting to ignore. The opportunity came, and I grasped it with both hands. Initially it gave me the excitement I was looking for, and quite a large sum of money. But it also gave me something I could have done without: my biggest stretch inside, four years for burglary, safe-blowing, larceny and handling explosives.

I spent the bulk of my sentence at HMP Kirkham in Lancashire, soon learned the ropes, and I was into every scam going. By the time I had spent two years at Kirkham all the inmates knew where they needed to go to buy cigarettes, tobacco or even booze. My contacts on the outside ensured there was plenty of booze and fags finding its way into the prison.

I escaped from Kirkham once; to a large extent I enjoyed my time there, but one lag managed to spend two weeks on the outside, in quite an exotic location ... Tenerife!

Derek Tyson was an identical twin, and during a visit he swapped places with his brother. I was given the task of instructing his brother in prison ways, and that meant getting him to follow the strict routine and keep his head down. Derek worked on the weaving machine at Kirkham and had become quite skilled. His brother, on the other hand, hardly knew what a weaving machine looked like.

Keeping the cat in the bag, for that fortnight, proved a big challenge, and Derek's brother ended up in some tricky situations, where bluff and bluster were the only ways of getting him through what turned out to be a bit of an ordeal for the lad. But worse was to come, on Derek's return, when the second switch-over was complete.

The prison warders noticed that Derek was strangely off-colour, or should I say on-colour, and he was ordered to see the prison doctor. It was feared he had yellow jaundice. He was given all kinds of medical tests; the medics even took a sample of his skin tissue to try to discover what had brought about the sudden and dramatic change in his pigmentation.

When Derek stripped off, he told me, his full body was a deep, golden brown. But when he stripped off his underpants, his arse was lily white.

'It's sunburn,' the doctor declared.

'Impossible!' said one of the screws. 'It's the middle of bloody January!'

A massive search of the prison got under way for what the screws believed must have been a sunlamp stashed away somewhere. They never found it, and the story of the sun-tanned prisoner went down in prison folklore.

My one escape, more of a walking out really, happened one night when Derek Tyson and I decided we could do with some air. We headed for Blackpool and spent a night walking along the promenade, tucking into a very large portion of delicious fish and chips. Two plain clothes CID officers spotted me and let the authorities know at Kirkham but when they arrived at the prison after us the next day, the Governor just couldn't believe their story.

Nearing the end of my sentence, during which I had kept my nose clean and kept one step ahead of the screws in my tobacco- and beer-smuggling activities, I secured myself one of the cushiest jobs in the nick; working in the chapel, cleaning and helping the priest prepare for Mass. The prison authorities may have been impressed by my Roman Catholic background, such as my time at St Benet's RC School and even Besford Court.

The priest was a wise old man, and he and I would spend much time in conversation. I'd tell him about my safe-blowing career, my time in Sambourne and Besford, the Merchant Navy, how I had always struggled with learning to read and write and how I had many little earners running in

Kirkham, through the baccy – the main currency inside – and booze.

The priest suggested I should mix with some of the more 'respectable' cons in the nick, such as the bent lawyers and the crooked accountants. I took his advice, got to know many of the middle-class professionals who had fallen from grace, and I also immersed myself in books, hoping, at least, to improve my literacy skills. In some ways it paid off, as I taught myself how to read and write as best I could. There was still the problem of my dyslexia, which was later diagnosed by a psychologist friend of mine who worked with children with special educational needs. But that was a problem that would never go away.

I also immersed myself in law books, *Stone's Justice Manuals*, on the criminal side, and learned a great deal about company law. Some of the bent lawyers and former company directors were only too willing to teach me some of their skills in exchange for ten cigarettes, a bottle of whisky or a half-ounce of tobacco.

Just before I left Kirkham the priest, impressed with how I had applied myself, and the little businesses I was running, said to me: 'George, why don't you apply your shrewd, sharp mind, and undoubted common sense, to the business world?'

'Why should I do that?' I asked.

'Because you're no bloody good at crime, George,' he said. 'You're always getting caught.'

CHAPTER 15

The Scrap Man

The flatbed truck was stationary in the old London square, as stressed commuters hammered away at their car horns, venting their frustration at being held up by a wagon overloaded with off-cuts of plywood and laminates.

'Put your fucking foot down!' shouted one of the cockney motorists who had wound his window down and started giving us the two-fingered salute. Big Stevie Molloy and I couldn't move; we didn't know where the hell we were, and we weren't about to start a tour of the capital knowing full well the road for the motorway heading north couldn't be that far away.

'Get out of the road, you fucking idiots!'

I put my head out of the passenger window, looked back and saw a smart business type driving a new-style Volkswagon. She, too, was very hot under the collar and extremely anxious to get on her way.

'Shall we just head straight on?' asked Stevie.

'No,' I said, 'that road might be heading south. We want to get home, not end up in Brighton.'

A City of London police officer approached, as fed-up motorists continued sounding their horns, sounding their anger and gesticulating towards us.

'Can I see your driving licence?' said the officer to Stevie.

'Ce cui bfuil,' said Stevie, smiling.

'I'd like to see your driving licence,' the officer said. 'Are you the owner of this vehicle?'

'Ce cui bfuil,' said Stevie in his deepest and best Gaelic.

'Ignore him, officer,' I said. 'He can't speak a word of English. All we're looking for is the motorway north.'

'Are you the owner of this vehicle?' the officer asked.

'I am,' I said.

'Do you have a driving licence and a log book that covers your mate there for driving?'

'I do. But, unfortunately, all my documents are back at the office. We're down here on business, you know.'

'Move the fuckers on!' shouted one of the irate motorists, whose exit we were blocking.

'Get the idiots on their way!' shouted the smart-looking business type.

The police officer went to a bin on the roadside, tore a piece of cardboard from a box and started drawing a map. He showed it to Stevie and me. The map showed a roundabout, straight ahead, a road and an arrow pointing to the A1 north.

'That's where you want to be heading,' the officer said. 'Now, get the hell out of here, and I hope to never clap eyes on you again.'

'Thank you kindly, officer,' I said. 'We'll now be on our way.'

'Ce cui bfuil,' said Stevie, smiling again.

Steve put his foot down, a plume of smoke flew out of the exhaust, enveloping the business type and her smart Volkswagon car, and we headed for home.

'What were you saying to the cop?' I asked Stevie, as we headed out of London.

'I asked him how he was,' Stevie said. 'It's one of the few Gaelic phrases I still know.'

We'd had a good day down south, delivering the cut-offs to hundreds of small, family-run DIY shops, and I'd managed to obtain a number of new addresses for my little brown book; all new customers of George Reynolds, supplier of plywood and laminate off-cuts.

After moving to Shildon, and with a substantial prison record behind me, it had been difficult finding any kind of work. Rehabilitation, for most employers, seemed to be a dirty word and I knew from my first days of freedom that I would have to fend for myself in some way through self-employment or living off my wits.

My first break came when I bumped into an old friend called Vince Taylor who had given a contract to a businessman called John Wade to move an old slag heap in Tindale, County Durham, a leftover from the local colliery which had to make way for new development. Vince and John pulled up in a wagon and we got cracking. I really was on the bones of my arse and John gave me ten bob to get a cup of tea at a local transport cafe. It was a kind gesture from a man who became another good friend over the years. I have never forgotten it.

The idea to start up dealing in wood and laminate off-cuts had come to me one day when I was passing a firm called Perstorp Warewrite in Newton Aycliffe, who were just chucking the off-cuts away, destined for fires or some landfill site. When I asked if I could take them, they agreed on the basis that I couldn't take a few, I had to take a lorry-load. As well as off-cuts, some of the laminates were seconds, and some water-damaged and would need bits cutting off. The bosses at Perstorp Warewrite, and other laminate producers I started collecting from, always seemed to look down their noses at me, like I was some kind of scavenger, feeding off their leftovers. They called me the scrap man, but I believed from the scrap wood I was buying for pennies I could start building a little business empire. How I longed to prove the doubters wrong.

The off-cuts Stevie and I loaded on to the wagon were sold cheaply – a pound here and a pound there – but as I'd paid only pennies for them in the first place, our journeys across the country proved very profitable. I was looking after the pennies, and I knew the pounds would soon be looking after themselves.

I had been running the off-cuts business for two years before Stevie joined me in the venture and, over that period, I had amassed what I considered to be a small fortune, enough to expand the business from supplying bits and pieces of wood to DIY corner shops to establishing Shildon Cabinetmakers. Our aim was to fit out working men's clubs and bars, and we intended to be the best in the business.

My cousin from Sunderland, Richie Tennick, a jack-of-all-trades and master of most, moved over from Wearside to join me. We took over a former ice cream factory-cum-warehouse in Shildon, which used to be known as Boddy's Buildings, found the machinery from wherever we could and, full of hope, energy, optimism and enthusiasm, started touting for business around the working men's clubs in County Durham.

At our office in Main Street, Shildon, was sown the small acorn which we hoped would grow into an oak tree of a business, branching out in all directions. I was still running the lorry-loads of off-cuts to destinations across the country, and the names and numbers in my little brown book were growing apace.

I was determined to succeed in business and one of my old masters at Besford's ten golden rules – never take no for an answer – kicked in many times, once to the point where the managing director of a big DIY firm would have been right to believe I was stalking him.

He was buying four by two laminates from a supplier for £1.50 and selling them off for about £2.50, but the supplier was buying each four by two for as little as 25 pence from me. I contacted this MD several times by telephone to tell him I could sell him the same product of the same quality much more cheaply but each time I tried to get through to him he was either in a meeting, out to lunch or otherwise unavailable.

I set about finding the MD's home address, discovered what time he left for work each morning and what car he drove, and, with the help of Stevie Molloy, followed him for three whole days. On the third morning I walked up to his house, picked his two milk bottles from the step and held one in each hand, and pulled his newspaper from his letter box and put it in my mouth. Then I rang his doorbell.

The MD appeared at the front door in his dressing gown, pulled the newspaper from my mouth and said: 'I know you've been following me. Now, perhaps, you can tell me why.'

'You're buying four by two laminates from a company for £1.50 each,' I said.

'That's right,' said the MD.

'Well, I can sell you exactly the same four-by-two laminates for 25 pence each,' I said.

'Why don't you go to my buyer?' the MD asked.

'Because he won't do business with me,' I said. 'All I want to do is to sell you some four by two laminates cheaply, which will increase your profit margins.'

The MD smiled, and then laughed. 'I don't know about your direct approach,' he said, 'but I've got to admire your persistence.'

The direct approach, I thought. Now there's an idea. Cutting out all the middlemen who were raking in vast profits by doing nothing else but buying in bulk and selling out in bulk. The direct approach, up-front, no nonsense, no hassle, no middlemen, direct from the manufacturer to the customer, cutting out all that unnecessary and time-consuming waste and expense in between.

The MD handed me a business card, wrote his name on the back of it and told me to go and place my order with his firm, something I had been trying to do without success for weeks because I had my way blocked by the gatekeeping middlemen who saw me as a scrap man with ideas above his station.

This direct approach could work extremely well, I thought, not just in my embryonic business but in many more. I left the MD's house with the order secured and put his name, address and direct telephone number in my little brown book. Things were looking up, at last, and all I needed to do was follow my instincts.

At Shildon Cabinetmakers one of the first fitting-out contracts we secured was quite a major job at the Evenwood Working Men's Club and Institute in County Durham. In truth, our Richie, Stevie Molloy and myself approached the job with a little trepidation. We had told the committee we were the best in the business, and would have to deliver on that promise, otherwise we would be out. The specification was quite wide-ranging and ambitious for the club committee, who saw it as a 'thank you for your custom' to all the members and bona fide guests, and as an investment for the future.

A whole new lounge, a new foyer and the complete renovation of the old bar was the job in hand. Our Richie designed the colour scheme, and we fitted the place out with deep, luxurious upholstery, fixed and loose leather-look seating, deep-pile carpets and tapestry curtains. The finish was impeccable, and the club members were over the moon.

Word soon spread around the working men's clubs in the north-east and the work started to come in thick and fast. But Shildon Cabinetmakers did not restrict itself to club and bar work, we'd take any kind of work on. What with my contacts within the small DIY shops growing, and securing more contracts for fitting out, business was booming.

But in a world where success breeds envy, our thriving enterprises were attracting the attention of the powers that be: the local councils, which seemed to do everything possible to put obstructions in our way; and the local constabulary, who did not want to see an old lag like me doing well.

Across from our offices in Main Street stood a building with an attic and a lattice-style small wooden round window in the apex of the roof. It was the old Hippodrome Picture House, and a friend had tipped me off that I was under surveillance. Sitting at my desk doing paperwork into the small hours, I often got the sneaking suspicion that I was being watched.

Late at night, I sneaked into the building and slowly climbed the attic steps, hiding at the rear of the room. In front of the attic's round window sat two police officers, drinking tea. From the attic, they could see directly into my office window. I don't know how long they had been there, watching me, but I got the impression, from the amount of empty sandwich packets dotted around, it must have been some time. Behind the officers, on a small table, sat a pair of binoculars and what looked like a torch.

'Whatever you might think of Reynolds,' said one of the cops, 'he doesn't half put the hours in.'

'Aye, but it's what he's doing during those hours that counts,' said the other cop.

'He's done time for safe-blowing and all sorts,' said the first cop.

'And a leopard never changes he's spots. Where's he at now?'

'Must have gone to the bog.'

Slowly, I sat behind the two cops on an old tea chest. 'Evening,' I said quietly.

'How do,' said the cops, without turning round. They must have been expecting a colleague.

The second cop took hold of the teapot, and poured his mate a cup. I grabbed a spare empty cup and put it between them. The cop poured me a drink of tea. 'Thanks,' I said.

'Still no sign of him,' said the first cop.

'Must be constipated,' said the second.

I sat watching the cops watching out for me for a full five minutes. It was almost surreal. One of them passed me a sandwich – very nice it was too. And there was no sign of life inside my office.

A double-decker bus pulled up outside the building, and the lights from the top deck illuminated the darkened room we were sitting in. One of the cops turned round to look at me, turned back and, in a quick double-take, turned to look at me again, his eyes wide with amazement.

'What the fuck are you doing here?' he asked.

'What the fuck are you doing here?' I asked.

'We're carrying out surveillance,' said the second officer.

'On who?' I asked.

'On you,' he said.

'Well, you couldn't be. I'm stood here, looking at you.'

'We've been watching you all night,' said the first cop.

'Well, you couldn't have been doing your job properly,' I said. 'Otherwise I wouldn't be standing here, looking at you. Would I?'

The two flustered cops packed their gear, and climbed down the attic steps. 'We'll have you Reynolds,' said the first cop, his head just above the attic hatch.

'You might,' I said. 'But you'll have to do a lot better than that.'

That run-in with the cops wouldn't be my last as I started to build up my business, but I was about to collide with yet another form of authority – local councillors – who would try everything within their power, by fair means and often foul, to ensure George Reynolds failed.

The police, and the local councillors, were in for one long bitter and often acrimonious fight. I have always liked a good battle, and I wasn't about to give in, when my business plans were just starting to take shape.

CHAPTER 16

The GR Club

The basket meals at the GR Club, my first venture into the world of nightclubs, were substantial: heaps of scampi and a couple of chips.

The club had been fitted out luxuriously with mustard-coloured, thick carpets, the latest modern seating and a well-stocked bar. On the wall hung an impressive, eye-catching picture of Durham Cathedral, all lit up, which was made by a firm in Newcastle. Shildon Cabinetmakers – myself, my cousin Richie and Stevie Molloy, as well as a couple of casual labourers – had fitted out the club, and business was very brisk indeed.

The building – formerly known as the Snowplough Hall because it was shaped like a snowplough, coming to a sharp point at the junction of Harker Street and Main Street, Shildon – was the only nightclub in the town, and the place to be.

There was a small dance floor at one end, the bar running along the main length of the club and then an eating area, with tables and chairs, where the bar meals were cooked and served by a dark-haired Italian beauty called Theresa Ross.

On the ground floor of the building, below the club, I had opened a milk bar – the Dolphin Milk Bar. Theresa Ross, from Spennymoor, County Durham was only 17 when she came to work with me in the milk bar. She had been recommended to me by a friend. We worked together closely, working long hours, and romance blossomed. Theresa moved into my two-roomed house in Harker Street, only yards from the Milk Bar and the nightclub, and we proved to be a winning team, both in business and on the domestic front.

The Harker Street house was a little cramped, with my Alsatian dog, Dolph – named after the milk bar – always insisting on sitting and sleeping on the settee. Richie was always a bit wary of the dog. Things would improve, I knew, because I intended to buy up some of the properties in Harker Street and fully renovate them. I also had big plans for a patch of land opposite, on which I intended to build a nice modern bungalow.

When the Dophin Milk Bar was opened, I slipped the reporter from *The Northern Echo* a ten-bob note. 'Give us a good write-up, son,' I said. It turned out it didn't need the publicity, business took off from day one.

The milk bar had a kind of American theme and Theresa served cappuccino and the like, milk shakes and meals. Scampi and chips was always very popular. Lorry drivers passing through, sales reps, locals and even members of the local constabulary frequented the milk bar. For the police there was a special ingredient in the cappuccino – laxative.

I preferred payment in cash, but was never one to turn an opportunity away, and when one lorry driver suggested he could pay for a breakfast with a box of scampi, I agreed. He would turn up at the milk bar virtually every morning for bacon, egg, sausage, beans, toast and a pot of tea. We were making a healthy profit. The currency: boxes of scampi. The same thing happened with a sales rep selling shoes, a lorry driver delivering 21-inch television sets and a bloke who worked for a tea company.

In one corner of the milk bar stood a pin table, in another a couple of one-armed bandits and there was a juke box packed with all the latest hits. My links with Vince Landa secured the bandits, which were imported through a mafia contact in the United States. A container load of bandits had been shipped to the north-east and I set up another thriving little enterprise, Dolphin Automatics, and managed to get the fruit machines into several pubs and working men's clubs in County Durham. They provided me with a healthy return. Initially, my applications to get licences to operate the bandits for the milk bar and the nightclub had been rejected by the local council, so I had to operate them illegally without licenses for a spell.

As the storerooms in the milk bar became crammed with television sets, boxes of Hush Puppy shoes and boxes of tea, and the freezers were packed to bursting with boxes of scampi, it was obvious that something needed to be done.

'What are we going to do with all this scampi?' asked Theresa, when I arrived at the milk bar after a shift at Shildon Cabinetmakers.

A gala night, I thought, was a great idea and would certainly shift our surplus stock. But I had one small obstacle to overcome – finding a drummer for the resident band. We had a decent singer, a guitarist and a pianist. I made a few phone calls and was told a talented young drummer would call me in the morning.

The lad called early, as I was promised, and later arrived in the milk bar. 'I'm Stuart Johnston,' said the lad. 'I spoke to you this morning about the drummer's job.'

Stuart had ridden his bicycle to Shildon all the way from

the family's home in Gainford, ten miles away. He could have done with losing a bit of weight. He was not the athletic type.

We went upstairs to the club and Stuart started rattling off his quite impressive track record. He had been recommended to me by Maxi Temple and he told me he had studied drums under Frank King in London. Another one of King's students, he said, was Phil Collins. 'Never heard of him,' I said.

Stuart took to the Premier drum kit, started off his routine: a paradiddle here and there, a straight eight, two beat, a roll, then a final flush finish. Even without any backing tapes, or anyone on the piano, I had to hand it to the lad; he could make that drum kit sing. I gave him the job.

The special gala night was well advertised on flyers throughout the town and, when the night arrived, the GR Club was packed to the rafters, with standing room only. On one side of the club stood some local bad lads and on the other some members of the local constabulary. They spent most of the night avoiding each other, as might be expected. The lure of the free spot prizes must have been what had attracted so many people. A group of hawkers, or gypsies, were also in the club, and they looked pretty mean. If there was to be any trouble, I was expecting it to be from their quarter.

In the kitchen Theresa was working like a Trojan, preparing the bar meals. The menu was quite extensive: scampi and chips, scampi and peas, scampi, chips and peas, and ... scampi.

'You want plenty of salt, plenty of salt, on the scampi,' I told Theresa.

Stuart took to the stage, Dave Buxton was on the piano, our Richie, who played a mean guitar, also jumped up and Peter Topping was the lead vocalist, a very talented young lad. The band struck up, playing a medley of hits by The Shadows, and the multicoloured lights in the ceiling shone on to the empty dance floor. This was going to be a very successful night, I thought.

Within an hour, the barman, Mick Riley, approached me as I was putting my monkey suit on, getting ready to MC.

'The light ale's gone off,' he said.

'Shove the hose pipe in,' I said.

With the mic in my hand, I took to the stage to announce the first spot prize. 'A big hand for the band,' I said, and the crowd applauded.

'Tonight, as you know, is gala night at the GR Club,' I said, 'and, as you know, we have some wonderful, wonderful spot prizes to give away. So, without much further ado, can I ask you all to please take to the dance floor.'

The band struck up: 'I remember when rock was young, Me and Suzie had so much fun ...'

A few couples took to the floor, some couples jiving, some women dancing around their handbags, the lights flashed and the red spot landed on one of the women. I took to the stage.

'It's your lucky night, Madam,' I said, as one of the lads handed me a few boxes. 'You've won a box of tea.' I handed it to the woman. 'A nice box of scampi ... ooh, it's as cold as a block of ice, that.' I handed the box over. 'A pair of Hush Puppy shoes, for the man in your life,' I handed the shoes over. 'And,' I said, as Stuart played a roll on the drums. 'A nice, new, 21-inch television set.' The TV, I handed to one of the women's friends, as she was overloaded, and the group of them went to sit back at their seats, delighted with the prizes.

The band struck up again: 'I remember when rock was young, Me and Suzie had so much fun ...'

As the night progressed, many people collected spot prizes; the salt in the scampi kept the punters crying out for more beer, so the hose pipe had to be put into another tank ... and the band played on. Theresa and I, and the barman, were run off our feet.

Members of the local constabulary kept to their side of the room and the local bad lads kept to their side, but the travellers, it appeared, were edging for a fight. I could see it in their body language. The locals stared at them with disdain.

It all erupted when the band struck up the Cher hit 'Gypsies, Tramps and Thieves': 'We hear it from the people of the town, they call us ...' Coincidence or not, all hell broke loose, so I grabbed my baseball bat, threatened to bang a few heads, and threw the gypsies, one by one, down the narrow club stairs.

After the night was over, and the last of the drinkers made their way home under the impression that they were a lot more intoxicated than they were, I made my way to the gypsy camp site on the outskirts of the town, set fire to an oily rag protruding from a drum of petrol and sent it careering down an embankment, rolling towards the gypsies' caravans. They must have got the message that I wouldn't tolerate any bother in my club, because I never saw them again. I had always liked to think the GR Club was quite exclusive.

Playing with fire, as the old saying goes, can result in getting burned, but when fire broke out at the GR Club it wasn't me who was playing with it, it was an exotic cabaret star with an eight-foot-long python, whose speciality was encouraging the fearsome-looking reptile to curl around her body while she threw flames from her gob.

It was all going swimmingly until a flame set light to the stage curtains, which sent a magician's rabbit jumping out of the top hat and his doves flying around the room, as well as singeing the eyebrows of the male punters in the front row who had sat so near to catch a glimpse of the artiste's very long legs. Thankfully, the damage to the club was limited to the stage and the front row of seats and the snake and the rest of the animals escaped unscathed.

I was able to attract some top acts to the GR Club, among them Billy J Kramer, who restarted his career there, comedian Roy Walker, Dustin Gee, The Krankies and comedian Freddie

Starr. But my greatest coup was attracting the popular duo Peters and Lee at the height of their success, when their hit single 'Welcome Home' was at Number One in the charts. They played the GR Club for the princely sum of £12.50. I had struck a deal with John Wray, who ran the Spennymoor-based artiste's agency AIR International. The artistes would play the working men's clubs in the first part of the night and then travel on to a nightclub for the remainder.

Peters and Lee – Lenny Peters was blind and the female half of the duo was driving – got lost on their way to the GR Club and had to ask for directions. They asked none other than Mike Amos, a resident of Shildon and one of the top newspaper reporters in the north-east who was working for *The Northern Echo*. As sure as night follows day the incident with the geographically challenged Peters and Lee made the columns of the newspaper. After they finished their spot, which attracted a capacity crowd to the club, the pair asked for a bonus, as their song was the top of the hit parade and they had only recently appeared on *Opportunity Knocks*. They even tried to get out of the contract they had signed with John Wray – but I was having none of it. The top stars left Shildon feeling slightly short-changed.

The GR Club was packing them in, night after night; the Dolphin Milk Bar was the most popular eaterie in Shildon, and Shildon Cabinetmakers were securing new contract after new contract fitting out working men's clubs. Theresa, myself and the other lads in the business were working from 8am every morning often until 2am the next day. Business was absolutely booming.

Theresa and I moved into a brand new bungalow I had built to my own specifications on a plot of land in Surtees Avenue, not far from the milk bar and nightclub. The bungalow was a little palace, with marble floors throughout, including the garage, a nice cocktail bar and heavy, drape curtains that opened and closed by remote control. We bought all mod cons for the kitchen and everything in the house, as always, was finished to perfection.

Some of the cash I had made I invested in buying up all the houses in Harker Street – there was eight in all – and I set about refurbishing them to sell off at a profit. A slight problem emerged when I asked contractors to move in to demolish one of the houses, and they demolished the wrong one.

As I stood in the bungalow late one night, looking out on Surtees Avenue and Harker Street, which was on the opposite side, I noticed a Mini car pull up. The driver got out, walked into one of the houses I was having renovated and pissed all over the new staircase I had just had fitted. I was absolutely livid and grabbed my coat to confront him.

By the time I got to the Mini I noticed the driver, another bloke and two women they had in tow enter the nearby Indian restaurant. I went into the house under renovation to inspect the stairs, and the smell of fresh urine filled the air. I ran back to the bungalow and phoned big Stevie Molloy, asking him to come down to Harker Street.

When Stevie arrived I told him what had happened and asked him if he wanted a piss. He said no, so we both walked over to the pub and downed three pints of bitter in about eight minutes, came back to the house under renovation and relieved ourselves in an empty paint tin.

I opened the window on the Mini and poured the piss all over the four seats. Stevie and I then went into the bungalow and waited for the Mini driver and his friends to come out of the Indian restaurant.

We watched as the two men and their girlfriends came out, every one of them smiling and chatting away. They all got into the Mini, then quickly jumped out.

'Oh, God! Can you smell piss?' asked the shocked driver.

'Oh no, my dress is soaking,' said his girlfriend, dressed in a white dress which now had a yellow streak on her arse and up her back.

Stevie and I came out of the bungalow and walked over to the Mini.

'Excuse me,' I said to the driver. 'I hope you don't mind, but I've just had a piss in your Mini.'

'You fucking what?' said the driver. 'You fucking what? Are you off your fucking head, or what?'

'No,' I said. 'I was just busting for a piss, so I had one in your car. He did as well.' I pointed to big Stevie.

'Aye. I've had a piss in your car,' said Stevie. 'I was busting as well. I hope you don't mind.'

'We'll see who fucking minds,' said the driver. 'I'm phoning the cops.'

Stevie and I went back into the bungalow waiting for the cops to arrive, and when they did we walked out into the street as the Mini driver, his face still full of shocked anger, explained what had happened.

'George,' said the cop, who knew me. 'Is it right that you have just pissed in this man's car?'

'Yes, that's right, officer,' I said. 'I was busting for a piss.'

'This isn't that *Candid Camera*, is it?' the cop asked, but he could see it was no joking matter.

'Why the hell did you piss in his car?' he asked. 'Your house is just there.'

'Because he pissed on my stairs,' I said, and I explained to the officer how the man had entered my property under renovation without my permission and had slashed all over the staircase.

'I want him fucking charging,' the Mini driver said.

'Hang on, hang on,' I said. 'I want you charging as well, and I can just see the both of us arguing in court. You pissed on my stairs and I pissed in your car. The press will have a fucking field day.'

After yet more argument, the police officer decided not to press charges against either of us. Stevie and I went home, and the Mini driver and the rest of his party picked up some pieces of cardboard, put them on the Mini seats and went on their way.

The run-in with the police was by no means my first and it would not be my last, but it was probably the funniest alleged crime the officer had had to investigate in his career.

My run-ins with the local councils, however, were not as straightforward and they were becoming more frequent. I had built a second bungalow, identical to my home, on a plot of land a few yards further down Harker Street, but trying to gain planning permission retrospectively became quite a headache.

I was soon to learn that, unknown to me, I had made some enemies at Shildon Town Council and Sedgefield District Council, who appeared to be envious of my success. I decided to apply another one of my old master Mr Martin's ten golden rules: Keep your friends close, but your enemies closer still.

I had to get someone in the know in my pocket and get as much information as possible on who was blocking my path, and why. It would mean greasing a few palms, and laying out some hard cash on a state-of-the-art transmitter and receiver and tapping into a few telephone calls.

Fully equipped, I entered the shadowy world of industrial espionage.

CHAPTER 17

The Spy

The heels of my boots cut into my backside, as I clipped the wires from the field engineer's telephone to the cables at the top of the 20-foot-high telegraph pole, to call up one of my local council representatives and give him a piece of my mind, and a little verbal abuse, anonymously.

The pillar of the community had been slagging me off behind the closed doors of the council chamber, but I had heard every word of it. An out-and-out conman, he had called me, a convicted criminal, a loudmouth and a villain. The man didn't even know me.

I dialled his number on the engineer's telephone, which I had been able to acquire – quite illegally – from a site in Bishop Auckland.

'Ring, ring ... ring, ring,' his telephone went at the other end of the line.

'Hello, councillor,' I said.

'Hello,' he answered. 'Who is this?'

'A friend,' I said. 'A friend who is a little concerned about the rumours that are being spread about you down at the old town hall.'

'What rumours?' he asked.

'Oh, just about your regular visits to Middlesbrough to see that very young girl. You know, the one with the thigh-high leather boots and the mini skirt so short it resembles a belt?'

'Who is this?' the councillor demanded. 'Who is this?'

'I bet your wife doesn't know about her. Does she?' I said.

'I demand to know who you are!' the councillor shouted down the line.

'Oh, you don't know me. I'm just a conman, a criminal, a loudmouth and a villain.'

'Reynolds? It's you, Reynolds, isn't it?' the councillor said. 'I'm getting straight on to the police to have this call traced.'

'Do what the hell you like,' I said. 'You fucking old pervert.'

As I unclipped the wires, I spotted a police officer walking along the street, torch in hand. I grabbed hold of the metal bars at the top of the pole, clung on and shifted my feet further up the pole. For some reason – he couldn't have heard me – the officer shone his torch on the pole and the beam slowly moved up towards me. I moved my feet still further. The heels of my boots were now dug so far into my backside the pain was shooting up my back.

The constable lowered the beam, switched off his torch, and went on his way.

After a few minutes, I climbed down from the telegraph pole, my bones aching, and walked off along the street with my gear. I must have looked like the hunchback of Notre Dame.

Since my first run-in with our elected representatives, I'd managed to bribe a councillor to wear a listening device – a small microphone – on his tie when he attended council meetings. I was able to hear who was winning tenders for work, who was likely to win planning permission and who – more importantly – was slagging me off.

The receiver I used was in a briefcase, and I would drive and park near to the town hall, as the meetings got under way. The listening device was surprisingly clear: you could hear every cough and splutter in the council chamber. When police raided my home later, they said their surveillance gear was obsolete compared with my state-of-the-art equipment.

I was listening in when my application for permission to build a warehouse next to the Spanish-style bungalow Theresa and I were now living in, in Surtees Avenue, came to a committee that met behind closed doors. Not that I needed permission: the 'poshest warehouse in County Durham' as it was described in the local paper, *The Evening Despatch*, had already been built.

I had a letter from the local council when I first applied to build a second bungalow, stating that the land I had bought was earmarked 'for industrial purposes only'. So I built the second bungalow, on the same design as my nice home, with the same style of windows, doors and everything. It was the best storage facility in the county.

As I tuned in the receiver, the local councillors spared no thought for who might be listening in.

'This man is a convicted crook who is riding roughshod over the people in this town. He can't get away with it,' said one councillor.

'The man is an aggressive, despicable bully. He walks around in that silly, leather trilby hat, with that awful Alsatian dog of his, as if he owns the town,' said a mealy-mouthed female councillor.

'We must take a stand against this man,' said another. 'If he gets away with this, we will be made to look a laughing stock.'

Later, a second committee granted planning permission for

the poshest warehouse in County Durham. And, in the laughing-stock corridors of power, I knew who my enemies were, thanks to the councillor – who I could name but I will spare him his blushes – and my own hi-tech bugging equipment.

The councillor, who could well handle himself, came in useful for some strongarm work, too, but more of that later.

Shildon Cabinetmakers had become so successful and profitable, with contracts to fit out Spennymoor Working Men's Club, Stanley Social Club, the Wheelcroft Club and the Railway Institute, to name but a few, we were rolling in it, so I decided to close down the equally successful GR Club after it had been running for three years. I donated the fantastic illuminated picture of Durham Cathedral from the GR Club to the club in Spennymoor and it took pride of place on one of its walls for many years. I decided I needed to concentrate on my other business interests. By this time, Shildon Cabinetmakers was turning in a very respectable £2 million profit every year.

The GR Club, and a few other properties of mine, stood empty for a while, but that did not stop Sedgefield District Council, which had its main office in Spennymoor, charging me rates. Furious, I barged into a private meeting of councillors to ask them why I should pay rates on an empty nightclub, and found them all sitting in luxury, eating nice sandwiches and drinking tea, cold beer and whisky – at the taxpayers' expense. I was more livid than ever, told all the councillors what I thought and the police were called. I called on a few selected councillors personally at their homes over the next day or two to give them another dressing down. The police were called again.

As my run-ins with councillors became more frequent, so did my confrontations with a police officer who appeared to have taken over where Detective Inspector Graham Knott, in Sunderland, had left off. His name was Detective Inspector

Peter Eddy and he chased me around County Durham like a man possessed.

One day we were working on fitting out a club and we had to dismantle a metal fire escape. Once we had taken it down, the fire escape was ours to do with as we pleased. Peter Dexter, a local businessman, was doing out the Park Head Hotel and, when we passed the pub, I thought the fire escape we were going to scrap would fit the hotel like a glove, so I sold it to Peter Dexter for its scrap value of £2,000.

That night Peter Eddy and two other police officers called at my house, intent on arresting me for the alleged theft of the fire escape. He locked me up for 12 hours. It only took a call to the club we were fitting out and for one of the committee men to explain the fire escape was ours once we took it from the building for me to be released from the vice-like grip of Det Insp Eddy. Later, I called Peter Dexter and asked him what the hell was going on. Peter Eddy turned up on my doorstep yet again, claiming I had threatened Peter Dexter. The episode taught me that Det Insp Peter Eddy was like a terrier with a bone and he was on a mission – to put George Reynolds behind bars.

Shildon Cabinetmakers secured a lucrative contract to fit out The Zodiac Club in Whitehaven, Cumbria, owned by millionaire coal haulier Mike Morgan. Richie Tennick and a few of the other lads went over to fit it out, and did a fantastic job as usual, and we were paid about £250,000 in total.

Stuart Johnston, the drummer from the old GR Club, went over to The Zodiac – I was acting as his kind of manager – and put a band in. A visiting group later spotted a number of very classy, custom-built guitars, which happened to be stolen. I was arrested and convicted of handling the stolen guitars and sentenced to 22 months, spending my time in HMP Gloucester. It was an offence I still deny – I had receipts for the instruments. I was later released on appeal.

It was while serving my time at Gloucester, where the Governor had heard of my building skills and got me to put a team together to build the prison gymnasium, that I was brought back to the north-east, at taxpayers' expense, for a trial over some allegedly stolen wire mesh.

I had taken the welded mesh from a skip in West Auckland, and the fella who runs the builder's yard knew I had done the same in the past, but paid for the material the following day. Peter Eddy got wind of it, and I was charged with theft. While he was questioning me, a load of ready-mixed concrete I had ordered was delivered and had set by the time I was released.

After that incident, I was sent to HMP Gloucester for the handling offence in connection with the custom-built guitars, while the police – Peter Eddy – built up a case against me for the allegedly stolen welded mesh. I was convicted of the theft and sentenced to one day's imprisonment concurrently with the sentence I was already serving. It was hardly worth the effort and the expense, but that's the criminal justice system, and the police, for you.

It was not long before I was back in jail – though Peter Eddy played no part in my arrest or conviction. It was my most hapless crime, which would have put even the most inept detective hot on my trail, and it happened when I stole explosives from a quarry in Richmond, North Yorkshire.

I'd left my getaway van parked nearby, and I stood in five feet of water, breathing through a reed, while the police looked for me. They knew they were looking for me – a sign on the van used in the burglary was a dead give-away, really. The Dolphin Milk Bar, Shildon, it read.

My lapse back into crime – and it was the only lapse, I was trying to go straight – cost me dearly: a further 21 months behind bars. I knew, however, that in Stevie Molloy, Richie Tennick, Harry Pincher and the other lads at Shildon

Cabinetmakers, I had a strong and loyal team who would look after business, the business I could not handle while behind bars.

CHAPTER 18

'The Devil Herself'

The door of the bungalow in Surtees Avenue, Shildon, burst open and in marched officers from the North East Regional Crime Squad (NERCS). They frisked me, searched the house, and then led me away to the station. From the house they took an air rifle, a field engineer's telephone worth £54 and a few other bits and pieces.

After a grilling at the local police station, I was taken handcuffed to the magistrates court in Newton Aycliffe to face charges. One of the magistrates on the local bench was Carl Williams, who ran a haulage firm in County Durham, working alongside his young wife Susan, from Byers Green.

I knew of Carl but had never met him, and though – as far as I can remember – he wasn't sitting in my court that day, my appearance before the magistrates, I later learned, was a topic of conversation around his and many other people's dinner tables that night.

By this time I had been living in the bungalow with Patricia

Smitheram, a hard-faced woman who had been running a boarding house in Darlington before I met her, and her niece Karen Brown. Theresa Ross and I had parted company several months before the other women arrived. She had fallen for another man, a man I had helped by giving him a job. I was sad, but these things happen.

Smitheram, who had basically taken me for a ride, had done a runner to a bloke she had been having an affair with in Shrewsbury, leaving Karen and I in the bungalow. With Smitheram gone, romance blossomed between Karen and I and we would later marry. Her aunt, however, was a woman scorned, and hell, as I found out that morning, hath no fury ... She had a track record of attaching herself to wealthy businessmen.

Before our acrimonious, but inevitable, parting, she had planned on flying out to Spain for a holiday with a female friend. The friend, I discovered, was male and it was not long before someone – an associate of mine – flew out to Spain to have a word, as it were, in this man's ear. It must have been a bloody loud word, as the man ended up in hospital. He claimed he had fallen down the stairs.

Smitheram, whom I later decribed in court as 'the devil herself', had a friend by the name of Billy Bell, who owned a flat within Morpeth Castle, Northumberland, to whom she fled on the night she did a runner from the bungalow.

I had lavished on her – foolishly I know now – very expensive jewellery and clothing and the high life suited her. When she fled the bungalow she loaded a TR7 car – my TR7 car – with the goods I had bought her and drove across the border into Northumberland.

We all know that an Englishman's home is his castle, but I travelled to Morpeth and scaled the castle walls to retrieve the property she was holding that was mine. Once inside, I picked up a telephone and rang Mr Bell.

'Mr Bell,' I said. 'George Reynolds here.'

'This is a castle,' said Mr Bell. 'It has kept marauding Scots out, so it will keep you out. You might as well go home, because you'll never get inside.'

'But I am inside, Mr Bell,' I said. 'In fact I'm just outside your apartment.'

I tried to cause as little fuss as possible as I retrieved my property and, later, my TR7 motor. After that little incident, Smitheram went back to her regular lover in Shrewsbury – and then hatched a very elaborate plot to fit me up. With her information, police were to charge me with thirty-eight separate offences, which landed me in Durham Jail, on remand, for nine long months. If convicted I was facing a long, long time behind bars.

Smitheram had approached a regional crime squad officer, Detective Sergeant Ken Mason, telling him she had a lot of information on my alleged criminal activities. She sang like a canary, but she was way out of tune. The fact she had been arrested in connection with an alleged burglary on a doctor's house, in which antiques were stolen, was no coincidence. She was obviously trying to use the 'information' she had on me, as some kind of bargaining tool on the burglary arrest.

I had shown Smitheram the high life, taking her to the fanciest restaurants, buying her expensive designer clothes and jewellery. I took her to visit my old friend Tommy Robson, who had bought a nice bungalow in Washton, North Yorkshire. I had bought a nice bit of property myself from Tommy, a cottage in Dalton. The one thing I was guilty of was breaking one of my old master Mr Martin's ten golden rules. In her case I had let my heart rule my head, and she was intent that I would pay a heavy price.

She told detectives I had bugging devices, a field engineer's telephone and an air rifle in the bungalow and claimed that I had set a cafe on fire in Croxdale, a scrapyard on fire in

Hendon, Sunderland, and had caused criminal damage to a number of cars, among other things.

I appeared before Sedgefield magistrates in handcuffs and an application for bail was refused. Magistrates are known to have friends among councillors – and are often JPs themselves – I often wonder whether that had any bearing on my refusal for bail.

Not long before my remand to Durham Jail I had been contacted by the vicar of St John's Church in Shildon, who had a problem. The key to the church safe had been missing for some time, and marriage lines were locked inside.

The couple wanting to get their hands on their marriage lines planned to go to Somerset House in London – until the vicar remembered George Reynolds and his safe-blowing days. He called me, asking for my assistance.

I took my tool wrap, containing detonators, gelignite, wire, pliers, crowbar and my little pen torch over to the church and met the vicar. A nice chap, he was. He took me into the room containing the safe, a large Chubb which, if I remember rightly, was one of only about fourteen ever made.

'Could you draw the curtains, please, vicar?' I asked. The vicar drew the curtains.

'Could you turn out the lights, please? I can only work in the dark.' The vicar turned out the lights and left the room.

I sorted my tools out, placed the gelignite and connected the detonator, and I could feel the old adrenalin rush as I triggered the detonator. The tumblers purred like a kitten, I turned the handle and the safe door opened.

The vicar came into the room. 'That is marvellous,' he said. 'It only took you three minutes.'

'Three minutes. I must be getting rusty,' I said.

The vicar invited me to open a garden party that weekend and during a kind of sermon he said: 'Brethren, sometimes the bad guys are the good guys,' and he related to the gathered crowd how I had saved the day for the local couple by opening the church safe. The good guy, turned apparent bad guy, now locked in Durham Jail didn't have much to look forward to. It appeared the police were going all-out to make these charges stick.

While I was on remand, Det Sgt Ken Mason, and many other police officers, including my old sparring partner Det Insp Peter Eddy, went on a fishing expedition, contacting anyone, anywhere with whom I might have been in contact and who might have something to say about me, something I had done or something I had said, which would give them a scintilla of evidence that a criminal offence had been committed by me.

It resulted in the charge sheet containing thirty-eight indictments. According to the prosecution, I was one of the biggest villains in the north-east. The charges ranged from criminal damage to theft, arson, unlicensed possession of a firearm and assault. It was obvious they wanted to throw the book at me. And this entire very, very costly police investigation and prosecution case had been sparked by one person: the 'timeless courtesan', as she was described in the newspapers, Patricia Ann Smitheram. In a complete travesty of justice, police had even put Smitheram together with my fiancée, Karen Brown, in the same cell; a point not missed by the trial judge.

It was alleged I had assaulted councillors, caused damage to cars belonging to the relations of councillors, damaged cars belonging to the family of my one-time partner Theresa Ross, because I had a vendetta against her family, set a scrap yard in Hendon, Sunderland, alight, set a cafe in Croxdale, County Durham, on fire, slashed tyres on vehicles ... the list was so long it appeared I had spent all my time waging vendettas and settling old scores. I must have had very little time for other business, if the charge sheet was to be believed.

The charges were split into batches of eight and the cases

were to go to Teesside Crown Court, Durham Crown Court, Newcastle Crown Court, and drag on for a full nine months.

And while the wheels of justice turned at their almost comatose pace, I was ordered to see a prison psychologist. I was sharing a cell with Keith Bell, who was involved with a notorious north-east punk rock band called the Angelic Upstarts; their biggest hit single was titled 'Who Killed Liddle Towers', about the death in police custody of a man by that name. The band were notorious because of their gimmick of kicking a pig's head about the stage while they sang the song.

Keith Bell, who I got on with very well, was a kind of unofficial bouncer for the band and was well known in the region as a hard case. Keith had just been to see the prison psychologist when he told me it was my turn. I was quite surprised. It was bad enough me having to share a ward in the prison hospital for a spell – because my charges included alleged arson – next to murderers and criminals bordering on the mentally insane, without having to be put under the spell of the local headshrinker.

The psychologist turned out to be a young woman – she looked like a young student – and she told me she was there to help me and wanted to test my mental dexterity.

'Your name?' she asked, after I sat myself down and made myself comfortable.

'George Reynolds,' I said.

'Right, George,' she said. 'I want you to imagine you are in the middle of a jungle, completely lost and on your own. How would you find your way out?'

'Well,' I said, 'I'd climb the highest tree I could find and look out to see if I could spot a road, a footpath or a railway line.'

'No,' she said. 'You couldn't climb a tree, because you have a bad leg.'

'Right,' I said. 'In that case, I'd use my compass.'

'But you don't have a compass.'

Top left: Me during World War II – aged 6!

Top right: Outside Grandma Tennick's shop in Sunderland.

Bottom left: My sister Cathy, Grandma Tennick and me in the rear yard of the shop.

Bottom right: Aged 17 at Seaburn with my dad's boat *The Windfall*.

A cheerless scene: the windowless dormitories at Sambourne – snow had fallen outside – and the dining hall at Besford Court School.

BESFORD COURT, WORCESTER.

A RESIDENTIAL SPECIAL SCHOOL CERTIFIED BY THE BOARD
OF EDUCATION.

Telephone
and
Telegrams
PERSHORE
74

Stations
DEFFORD
L.M. & S.R
2 miles.

PERSHORE
G.W.R.
4¼ miles.

NAME OF PUPIL........ GEORGE REYNOLDS ....

Form of Guarantee.

I/WE hereby guarantee

The above named child will be purchased from you for the sum £100 : 0 : 0 and we will from that point be responsible for the treatment , maintenance and training of the above whilst a pupil of Besford Court School.

We will pay, on admission , the sum of £10 to cover the cost of the child's clothing outfit for the full course.

To pay the return fare and any travelling expenses incurred in connection with leave of absence granted at any time.

From 8 yrs of age we are allowed to work the boy for 8 hours a day and no more, Saturday and Sunday are to be used for education. When he reaches 12 yrs of age we are allowed to work the boy for 12 hours a day and no more, Saturday and Sunday to be set asside for basic education.

To remove the child from the school when such a course becomes necessary, free of all cost to the Managers.

To defray, in the event of the decease of the child, all funeral and other expenses incidental thereto.

If this child does not come up to our expectations we may return him and all incombrances will remain valid.

Signature — *J. Thompson*
Director of Education.

Address .. Education Offices, 15 John Street,
Sunderland.

Public Authority responsible .... Sunderland L.E.C

Address ..   As above

Name of Witness   R S Bower

Address   15 John Street, Sunderland.

Date 10th April

The official form revealing how I was bought for £100. (*Inset*) The notorious 'punishment wall' at Besford Court School.

The Besford Boys are back in town

Jimmy McEvoy of Red House. Sentenced to five years at Sambourne and Besford. His crime: Playing truant.

Jimmy Conley of Red House. Spent almost nine years in the approved schools. His crime: Theft of a purse (which he denies).

Danny Lavelle of Pennywell. Spent seven years at Croombe Court (after Sambourne closed) and Besford Court. His crime: Playing truant.

Geordie Lavelle from Pennywell. Sent to Sambourne and Besford for seven years. His crime: Playing truant.

George Reynolds formerly of Sunderland. Sentenced to eight years at the approved schools. His crime: Playing truant.

Joe Mather of Farringdon. Sent to the approved schools for six-and-a-half years. His crime: Stealing cigarettes and a box of chocolates from a van.

Davey Hopper of Red House. Spent six years at Sambourne and Besford. His crime: Stealing a cricket bat from Monkwearmouth School.

Dempsey Green from Castletown. Spent two years at Besford. His crime: Playing truant.

Top left: In my merchant navy uniform.

Top right: The old Sunderland football team at Besford Court School circa 1947. The picture includes Joe Mather and Davey Hopper (*top row second and third from left respectively*) and Jimmy Conley (*front row second from right*).

Bottom: The Besford boys as they are today.

Top: Hard at work renovating the GR club.

Bottom: Revisiting the Bungalow Café in Sunderland.

Top: Sylvia the pig's old sty at Besford.

Bottom: Revisiting the mine made into a charity box that I used to steal from as a boy.

Fame and fortune at last! With my Rolls Royce and personalised number plate outside my luxury home in Durham. (*Inset*) More trappings of wealth – a picture of my yacht, *Secret Love*.

Top: With my beautiful wife Susan and the Worthington Cup – Feethams Ground, Darlington Football Club.

Bottom: The only way to travel – my helicopter!

'Then I'd dig a trench and tunnel my way out.'

'But you haven't got a spade.'

'You're making things awkward for me,' I said. 'I'm in the middle of a jungle, with a bad leg, no compass and no spade.'

'That's right,' she said. 'How would you find your way out?'

'Well,' I said. 'I'd dig a trench with my bare hands, start a fire and burn the jungle down, jump in the trench and get out when all the jungle had been burned.'

'But you don't have any matches,' she said.

'Then I'd start the fire by rubbing two dry sticks together,' I said.

'Thank you, George,' she said. 'That little exercise was to test your survival instincts. Now, I want you to imagine you're at the top of Newgate Street in Bishop Auckland and you see a giant battleship heading towards you on a collision course. What would you do?'

'I'd sink it with my torpedo,' I said.

'Ha, ha, ha,' laughed the psychologist. 'And where did you get the torpedo?'

'From the same place you got the battleship,' I said. 'Peter's Army and Navy Stores.'

'Ha, ha. You're quite dry, aren't you, George?' she said. 'Now, what do you do for a living?'

'I'm the managing director of my own company,' I said.

'Really?' She seemed genuinely surprised.

'Do you like cars?'

'I do,' I said.

'And what type of car do you have?' she asked.

'I have two: a Rolls-Royce and a Mercedes Benz.'

'Really,' she said. It was obvious to me the psychologist had not been fully briefed, if she had been briefed at all.

'And do you have your own house?' she asked.

'I do,' I said. 'I have a beautiful detached bungalow with all mod cons, even the curtains close like the curtains do in a picture hall by remote control. All the floors are marble, even the garage floor.'

'Well,' said the psychologist. 'You must have plenty of money to be able to afford all that.'

'I have,' I said. 'I'm a millionaire.'

'Really,' she said. 'Then what are you doing in here?'

'I shouldn't be in here,' I said. 'I've been framed.'

The psychologist terminated the interview there and then and later she contacted my lawyer – and good friend – Neville Fairclough to give him her assessment of my mental state. She said I was suffering from delusions of grandeur, living in a fantasy world where I believed I was the millionaire director of my own company. Neville explained my background and then got my agreement to call in an independent expert psychologist from Durham University, who just happened to be the young student psychologist's tutor. He was not impressed that she had failed to check my background, and any report she would produce in court – which, left unchallenged, would have painted me as a barmpot – could be quickly and effectively challenged by the independent report from our own top expert.

The court cases, remands and trials dragged on and on, and during all the outlining of evidence, the cross-examination, the calling of witnesses, the flowery closing speeches by the barristers and the judges' summing ups, the public gallery was packed with George Reynolds' supporters.

Even in the witness box, a number of witnesses called by the prosecution were on my side. Romana Ross, sister of Theresa, said in open court: 'Why are you a doing this to George? He is a fine man.'

'This man had a vendetta against your family,' said the prosecution.

'George has never had a Lambretta. What are you a talking about?' Romana replied.

The vicar of St John's took to the stand: 'Sometimes the bad guys are the good guys,' he said, the Bible not far from his hand, as he outlined the favour I had done by opening the church safe.

During the initial stages of the case, I had turned to Det Sgt Ken Mason and his colleagues and told them: 'You will never pin all this on me. My boss will make sure you don't pin all this on me.'

'Who is your boss?' Det Sgt Mason asked.

'It's him upstairs,' I said, tongue in cheek. 'The great judge in the sky. I have his direct telephone number, and he's ex-directory, you know.'

The wheels of justice turned very, very slowly and sometimes ground to a halt, but at the end of the long nine months I was found not guilty on almost all charges, convicted of only a couple of minor criminal damage charges, possessing the field engineer's telephone – which I had used to call my councillor friends after climbing up the telegraph pole – and possessing tear gas cartridges and an air rifle. I was given a jail sentence and fined, but having spent nine months on remand, I was a free man.

The trials had been the biggest waste of police and court resources – and taxpayers' money – I had ever come across.

And it was all started by 'the devil herself', Patricia Smitheram, a woman scorned.

CHAPTER 19

The Contract

Convicted killer Dennis Stafford had not long been out of prison, after serving 12 years for the murder of Angus Sibbet, and was still on life licence, when I received a call.

'Do you know there's a contract out on you?' he asked.

'No,' I said. 'But that's wonderful. Who's doing it?'

'I am,' he said.

'Oh. So when are you doing it?' I asked.

'I'm not,' he said. 'I don't want to end up the richest killer in the graveyard.'

Strange that, I thought, Patricia Smitheram was alleged to have told the police: 'I want to shoot Reynolds right in the bollocks', and now she was appearing at Wakefield Crown Court on a charge of possessing a sawn-off shotgun with intent to endanger my life, and the tables had turned. She told the court I had put out a contract on her, and had hired Dennis Stafford and my old friend Vince Landa as the would-be assassins. It was all a load of crap.

Smitheram, her father John Gavin, and yet another boyfriend of hers were all charged with the same offence. They claimed to be in fear of their lives when found in possession of the sawn-off shotgun.

'A gangster with killers as his henchmen' was how a barrister described me in court. Smitheram's father was said to be 'an elderly man, well and truly frightened by a villain from the north'. It was all very unfair that these nasty things were being said about me in a court of law, and I was not given the opportunity to defend myself. But I was not on trial.

True, I had met up with Vince Landa again. He had been on the run for ten years, after failing to appear before magistrates in Houghton-le-Spring, near Sunderland, on fraud charges relating to his one-armed-bandit empire. He had been on Interpol's most wanted list and spent some time in a Sicilian jail after his yacht sank off Syracuse.

Vince got in touch with me, telling me he wanted to give himself up. He said I was the only person he could trust, and I was able to put him up at the cottage in Dalton, North Yorkshire – the property I bought from my great friend Tommy Robson – so Vince lay low for a while, but not for long enough, while he prepared to hand himself over to the police.

For many years, various MPs had called for action to get Vince extradited. Questions were even asked of the Director of Public Prosecutions. But where police, MPs and even Interpol had failed, George Reynolds had succeeded, helping to bring a fugitive to justice. Vince Landa had always been very kind to me, showed me a different world really, so helping him get this problem sorted out was the least I could do.

Vince was as surprised as Dennis Stafford was to learn that I had hired them both as hitmen to bump off Patricia Smitheram. 'Doesn't that give you the fucking raging needle?' Vince would say, one of his favourite sayings.

After a bit of a media circus, with everyone scrapping for an interview with Vince, he gave himself up and I travelled to the magistrate's court for his first appearance in connection with the fraud charges laid almost ten years earlier.

His case went the distance and, after almost 11 years of self-exile in the Mediterranean, he was eventually dealt with. He was fined £2,750 on seven fraud charges, ordered to pay £1,000 costs and walked away from Teesside Crown Court a free man.

At her trial in Wakefield, Smitheram had by now become a bit of a drama queen in the witness box; she had had plenty of practice, and for her performance she should really have been given an Oscar for best supporting role. It was alleged that her father had bought the gun to seek revenge on me for splitting up his family. Smitheram's boyfriend admitted turning the shotgun into a sawn-off.

The assassination plot, for which I had supposedly hired Stafford and Landa as hitmen, was outlined to the court by Detective Sergeant Dennis Clarkson, who also claimed that Stafford and Landa were my employees. It was an outrageous statement to make in open court, and it ended up in the newspapers. All I could do was sit in the public gallery, watching the proceedings, and not utter a word in my own defence. Not for the first time, I realised that the law is indeed an ass.

John Gavin, Smitheram's father, and her boyfriend were convicted of sawing down the shotgun barrel. Gavin was sentenced to nine months jail, suspended for two years, and Queen was given 120 hours of community service. Smitheram, who was rapidly turning into a Teflon madam, and who had been described in a previous case as 'a locust', feeding off other people, was acquitted.

After the case she boasted in print that, during some of the time she lived with me, she was being heavily bankrolled by a millionaire Leeds businessman whom she called her 'sugar daddy' and whom she shagged frequently.

Business was still booming at Shildon Cabinetmakers, and I had a number of irons in the fire to expand the business, or branch out into a new direction, focusing, in the main, on producing kitchen worktops. I had analysed the worktops business, and was sure I could do it better. My contacts within the DIY trade were extensive, my experience invaluable and my desire to succeed burning more brightly than ever.

Karen Brown and I were married, and we produced two wonderful daughters: Victoria and Alexandra. Eventually, we would move into a fantastic mansion in the heart of the most scenic countryside in County Durham, Witton Hall in Witton-le-Wear. The palatial house was on the market for £100,000 and, rumour had it, Kevin Keegan was interested in buying it when he returned to Newcastle United.

I still had a great deal of work to do building up my business. I was still very keen on the idea of some kind of direct manufacturing, probably in the laminate business. I was learning more every day about the DIY trade – the producers, the distributors, the suppliers and the changes in the markets. And my little brown book was now bulging with so many contacts I would soon have to buy a new one.

A lot of what I had in mind for the business was nothing more than good old-fashioned common sense.

For a while, things on the domestic scene quietened down. Despite Karen's familial relationship with the 'devil herself' Patricia Smitheram, we had little contact with hertter, and I thought, and hoped, that her name would not feature in my life again.

But, like the proverbial bad penny, Smitheram's name did turn up when one of my best friends – a man who had helped me on my way in business – was tortured and beaten to death in one of the worst murder cases ever dealt with by police in North Yorkshire.

Smitheram's name cropped up because I was sure she had

some involvement with the passing of information. Proving it was another thing; so George Reynolds, convicted safe-blower, ex-merchant seaman, millionaire entrepreneur, maker of money and utter genius, turned his hand to the most unlikely of professions – that of detective.

CHAPTER 20

Detective Inspector Reynolds

Antiques dealer Tommy Robson, a great friend of mine from my early days in Sunderland when he ran a workshop lock-up in Gladstone Street, had done well for himself over the years, building up a solid business. He had run an antiques shop in Whitburn, near Sunderland, and retired to a nice cottage in the hamlet of Whashton, North Yorkshire, but he still had a hand in the business of antiques. I had visited Tommy regularly many times over the years – more than a dozen of those times with Patricia Smitheram. I had also bought that cottage in Dalton from Tommy.

He was a trusting old soul, never closed his curtains and hardly ever locked his door. He was very active in village life: cutting the village green and mixing with the sixty or so villagers who lived in Whashton. He even made two benches for the local quoits pitch, as well as presenting a trophy to a winning team. The village appeared idyllic: tidy lawns, colourful flowerbeds and peace – so far removed from the cobbled streets of Roker where I first met him.

News reached me that robbers had burst into his home, tied him up and tortured him in the most cruel and sadistic way imaginable, using piano wire and a crocheting hook as their weapons of evil. The raiders, who had obviously tortured Tommy to find out the combination of his safe, had killed him. Their information was specific – too specific for anyone who had not been in the house to know – that the heavy metal safe had double doors and contained £50,000, sovereigns, gold krugerrands and watches. Tommy, as well as being trusting, was also not the kind of person to give in easily, and the killers must have caused him untold pain before he released the combination to the safe.

I was absolutely devastated by Tommy's killing, and the nature of his death. In truth, he had been something of a surrogate father to me and I really felt like I had lost a member of my own family.

I put the feelers out around the north-east underworld for information, but I had more than a gut feeling that Smitheram knew something about the events leading up to Tommy's death. Not only had she been in his cottage several times, she had even stored jewellery in his safe.

I contacted Detective Sergeant Ken Mason, of the North East Regional Crime Squad. Despite him having been part of the prosecution case against me after the Smitheram fit-up, I had a lot of time for Ken. I always got the impression he would have liked me as his snout, though I could never be a copper's nark. The only time I had ever helped police with information was in the case of the murder of my pal Tommy Robson.

Det Sgt Mason was intrigued when I told him Smitheram had visited Tommy's house several times. He put a lot of work into the case, and liaised with the senior officers in North Yorkshire investigating the robbery and murder.

The police investigation lasted three weeks, and detectives were soon on the trail of the killers, thanks, in part, to my own enquiries that linked Smitheram to three men. Tommy's red Mercedes was found abandoned in the dockland area of Liverpool. Detectives from North Yorkshire travelled to Merseyside.

The big break in the manhunt, however, came when details of Tommy Robson's Access account arrived in the post at his son's address. It transpired that someone had used the credit card to buy alcohol only hours after Tommy's savage murder.

Detectives in Liverpool were able to point their counterparts from North Yorkshire in the direction of a man known locally as Willy Woodbine, real name William Taggart. He was identified as the man who had bought drinks at an off-licence shortly after Tommy was killed and he was the first of three men to be arrested.

Other clues were unearthed: fingerprints in the Mercedes and a palm print inside Tommy's cottage in Whaston. Two other men, Jack Mulliner – known in his home town of Dewsbury as Batley Jack – and a father-of-four called Raymond Bowler, who had only been out of prison for four days before the raid on Tommy's home, were soon in custody.

It turned out that the three of them – Mulliner, Taggart and Bowler – had prepared themselves for the raid on Tommy's cottage. The information about Tommy's wealth, his house, the safe, and all other details, were known by Batley Jack – Mulliner. Batley Jack had shared a cell with both Taggart and Bowler when doing a 12-month stretch and had boasted to another prisoner that a woman on the outside was providing him with information on houses ripe for burglary. That woman was Patricia Ann Smitheram.

The judge in the murder trial, Mr Justice Glidewell, said during his summing up that it was 'a deduction and not an assumption' that Smitheram had passed the information about Tommy's house, his wealth and the safe on to Batley Jack, who, in turn, shared it with his associates in the vile crime. The three were jailed for life, but Smitheram, the Teflon tart walked free.

Her 'information' had led to me spending nine months on remand in Durham Prison on more than thirty trumped-up charges and I was eventually acquitted of them all, bar two or three minor offences.

During my time in Durham Prison, it has to be said, I had made friends among inmates and in the ranks of the prison warders. Some of them were all right. I knew the prison like the back of my hand: the best cells; the little bits of knowledge that could make a prisoner's life just that bit more bearable.

It is true that while Mulliner, Taggart and Bowler were remanded to Durham Prison, awaiting trial, I did visit the jail once or twice to renew old acquaintances, and chat about the old times. During their preliminary court hearings at least two of the accused claimed they were being held in 'inhumane' conditions. They were held in one of the coldest cells in the nick, it was claimed.

Why that should have been, I really don't know. But whatever influence a former safe-blower, seaman, street-fighter and millionaire might have, it couldn't extend to what goes on in the fortress-like environment of a jail. Could it?

With my old mate Tommy's killers behind bars for life, and Smitheram well and truly out of the picture, it was time for me to put the criminal past behind me – as criminal and then detective – and concentrate more fully on the business in hand: making a few more millions.

I set about the task with my usual single-mindedness, enthusiasm and aplomb.

CHAPTER 21

The Midas Touch

The market for kitchen worktops was dominated by half a dozen big companies, and the market for the raw material roundwood, which made chipboard to make the worktops, was dominated by one group of companies. Not one of the companies wanted a new face muscling in on their territory; a territory that provided them with huge profits and was therefore worth protecting. The big boys, however, had never heard of George Reynolds, but they soon would. It was my biggest challenge, taking on the world's kitchen-worktop manufacturers and, like my past duels with the authorities – the police and the local and district councils – there could only be one winner in the end.

Shildon Cabinetmakers was thriving, under the managerial stewardship of my old mate Stevie Molloy, and I had brought in a man with a sharp intellect and finely honed business acumen, George Rae, to make the company even more profitable. George would admit himself he was on the bones of his arse when I threw him a financial lifeline. The Shildon Trade Centre, where we made kitchen carcasses – the doors and framework for fitted kitchens – which I had also set up, was also thriving. As ever, though, there was room for expansion.

Many of the thousands of small, corner-shop DIY stores, which I had supplied with off-cut plywood and laminates for several years, had closed down, through no fault of their own. The world had gone DIY crazy and big stores, with vast storerooms and shelves full of everything from a panel pin to a put-it-up-yourself conservatory, were springing up all across Britain.

Some of the big guys running the new, massive DIY stores had been the little guys I had dealt with when travelling with Stevie Molloy in our big yellow, flatbed wagon, delivering the off-cuts of plywood and laminates we bought from the likes of Perstorp Warewrite, in Newton Aycliffe. And in my little brown book I had these little-guys-turned-big-guys' home telephone numbers – many of them ex-directory.

But there was something else, and it was something that was bugging me.

I had carried out quite a bit of research on these kitchen-worktop manufacturers, and, as well as the market being dominated by the big half-dozen, and the raw materials supplied by a group of companies, the manufacturing end was sloppy – full of waste and inefficiency.

To me, the inefficiency was plain to see. At the average kitchen-worktop manufacturing factory, one man placed the wood at one end, another man cut it and stacked it up, another man took it to glue it, another man got hold of the glued wood to stick the laminate on, another put it through the press, another stacked it, another picked it up and shrink-wrapped it, and stacked it, another picked it up to load on to a wagon, another loaded it on to the wagon, then it was off, slowly, to the buyer. And that was only on the factory floor.

GEORGE REYNOLDS

In the office, a sales manager would call round his forty or so sales reps to give them their orders for the day, as they ate toast and marmalade after their cornflakes, listened to Tony Blackburn on the radio, and prepared to take the children to school in the unwashed company car. The sales reps would drive off on their rounds, after dropping the children off at school, to try to pick up some orders.

Then there were the unions to consider, the dinosaurs of British industry living in the past who had buried their heads so deep into the sand that, if you showed them the door to enlightenment, they would claim it was oppression, an infringement of their civil liberties. And Brother Bill and Brother Bob and Sister Felicity bleated on about capitalism and the evil of Maggie Thatcher's enterprise culture, as they took an extended tea break and complained at the lack of chocolate chip cookies the management had failed to provide.

The unions were a good thing in the days of mass unemployment, the Jarrow March and real deprivation – the deprivation I had known and felt myself – but in the early Eighties it was clear that they were just full of agitators green with envy, who didn't have a pot to piss in and envied the boss because his piss-pot was engraved in gold. The union activists, the agitators, were always those who made the most noise, but they were empty vessels who begrudged pressing an automatic button on the assembly line, because every depression of the button was another bit of profit for the company.

They reminded me of the old capitalist vs. communist story of an American factory boss who turned round to one of his workers and asked: 'What do you do at night?'

The worker replied: 'I usually buy a six-pack and watch the TV. I've no time to do anything else, the hours I put in.'

'We should all be communists,' the boss replied. 'Then, if I had two houses, I'd give one to you, and if I had two cars, I'd give one to you.'

'What about if you had two pairs of shoes?' the worker asked.

'Now fuck off,' said the boss. 'You know I've got two pairs of shoes.'

Before embarking on an enterprise as big as I imagined this would become, I needed to do some spadework, so I approached one of the top men at B&Q to ask how many worktops they bought in every week. I was told 3,000. I approached Formica and Perstorp Warewrite and asked them how much it would cost for them to supply me with 3.000 kitchen worktops a week. They only knew me as the scrap man, and told me I could take that amount at a certain price but they would all be the same colour, the same length, they would not be shrink-wrapped and I would have to pack them myself. They also told me that if I dealt with them, I would have to go through their sole distributor.

I knew I could do better, so decided to take them all on.

In Shildon at the time there was a firm called Direct Transport, which had about 100 wagons, but many of the wagons were lying idle as the firm had just lost a big contract for Thorn to a competitor. Direct Transport was owned by Dougie Holloway and run by his managing director, John Monk, both shrewd businessmen who became good friends of mine.

I told Dougie I'd like to rent his warehouse to make kitchen worktops that I already had customers, and that I could put business his way as his idle wagons could be used for distribution. It all made sense and, after a lot of haggling with the bank manager, I managed to get the finance needed to get up and running.

I had already secured a huge area of land locally, thanks to more than a bit of help from the landed gentry in the form of

Lord Eldon and his brother the Hon Simon Scott, the biggest landowners in the Shildon area. They had 40 acres of prime land in an ideal location for my new factory and I approached Simon Scott informing him I would like to buy the land. Simon told me he had heard a lot about me and he believed I would bring work to the local area. He said the land, with planning permission, would be worth between £20,000 and £27,000 an acre. He put his faith and trust in me by selling me the land at just £2,000 an acre. That was a remarkable and generous stamp of approval from a well-known local landowner, who acted more as a benefactor towards local people by giving me such a cut-price deal.

Direct Worktops was born and I called a meeting of the top men: John Monk, Dougie Holloway, George Rae, Chris Ingle were among them, and myself.

There was one other figure sitting at the boardroom table: a life-size cuddly toy pig that I called Sylvia. She was there to remind me of my days at Besford Court and the ten golden rules outlined to me by Master Martin.

We sat around the table and I outlined my business proposals.

'Right,' I said. 'We are going to do this the complete opposite of everyone else. They use rubber rollers on the line, we'll use stainless steel; they shrink-wrap off-line, we'll shrink-wrap on-line; they have sales reps, we won't have any sales reps; most don't offer post-formed tops, we'll manufacture nothing but post-formed tops; they give 90 days' credit, we'll give one month.'

'So, the whole world is wrong, and you're right?' asked Dougie Holloway.

'Got it in one,' I said. 'You've hit the nail on the head first time. I'm right, and everyone else is wrong.'

The warehouse was springing up, the wagons were waiting, it was now just a question of getting the machinery, the raw materials and the workforce in place.

GEORGE REYNOLDS

The workforce was easy; I had some good people working for me already and others I had met who I trusted and knew would work hard. Dave Powles, a cockney, was a fantastic electrician. I had met him initially when he came to fix a heating boiler at the bungalow. Many other engineers had called round to try and fix it, but Dave was the only person who could. He became an integral part of the team. Ian Robinson approached me for work. The lad had been working as a coalman. I was a little hesitant at first but, when he came to me a second time, I took him on. Stuart Johnston, the old drummer from the GR Club, had worked well for me in the past, so he came on board. The master of them all, my cousin Richie Tennick, who could turn his hand to anything, was part of the team. A time-served joiner, Luke Raine, who had done some contracting work for me, and proved a good worker, eventually also joined the team. These were the core of the workforce, but several others, too many to name, also helped start and build Direct Worktops. Initially, as with any new business, there was a hell of a lot of work to do.

The raw material, chipboard, we could bring in from the UK and from abroad. There were a number of suppliers: Swedespan, in Sweden; Caberboard in Scotland; Kronospan in Wales; and even a supplier in Russia. Initially, getting the raw material was going to be one of our biggest outlays, so that was something we would need to look at in future to cut costs.

The machinery was the key to the whole plan. What I wanted was a flowline, where raw material would be put in at one end, go through all the necessary processes, then come out the other end complete: glued, post-formed, shrink-wrapped, labelled and ready for distribution to the customer. Getting my hands on the right machinery in the UK was proving difficult. There was a firm in the Tyneside area which made woodworking machinery and said they would consider installing the machinery in my factory. While they were considering the business, I went elsewhere, to Germany and a firm called Wemhoner. UK firms, I was finding, seemed a bit slow on the uptake.

Representatives from Wemhoner visited our Lambton Street site in Shildon and told me they had just the machinery we needed. Along with my trusted lawyer, Neville Fairclough, I visited a machinery fair in Germany to look at Wemhoner's machines, and I was very impressed. I had never seen anything like it. The machines were super-fast and super-efficient. They had been made, I was told by company representative Lutz Harrat, for a firm run by Arabs who had paid thousands of pounds for research and design work, but had not followed the sale through. The asking price for the machinery was £2.1 million. I wrote an IOU for that vast sum of money on the back of a cigarette packet. The IOU was honoured in full – once you shake on a deal, that is it.

We designed the line ourselves, working with the German precision machinery, and within months the line was spitting out kitchen worktops. I could undercut our competitors very easily and within six months the company was turning a profit of about £2 million.

I called another meeting of the board.

'The whole world was wrong, and you were right, George,' said Dougie Holloway. 'What hairbrained scheme have you got next?'

'Now,' I said. 'Everyone else is manufacturing and supplying eight-foot long kitchen worktops, aren't they?'

'Yes,' said the board members.

'Well, what we'll do,' I said, 'is produce and supply ten-foot-long kitchen worktops.'

'You're fucking mad,' said George Rae. 'You think you can produce ten-foot-long worktops and the rest of the world, not just the UK, will follow you?'

'Got it in one, George,' I said. 'Within four years I

guarantee that most, if not all, worktop manufacturers will be making ten-foot-long kitchen worktops.'

'You're still fucking mad,' said George.

I put a challenge to the board, putting my assertion in writing. If, within 4 years, most worktop manufacturers were producing 10-foot worktops, then they could hand their shares to me. If they weren't, I would hand my shares to them. I was the majority shareholder.

It was a challenge some of the board members took up, and they signed the written papers which were put under lock and key.

'This is the easiest money I'm going to make in my life,' said one.

'I'll be the new managing director,' said another.

'We'll be rolling in it,' another doubting Thomas added.

But not all the board members saw my prediction doomed to early failure.

'I'm not fucking signing,' said Dougie Holloway.

I had big expansion plans, my aim was to dominate the kitchen-worktop market, and I wasn't going to allow the established big firms, using the traditional, laborious production methods, high labour costs and unionised workforces, to stand in my way. This was a time for entrepreneurs to flourish; it was the dawn of the enterprise culture, and I considered myself very enterprising.

The big firms didn't like it, because I was taking business from them. So within the market they painted me not just as a straight-talker with unorthodox business methods, but as a dangerous maverick with a criminal record to match.

I was still having my run-ins with the local councillors. I was accused of stealing a road, just because I had erected bollards at the end of Harker Street, near the workshop, to ease the parking problems on what was my land. I had the deeds, after all.

Then Sedgefield District Council sent me a rates bill for £73.88, a supplementary rates bill – I was already paying £6,000 a year in rates – and took offence when I asked them what the money was to be spent on. After asking the questions, and not getting any answers, I paid the rates bill by cheque – a cheque weighing 250lbs. It was made out on a kitchen worktop and the council had to accept it. They must have had a bit of a problem carrying it round to the bank.

Then something happened in Shildon which gave the council a change of heart: the closure of the rail wagonworks – the Shildon Shops – and the loss of thousands of jobs. It was devastating for the town, reported the local press, and every effort was made in Parliament to try and save the works from the axe. But the works were doomed. A cloud of gloom hung over Shildon as local people said the closure sounded the death knell for the town. It was all very, very depressing.

Every cloud, though, has a silver lining and I saw the closure more as an opportunity than a setback. I put plans into the council to open new factory units on a greenfield site to expand the worktops business. The plan was warmly welcomed. The council, which I had had more confrontations with than I care to remember, even agreed that the new factory units could come under the umbrella name of The George Reynolds Industrial Estate. A whole industrial estate named after yours truly? I was quite proud, though some councillors may have choked on their own breakfasts when they read about it in the morning newspaper.

The authorities wanted to chuck money at me, offering me lump sums to take on workers from the old Shildon Shops. But, to be frank, I would rather pay them for me *not* to take the former Shops workers on. It was common knowledge in Shildon that the person doing the briskest business, and making a lot of cash, from the Shops was the fella in the High Street who sold sleeping bags to the Shops workers on nightshift.

Elsewhere in County Durham, other businesses were going through tough times. A competitor of Direct Transport, W H Williams Haulage, based in Spennymoor, was losing business, and one of its directors, Carl Williams, who was also involved with a wood firm, the Spennymoor Pallet Company, was hit by a bill amounting to about £30,000 because of the collapse of the wood firm.

I had heard of Carl Williams – he was a justice of the peace on the bench at Newton Aycliffe – and more recently I had heard of his wife Susan, through my old friend Romana Ross, the Italian relation of my one-time lover Theresa. Romana, who was still running a Pizzeria in Spennymoor, had suggested I should meet Carl and Susan when I popped into her place for coffee.

Karen was away on holiday at the time and I decided to call Carl Williams up and invite him to Witton Hall. I called him at about 11pm and he seemed surprised, not only that I had called him at that time, but also that I had managed to get his ex-directory telephone number. I believed I might be able to help him out with some advice on the wood firm's debt, but I was also conscious of the fact that it made good business sense to get to know a competitor.

He arrived at Witton Hall within about an hour and I stood near the entrance gates, my open-necked shirtsleeves rolled up, beckoning him towards the drive and the front door. To my surprise his wife, Susan, was with him and when she stepped out of the car I immediately noticed how young she looked. And how attractive. She was wearing a pink leather suit and pink leather boots and she looked every inch a fashion model.

Carl Williams and I talked business, a lot of business, and I helped him with my knowledge of the law and, later, in the early hours of the morning, I took both of them on a tour of my factory. They were very impressed and Susan, who asked a great number of questions, appeared more interested in the workings of the machinery than her husband.

When they left and headed home I could not get Susan Williams out of my mind. She was stunningly attractive, with a perfect figure, an engaging personality and wit, the most charming smile and the kind of zest for life that can only be found in a few, special people. It was the first time we had met and she had set my heart racing.

Of course, here I was, a married man, whose wife was away on holiday, enchanted by a delightful young woman. I knew I had caught the bus, but I was only looking at the traffic, I told myself. But there was more to our meeting than that.

For the next few days I thought about Susan Williams a lot and decided the best way to get her out of my system was to immerse myself in work, and convince myself not to think foolish thoughts. It was more than likely our paths would never cross again.

I was, by now, with my thriving company Direct Worktops, almost on top of the UK market for kitchen work surfaces. It was time to expand further, convert the market to ten-foot-long worktops … and invade Europe.

CHAPTER 22

More Millions

The new worktops factory was more streamlined, more efficient, more automated, and we were churning out the product at a rate the business had never seen before.

A young lad from Tyneside, the son of a friend, turned up at the factory and asked me for a job.

'What job would you like?' I asked.

'Your job,' said the lad.

'Do you know something, son,' I said. 'I've been looking for someone like you since the day I started.' I started him on a salary of £30,000, on condition that he did the same amount of work that I did, and he agreed.

The lad turned up for work at 7am sharp on a Friday. I put him behind a desk and gave him a list of 700 customers who needed to be contacted by telephone for their orders.

'I'll never get through all them,' he said.

'Oh, but you will,' I said. 'I do it every day.'

As the lad started his calls, I called one of the top men at

B&Q. 'Good morning,' I said. 'George Reynolds here. We have been supplying you with eight-foot-long kitchen worktops. We are now going to supply you with ten-foot-long worktops.'

'Hold on,' said the man at the other end, 'but we're only paying £14 for an eight-foot top.'

'Yes,' I said, 'and you will still only pay £14 for a ten-foot top. That way you can put your prices up a little, and increase your profits instantly, without any further cash outlay.'

The buyer said he would ask the top bosses, and came back shortly afterwards, to say we had a deal. We were supplying B&Q about 20,000 worktops a week by this time.

I got a call from Wickes: 'We hear you are offering ten-foot-long worktops?'

'That's right,' I said.

'And how much are these worktops?' the man from Wickes asked.

'£14,' I said.

'£14! £14 for a ten-foot worktop. That's impossible,' the man said.

'No, no,' I said. 'This is possible, I have already struck a deal with B&Q, one of your competitors, to sell them 20,000 worktops a week.'

The man from Wickes said he would ask a buyer to visit the factory. Word was spreading, and I received a call from a buyer at one of the other major DIY companies.

'Mr Reynolds?' the man asked.

'Speaking,' I said.

'Is it right that you are offering ten-foot-long kitchen worktops for £14 each?'

'That's right,' I said.

'And what type of laminate are you offering?'

'What type of laminate would you like?' I asked.

'How many people do you employ?' the man asked.

'Twelve,' I said.

'That's twelve hundred?' he asked.

'No. That's twelve people,' I said.

I heard the man at the other end of the line start choking on his coffee. 'We'll pay you a visit,' he said, after clearing his throat.

The machines in the new factory were able to produce six worktops at a time, all going through every process at the touch of a button. I always stressed to my workforce that there were three key ingredients for business success: efficiency, efficiency and efficiency. To the management I always stressed there were three key elements in the approach to business: attitude, attitude and attitude.

The big DIY firms were being forced into a position where it would be in their best interests to deal with Direct Worktops, otherwise they would be buying in worktops at a more expensive price per unit than their competitors were selling them at.

It wasn't long before I had all the big players on board: B&Q, Wickes, Focus, Do it All and Texas Homecare.

Our new managing director, the lad from Tyneside, was still making calls. 'Do we get a tea break in here?' he asked. 'It's 10 o'clock.'

I sent for two pots of tea and a biscuit each.

'Have you secured any more orders?' I asked.

'Not yet,' the lad said.

I took a pile of the papers from his desk, and started ringing round the customers myself. As I put the receiver down after the first call the telephone rang.

'Mr Reynolds. Mr George Reynolds?' It was a woman's voice.

'Yes, this is Mr Reynolds,' I said.

'And you are the proprietor of the Shildon Trade Centre, are you not?'

'I am the proprietor, Madam, that's right,' I said.

'And as the proprietor, you are responsible for the behaviour of your workforce and your under-managers. Is that right?' the woman asked.

'I am the man in charge, Madam,' I said.

'Right,' said the woman. 'I wish to lodge a formal complaint against the manager of your trade centre, a Mr Molloy I believe his name is.'

'Big Stevie,' I said. 'Stevie Molloy?'

'Yes,' said the woman. 'That's the man, Stevie Molloy. He was very rude to me, you know.'

'Stevie Molloy, rude? I'm surprised at that, Madam. He is normally very approachable and polite to all the customers.'

'Well, I'm telling you,' the woman insisted. 'He was very aggressive and abusive towards me.'

'Are you sure you just weren't intimidated by Mr Molloy? He's a big chap, you know, Madam,' I said.

'No. It was his manner,' the woman said. 'He was very aggressive, impolite and discourteous.'

'Oh, I see,' I said. 'Now please forgive me when I ask this, but Mr Molloy did not tell you to fuck off, did he?'

'No,' said the woman.

'Then I'm telling you to fuck off. Do you hear me? Now fuck off!' I put the phone down.

The lad from Tyneside started to laugh.

'Have you got any more orders yet?' I asked.

'No,' he said.

'Then bloody get on with it,' I said.

'Don't we have a lunch break here?' he asked. 'It's 12 o'clock.'

I ordered sandwiches, two pies and tea to have at our desks.

We were taking in about 200 wagonloads of chipboard a week to produce the worktops, and the cost was phenomenal. There had to be an easier and cheaper method to get the raw materials we needed. The roundwood, the raw material to produce chipboard, was all sewn up by the rest of the industry, selling it on to the chipboard plants in the UK. All the chipboard plants had been set up by foreign companies. I decided we would build our own chipboard manufacturing plant.

As the day progressed, under our new managing director from Tyneside, I asked him how many orders he had secured.

'Nine,' he said.

'Well, I've got twenty-two, and you're being paid more money than I am,' I said.

I continued making my phone calls, trying to be as persuasive as possible to secure more orders, and thanked God I had the direct lines through to most of the people I needed to deal with. There was nothing more frustrating than having to deal with personal assistants, secretaries, or other people in the middle, who could attempt to block your way.

As I was on the phone I could suddenly hear a loud flip, flop, flip, in the marble-floored corridor outside my office. I tried to ignore it, but it came back flip, flop, flip.

'What the hell's that?' I asked Ian Robinson.

Ian Robinson went to investigate and said it was Ian Lamb, who was losing the sole on one of his shoes. I asked him to bring Ian Lamb into the office.

Ian looked a little run-down, I think he was having a few problems on the domestic front. I asked him about his shoes. He took his right shoe off and showed it to me. The sole on the shoe was just hanging by a thread, like a big tongue hanging out of a dirty mouth.

'Can you not afford a new pair of shoes?' I asked him, to which he replied that he couldn't.

I reached into my pocket and pulled out the wad of notes I always carry day-to-day, held together by an elastic band. Ian's eyes lit up in anticipation. I took the elastic band from the wad, rifled through the cash, and put the notes back into my pocket.

'Here,' I said, handing him the elastic band, 'put that round it, and that'll solve the problem.'

I didn't think what I had done should have caused any amusement. Ian Lamb was certainly not amused, but Ian Robinson could not contain his laughter.

After that funny interlude, I was back on the phones to secure more orders, without the flip, flop, flip ringing in my ears. Our new managing director from Tyneside was still struggling. Five o'clock arrived, and the lad asked what time we would be finishing. I told him we had hundreds of faxes to send out to arrive on desks the following morning, so we would finish when we finished faxing. He and I left the office at 20 minutes past midnight. He looked bleary-eyed, absolutely knackered. 'You don't need me in tomorrow, do you?' he asked. 'It's Saturday.'

'Yes,' I said. 'We always work on a Saturday, and tomorrow will be a lot harder than today. We've got loads of work on. I'll see you bright and early at 7 o'clock.'

Saturdays were inspection days at the factory. I insisted that the mornings were spent cleaning the machines and the factory floor. It was always so clean you could eat your dinner from it. The workers were happy to work on Saturdays, even though they were not paid any overtime. If they wanted overtime, I told them they would need to go on the union rates, and that would leave them about £100 worse off every week. They agreed to work for a flat rate – well above the union rate – for the actual hours worked.

My inspection that Saturday alarmed me. One of the new starters had carved a heart, with a little Cupid's arrow going through it, on one of the pristine machines, with 'Billy loves Carol' etched into the metalwork and finished off in brightly coloured felt-tip pen. It was a work of art, graffiti art, and I hit the roof.

I stormed out of the factory to a nearby garage, bought four cans of bright car-spraying paint, and sat on my haunches next to the worker's Volkswagon Beetle. 'George loves you' I sprayed in bright, dayglo orange on the side of his motor. 'George loves you' I sprayed in bright pink on the other side, and finished my artwork with a few squiggles here and a few scrolls there.

The worker ran towards me. 'What the fuck are you doing?' he asked.

'I'm spray-painting your car,' I said. 'Looks good, doesn't it?'

'You fucking can't do that,' he protested.

'Oh, I fucking can,' I said. 'And I'll pay for your motor to be re-sprayed, which will cost about a grand, and you can pay for my machine to be re-sprayed, which will cost you about twenty thousand. Do we have a deal?'

The lad looked shocked.

As the miserable worker went to the office, the lad from Tyneside – our new managing director – approached me.

'It's 12 o'clock,' he said. 'My eyes are stinging with reading those fax numbers, my fingers are numb with using the phone, I've hardly had any sleep, and I've still only managed to get ten orders.'

'You're not doing very well, are you?' I said. 'You told me you could do my job.'

'Well, I've made a decision,' said the lad.

'And what's that?' I asked.

'You can shove your job up your arse!'

Such workers I could do without. I had in my employment a number of real grafters who understood teamwork, and agreed with the Reynolds' business philosophy that things did not come easy; it took hard work and long hours to succeed.

One such worker was Barry Dunn, who, step-by-step, had managed to secure hundreds of orders for our worktops in

Europe. He was a real grafter, was Barry, and brought untold business our way, for which he was well rewarded.

Dave Powles and I had only recently returned from Europe, where we had attended a huge engineering fair in Milan. We had been invited over by a man called Stefani who had heard about the £2.1 million we had spent on machinery in Germany when we attended a similar event there and he hoped to put some business our way.

Dave and I had flown out and were dressed very casually. He was wearing a T shirt with a slogan on, something like 'Drink A Pint of Milk A Day', and I was wearing a plain shirt, open at the neck.

When the plane descended into Milan and landed we noticed a red carpet being rolled out. A number of smart-suited men and well-dressed women were lining up to the side of the red carpet. There was also a band, its members dressed in bright uniforms, ready to strike up.

Dave and I looked around the plane and could see no one who looked that important, but we spied a long-legged, attractive, blonde woman, who we assumed must have been an actress. The passengers alighted the plane one by one, and the band remained silent. But when Davey and I got off, the most unlikely-looking VIPs on board, the band struck up and the smart men and women started shaking our hands. 'Hello Señor Reynolds,' said one of the men. 'Welcome to Milan.'

We had not expected such a greeting party, which also included reporters and photographers from the local press, as well as a television crew, and Dave and I were quite overwhelmed by all the attention we received.

It became clear that our arrival had been written about in the local press and much speculation had arisen about just how many millions we were preparing to spend at the engineering fair. Like the Chinese whispers that grow legs, the sum we were expected to spend had jumped from £2 million to many more millions.

During our stay we were treated like royalty, staying at the best hotel and being chauffeur-driven to attend a meal arranged by Mr Stefani. A large, black limousine arrived at our hotel with four black Minis behind, and Dave and I sat in one of the Minis, which had bullet-proof glass that magnified everything on the outside. Mr Stefani, we were told, was very security conscious, as there had been a kidnap plot on one of his sons. The black Minis, therefore, were decoy cars, so that any potential abductor would not realise what car he was in.

We did end up spending quite a bit of money at the Milan Engineering Fair, but not as much as we had spent in Germany. Where Italian machinery, like their cars, was very stylish, I thought, it was the German machinery that was more efficient.

Back at Direct Worktops, I was making my way to the office when I heard a commotion in the factory, where the wagons were cleaned. George, one of the managers, was having a contretemps with a lad called Frankie. It turned out that George had asked him to go to the local shop and get him a half-ounce of tobacco for £2, and if he couldn't get the baccy for that price, he should get the next best thing. Frankie had come back to the yard with two pork pies.

At around the same time a chap called Simmons approached me for a job. It was the Mr Simmons who had stopped me working at his father's furniture company in Sunderland when I was 16 because I could not read or write. I gave him a job, because I believed that you should never treat people the way you have been treated in the past. That was another of my old master Mr Martin's ten golden rules.

With business at its peak at Direct Worktops, and turnover and profit now running into several millions per year, the only thing left for me to do was streamline the manufacturing process still further by building my own chipboard plant. There would, however, be a few obstacles put in my way.

CHAPTER 23

The Wheels of Industry

A private mini power station, the first of its kind in Britain, at Direct Worktops' £20 million, 200,000 square foot factory would slash electricity bills by about £20,000 a week on the George Reynolds Industrial Estate. Two gas turbines were to generate all the electricity the company needed.

On top of that I was beating the industry leaders, and going environmentally friendly at the same time. The industry had tried to keep me out by upping the price of roundwood. For those within the industry, roundwood could be bought at about £40 a tonne, but for George Reynolds it doubled to £80 a tonne.

But where I had one up on the rest of the industry was that Direct Worktops, my other company George Reynolds UK Ltd, Shildon Cabinetmakers and the Shildon Trade Centre were all cash-rich. We were blue-chip companies, which could pay for goods on delivery, unlike those within the roundwood industry, who would pay the suppliers within 90 days. Direct Worktops was the biggest producer of kitchen worktops in the world, so we obviously had some clout.

My first round with the industry was to install a type of weighbridge on one of our lorries. The wagon would pull up alongside a roundwood-carrying heavy goods vehicle and we would offer the driver so much per tonne, on the spot, weighing the wood on the back of our own lorry. It worked well, and word soon got back to the roundwood producers that when they dealt with George Reynolds they got the price asked for on the spot. No waiting for cheques or clearance.

The other method of beating the industry, and earning brownie points and Government cash for going green in the process, was to use old wooden pallets to produce the raw material for the chipboard. Companies wanting to dump old wooden pallets in landfill sites were charged, so it made perfect sense for me to take the material off their hands for a small fee and use it in the chipboard manufacturing process. We also collected waste wood from many sites and recycled it.

There was little waste at the site. The sawdust was compacted into heat bricks, which burned on open fires as well as coal and heated the factory, and some of these were donated to elderly people during the winter months. Others were sold off, and the profits made went to erecting the Christmas lights in Shildon town centre.

The industry had been hoping to squeeze me out of business, but all they did was force me to be more competitive and efficient. By squeezing me hard, they had really shit in their own nest, and, as far as I was concerned, they could lie in it.

Business was better than ever but, on a personal level, I was still having problems with the police, the council and the like. The bungalow was raided by police in connection with an alleged £50,000 raid on Teesside, which had naff all to do with me.

I had built my own nuclear fall-out shelter in the garden after watching that disturbing and realistic drama documentary about a nuclear bomb in Sheffield – *Shreds* it was called. My bunker upset some councillors.

I had kicked my 100-fags-a-day habit, and started chewing nicotine gum instead.

On the marital front, Karen and I decided to separate and then divorce. I offered her a £3 million divorce settlement, but she chose to go through the courts, and ended up losing out heavily. Not content with that, she and her family concocted bogus stories claiming that I had threatened Karen's mother, Pauline Brown, and that I had threatened to burn down the home of one of her daughters. It ended up with me spending 12 hours in a police cell, and then later appearing in court where all four charges against me were dropped. My brief, Gerald Johnson, told the court: 'The family saw the gravy train disappearing at the termination of the marriage so they fabricated the story of the threats to ensure a large financial settlement.'

On the council front, my chipboard power plant was upsetting quite a few local people, even though it was considered by a councillor from Hexham to be far more environmentally friendly than the Egger UK plant in the Tyne Valley, which emitted a blue plume of smoke from its chimneys and looked like a blot on the landscape.

Durham County Council's trading standards department took me to court on forty-seven – yes, forty-seven – charges of supplying goods, namely kitchen worktops, with false descriptions. I described the worktops as being recommended by Esther Rantzen's *Watchdog* programme, and advertised them as such in the local press, only for me to be hauled before magistrates in Darlington, to pit my legal wits, through a lawyer, against a high-flying legal eagle from the county council and a barrister from the BBC.

Direct Worktops kitchen worktops had won an award from the Furniture Industry Research Association (FIRA) and the BBC had put out a *Watchdog* viewers' information pack, which included an action plan from FIRA, which mentioned our award-winning kitchen worktops. Surely, that was Esther's programme recommending our worktops to BBC viewers, was it not? Magistrates in Darlington, wisely, agreed and all charges against me were thrown out. By now, if I'd had to count up how many trumped-up civil and criminal charges had been made against me, it would be nearing a hundred. All of them thrown out. Is it any wonder that it appeared to me that I was always having to fight battles with the authorities? There was a wholesale vendetta against me by the authorities, and there was one thread that ran through every trumped-up charge laid against me: envy. Envy of my success and of my wealth. The green-eyed monster, like Chad over the wall, was popping up everywhere.

To top it all, I had to go into hospital for an operation and, while I was under the surgeon's knife, a number of conspirators at Direct Worktops got together to oust me as managing director and launched a coup to take over the company themselves. I got to know about it through my loyal and trusted workers who smelled a rat in Shildon.

The conspirators, whom I called the enemy within, I discovered, had not only tried to get the bank to pass a vote of no confidence in me, but they were also behind the visits by the inspectors from HM Inland Revenue who had turned up regularly at the Direct Worktops factory for getting on for four years.

The tax inspectors could not understand how I could live in a mansion, own a £7 million super-yacht, drive a Rolls-Royce, run a £2 million helicopter, own an apartment in Marbella and a penthouse in London and yet I was earning just £30,000 a year as the company managing director.

Over the four year period, a team of eight tax officers visited the factory initially, interviewing me and writing down every cough splutter uttered, but gradually that was whittled down to two, when they could see I was not on the fiddle.

At Witton Hall I had a secret cupboard within which stood a huge vault and the entrance to this cupboard could only be gained by touching a gigantic mirror in front of it in a particular place. When that spot was touched the mirrored door would swing open, revealing the huge vault inside. Very few people were aware of the secret room, and if a surveyor measured the area of land Witton Hall covered, and every room inside, he would have great difficulty discovering there was a spare and unaccounted for small room in the mansion.

After what must have been their lengthiest inquiry, at least in the north-east, a full team of tax inspectors turned up at the factory one day, oozing efficiency and wearing the kind of smiles that demonstrated they believed they were on to me. But I had nothing to hide. We all sat in the boardroom, with Sylvia at one end and me at the other, and the taxmen pulled out their notepads and the grilling began.

'Do you have a safe at Witton Hall?' the head man asked.

'No,' I replied.

'Are you sure?'

'Yes,' I replied.

'Are you 100 per cent sure that you do not have a safe at Witton Hall?' he asked again.

'Watch my lips,' I said. 'I, George Reynolds, do not have a safe at Witton Hall.'

'Right,' said the tax inspector, 'then you will have no objection to signing a statement to that effect.' I signed the statement.

The taxmen asked me if I objected to them searching the house and, believing they would never find the secret room,

I agreed. We all jumped in our cars and headed for Witton-le-Wear.

At the house the taxmen looked in all the rooms and started tapping on all the walls. They even searched the greenhouse. I knew something was afoot, and I knew only one or two people could have tipped them off about the safe.

In front of the big mirror, one of the taxmen took out a comb and started combing his hair, as if it was the most natural thing to do. His elbow tapped the mirror, and the huge door swung open, revealing the big vault inside.

'Well, well, well,' said the head taxman. 'What have we here?'

'It's a safe,' I said.

'But you have signed a sworn statement declaring you did not have a safe in this house,' he said.

The safe was opened ... and there was nothing inside. But the taxmen had proven I had told an untruth, and they were more adamant than ever to squeeze money out of me – money they claimed was unpaid taxes.

About a week later the tax team arrived very early at the factory and the head man was wearing a grin as wide as a Cheshire cat. Again we sat around the boardroom table and again the taxmen got their notebooks out, and typewritten pieces of paper and forms.

'We've got you!' the head man said with gleeful delight. 'We know how you have been avoiding paying your taxes.'

'Oh, you do,' I said. 'Then perhaps you can enlighten me.'

The head man said they had inspected our company accounts and had found that the accounts revealed a five per cent wastage factor on worktops.

'You have a good, clean operation here,' said the head man. 'We've seen it all, and we know that your wastage factor could be no more than one quarter per cent.'

The head man was more shrewd than I had given him credit for. He had hit the nail right on the head.

'All right,' I said, with my back up against the wall. 'I will sign another statement, but I would like you to come back next week.'

The tax inspectors left the factory feeling elated that their long, protracted inquiry was about to bear fruit.

During the week, I acquired the company accounts for some of the biggest and most profitable companies in the country and analysed each one of them for their wastage factor. I was pleasantly surprised that most, if not all, showed a wastage factor far higher than that of Direct Worktops, one or two running into twelve per cent.

The next meeting with the taxmen arrived and we sat around the boardroom table. I laid all the company accounts I had acquired on the table in the shape of a fan, as the taxmen looked on.

'Right, gentlemen,' I said. 'You have checked my company accounts and have accused me of fiddling out of the waste factor and I have told you I am prepared to make a statement. Are your pens poised?' I asked.

'The waste factor for Direct Worktops is five per cent. Now what I have here are the company accounts of some of the biggest companies in the country. Some of them are household name plcs.'

I picked up the accounts and one by one dropped them on to the table. 'Seven per cent,' I said, 'six per cent ... ten per cent ... eleven per cent ... and look what we have here, twelve per cent.'

The head taxman appeared perplexed.

'By your own reckoning,' I said, 'Direct Worktops is the most efficient and well-run company in virtually the whole of Britain. More efficient – and you discovered this not me – than some of the biggest plcs in the UK with thousands of well-paid staff and multi-million-pound turnovers. Are you telling me that Direct Worktops, whose managing director is backward, mentally deficient and illiterate, is the best and most efficient company there is?'

All the taxmen were gobsmacked.

'Now that's my statement,' I said. 'And you can run this to court, but I can give you a little legal advice that will cost you nothing. Any barrister seeing this will rip your case to shreds within seconds. It will never run.'

The head taxman, looking rather sheepish, told me he needed to speak to his colleagues in private, and asked me to leave the room. A few minutes later he called me back in.

'Right, George,' said the head man. 'We want to put this to bed. Will you give us £1 million as full and final settlement?'

'Will I fuck,' I said. 'I've got a million-pound mansion to run and a £7 million yacht to keep. How the hell could I afford to give you one million pounds?'

'Right,' he said. 'What about £500,000?'

'No,' I said.

'£400,000?'

'No,' I said.

'We can't go any lower than £200,000.'

'Then take me to court,' I said. 'That way I will get something out of this.'

The head man asked me to leave the room again and, after more deliberations with his colleagues, called me back in.

'Will you give us £60,000 as full and final settlement?' asked the head tax inspector.

'Yes,' I said. 'Would you like it in cash?'

The tax inspectors left and the inquiry was finally over. I was now more clear than ever on the identities of the members of that little clique that made up the enemy within. Recovered, out of hospital, fighting fit again, and aware that most other worktop manufacturers in the world were now producing ten-foot-long worktops, I called a board meeting.

George Rae, the man to whom I had thrown a financial lifeline when things were rough, appeared to be leading the conspirators, along with another board member, Bill Berry, and one or two others.

As they all sat at the boardroom table, looking po-faced and sullen, I went to a filing cabinet and pulled out the photocopied forms they had all, bar one, signed four years earlier when I predicted most worktops would be produced in ten-foot lengths.

'Bill,' I said, showing him the document. 'Do you remember this?'

'Well, yes,' he said. 'But if I remember rightly, that was just a joke, wasn't it?'

'I never joke where money's concerned, Bill,' I said. 'Now most kitchen worktops are ten-foot long. Am I right or am I wrong?'

'Well, you're right,' said Bill. 'But, er ...'

'There's no fucking buts about it. We have it here, in black and white, that if most worktops are sold in ten-foot lengths, you'd resign and give me your shares. Am I right or am I wrong?'

'Well, you're right,' said Bill.

'OK then,' I said. 'You're sacked and I will buy your shares from you at the current market value.' Bill looked as white as a sheet.

'Hang on, hang on,' said George Rae. 'I'm not happy about this.'

'Well, you should be, George,' I said. 'Because you're fucking sacked as well. And I'll buy your shares, too.'

One by one I went through all the board members who had

signed the document four years earlier – all of them I believed to be the conspirators – and sacked them all. It took some time for me to clear out most of the board – it must have been the best part of an hour.

After the big clear-out, the court cases, the hospital operation, more run-ins with the police, more run-ins with the council over alleged dust pollution from the power station site, I believed things had calmed down, and business could be put back on an even keel.

But then disaster struck. A massive blaze in one of the silos at the power plant, sparked by a faulty extractor fan and fuelled by the raw material I had tried so desperately to get my hands on: wood chippings.

Sixty firefighters from across County Durham tackled the huge blaze for five hours. I stood watching the flames lick the night sky and was joined by my fellow workers and their families. Some of them had tears in their eyes.

The fire caused tens of thousands of pounds worth of damage, but when the workforce arrived and saw the charred remains of that part of the factory, they worked their socks off, working all the hours God sent to rebuild that part of the site. I was adamant that no jobs would be lost and production would carry on, so we again had to bring in chipboard for production. Not surprisingly the price of chipboard, at least for us, rocketed. We had a few problems claiming through the insurance on the fire, as, it appeared, we had been underinsured, but we came through in the end.

In little more than 12 months, thanks in no small part to the dedicated, loyal and supportive workers who made up the core of my business empire, we were up and running at full throttle again.

I decided that, in time, I would reward every one of them.

CHAPTER 24

Pretty in Pink

The moors at Hill End, above Frosterley in County Durham, were isolated, desolate and, during the winter, it was the most God-forsaken area anyone could have the misfortune to live in. The nearest neighbour was miles away, the only other sign of life was the occasional passing sheep; civilisation seemed to end at the dirt track leading up to the shepherd's cottage I found myself living in after my bitter and acrimonious separation from my second wife, Karen Brown.

Here I was, a multi-millionaire with a £7 million yacht, a million-pound mansion, a Rolls-Royce in storage, a penthouse in London and an apartment in Marbella, and I was living in a ramshackle cottage in the middle of bloody nowhere, without hot running water or electricity and with the poorest of sanitation. What I had done to deserve it, I couldn't fathom out. As always, thankfully, I was still spending a great deal of time at work.

I had to move out of Witton Hall, the atmosphere had

become too tense and hostile, during the initial stages of our separation. My estranged wife was still living there, and had moved some of her relations in. Solicitors had been appointed on each side, and the gradual breakdown of a 12-year marriage, which had produced two wonderful children, had begun.

Not long before the parting of the ways, and whilst I was still at Witton Hall, Karen had gone off on another foreign holiday and, desirous of some convivial company, I sat down and fingered through the little telephone book that listed the names, addresses and telephone numbers of the many friends I had made over the years. For some reason, perhaps it was fate, the book opened at W, and there were the names of Carl and Susan Williams, the couple who I had invited to Witton Hall about six years earlier and whom I hadn't seen since. I remembered Susan, in particular, and her wearing that bright pink leather suit and bright pink boots. She did, I recalled, look pretty in pink.

I got on the telephone and rang up Carl, asking if he and his wife would like to join me for a meal and we chatted for a while. It turned out that Carl Williams had lost his court case over the £30,000 debt left by the wood pallet company, and he and Susan had had to move out of their home at Denehurst in Ferryhill, which was once owned by John Davidson, of John Dee Transport, and were now living at Greenfield Farm at Byers Green in County Durham.

Susan, I was told, was working at a women's refuge in Bishop Auckland, as a welfare worker and, though she was meant to be attending a leaving do that night for one of the refuge workers, she and Carl decided they would like to join me for a meal.

I drove down to Byers Green in the Roller, spent an hour in the Williams' house, and then we jumped into the car and headed for the Ramside Hall Hotel near Sunderland, where I had booked us a table. At the hotel we had a delicious meal and laughed virtually all night. Susan looked radiant and, to be honest, I couldn't take my eyes off her.

The next morning I got a call from Susan, who thanked me for the nice meal at the Ramside. 'Now, don't leave it six years before you see us again,' she said.

'Why don't you leave that schemer?' I said. 'Come and live with me.'

Susan, perhaps, thought I was joking, as she didn't answer, but I was deadly serious.

'You don't understand, Susan,' I said. 'I love you, and I have loved you since I first clapped eyes on you six years ago. You're always on my mind.'

'Get away with you,' she said coyly. 'You're a married man, and I'm a married woman.'

A few weeks went by. I spoke to Susan several times on the telephone.

Many months later, Susan had left Carl Williams and had gone to stay with a friend. Karen and I had parted, and I ended up in the shepherd's cottage on the desolate moor overlooking Frosterley. Later, though, with a little help from myself, Susan managed to obtain a flat above an estate agent's in Crook and furnish it. It was our intention that we would eventually be together.

Susan and Carl, like many married couples who wed young, had been going through a rocky patch long before I arrived on the scene, and on one occasion she went to a women's refuge in Bishop Auckland, sleeping under curtains rather than blankets. It was the same refuge where she later found a job. Earlier in their marriage, she had been so desperately unhappy that she had tried to kill herself by slashing her wrists. It was a cry for help more than anything else. She had also suffered from agoraphobia and gone through the trauma of a stillborn child and, again early on in the marriage, had suffered the shock of discovering her son, Paul, had contracted bacterial meningitis. Thankfully, Paul got over the illness.

The age difference – 24 years – was remarked on many times, and people said our relationship would never last. Inevitably, Susan had to suffer the catcalls of 'gold-digger' and 'millionaire's moll'. But the bitchiness and hurtful remarks came from people who didn't know me, and didn't know Susan, and who were unaware of the strength of character we both possessed. I knew, and she knew, that we would do more than just ride the storm, we would rise above it.

During the early days, Susan began receiving the most obscene and lurid poison-pen letters, including some containing used condoms. They were full of hate and vileness. She was naturally frightened, so we had to call in the police.

Her flat in Crook was trashed and in the street she was threatened with violence: 'You're dead meat! You're fucking dead meat!' It was becoming unsafe for her to live in the flat and, eventually, she had to flee to a safe house in Sunderland, which I found through Wilfie Dixon, a good friend of mine, in the grounds of Burdon Hall at Silksworth, where she lived for four months. It was at Burdon Hall that we spent our first night together. Susan and I needed a break, so we flew to Palma, Majorca, where I stayed on my yacht, *Secret Love*, which was registered in Sunderland, and Susan stayed at a hotel.

It was during those few days together that I realised Susan did not have a clue about the extent of my wealth. I picked her up at her hotel and we walked along the jetty towards the deep water quays in Palma where *Secret Love* was berthed, next to a yacht owned by Robert Maxwell.

When Susan saw the yacht she was astounded. It literally took her breath away. The yacht was the size of a four-storey block of flats, with four decks, a sun-deck on the top, a jacuzzi, seven bedrooms, seven bathrooms, three kitchens, staff accommodation, huge lounges and two enormous hydraulic lifts at the back on which stood two big speedboats. Susan was stunned by the enormity and luxury of the vessel.

A few months later, we flew out to the United States to a yachting event in Fort Lauderdale for a ten-day break. Later still in our relationship we visited a super-yacht festival in Monte Carlo, hosted by a well-known yacht dealer called Merle Wood, and it was there that I spotted a yacht that looked strangely familiar; it was the yacht I had worked on as a young rigger on the River Wear in Sunderland and my initials, we discovered after chatting to the boat owner who chartered the vessel, were still inscribed at the back of the porthole-type door, behind a picture, where we had lowered the vessel's forecastle and filled it with pig iron.

After our holiday in Fort Lauderdale, during which time Susan's divorce came through, when we arrived back home we knew we did not really have a home, only temporary accommodation. We bought a lovely house in the Lake District, called Overmere, but we still needed a family home in the north-east. After looking through many brochures in estate agents, we bought a beautiful house known as South Hall, in Wolsingham in the Holywood area, and we made the house our first real home. It was my intention, however, to reclaim Witton Hall, but for that to happen I had to wait a long time for my divorce from Karen Brown to be finalised.

At Wolsingham Susan and I and the children could get busy living, and attempt to put the past behind us.

Eventually, Susan and I were married in Gleneagles, Scotland. As I had always done, I had a bit of fun about my criminal past by wearing a convict's uniform and a ball and chain at our wedding reception. It was a fantastic celebration, and we could finally settle down to married life.

CHAPTER 25

The Gunmen

A new band of conspirators, this time on the criminal side, was out to get me and my family, and to do us real harm. They intended to burst into my home, tie me up, threaten me, probably torture me if not kill me, and take as many of my possessions as they could get their hands on.

Our large, Victorian house in Wolsinghan, in the rural heart of County Durham, was the target for the robbers, who appeared to have planned their raid well in advance

The men conspiring to tie me up and rob me had tooled themselves up well, with two sawn-off shotguns, wooden staves, masks and masking tape, with which they intended to gag me. It appeared that they had planned the raid meticulously, casing the house and planning the best time to strike. An accomplice was to keep tabs on me on the night of the raid, to alert the gunmen to my whereabouts.

What they had not banked on was the police being tipped off about their plans, and lying in wait inside my house to catch them. It was a nice summer's night, and as darkness fell there wasn't a cloud in the sky. A bright full moon illuminated the grounds around the house. The police officers, some with hi-tech night-sights, kept watch inside the house, waiting for the gunmen to arrive. They pulled up in a car, and as one of the police officers raised his night-sight goggles he saw one of the men pull a sawn-off shotgun from the boot, then a second man pulled another sawn-off from the boot.

The police officer radioed for assistance; what they needed, in this isolated part of County Durham, was the Northumbria Police helicopter. The chopper arrived, but did not immediately hit on the location. It was a sight people in Wolsingham had never seen before. The hapless gunmen thought it was funny, and pointed their guns towards the chopper, as if to shoot it down. One of the gunmen also looked through the window of the house, and lifted his mask, allowing one of the police officers, thanks to the bright full moon, to get a full-on view of his face. Despite the meticulous planning, the raid was hardly the work of master criminals.

Only when the helicopter hovered nearer the house did the four hapless gunmen leg it. Before long, they were all arrested, and the sawn-off shotguns were found dumped in hedges. Two of the men were arrested in the house grounds, and the other two a short time later. I had to hand it to the police, they had done a great job.

At the later court case, Jason Mawson, of Raysworth House, Byers Green, Steven Hylton, of Upper Church Street, Spennymoor, and Shaun Freeman, of Byland Towers, also Spennymoor, all admitted consiracy to rob, and were jailed for eight years each. William Dunnett, of Wear View, Byers Green, who admitted the same charge, was jailed for five years.

At Newcastle Crown Court, Judge William Crawford said it was a 'wicked and evil plot' and he rightly commended the police team involved.

It was frightening to realise that there were people out there so envious of your wealth and riches that they were prepared to arm themselves with shotguns to get something that belonged to you. In many ways it reminded me what had happened to my old mate Tommy Robson, tortured to death by robbers who wanted something from him.

The incident had shaken me up, and it frightened Susan so much that the pair of us became a lot more security conscious. In the first few weeks, we would venture out only in the company of others. Although I had done crimes of my own in the past, they never involved tying people up and terrorising them; that type of crime was the crime of cowards, who had little imagination or criminal flair.

Susan and I shared the view that many people in the north-east, like the criminals who tried to rob us, hated success; if someone put their head above the parapet, others would be there to knock it down. It was the old tall poppy syndrome: people viewed life as a level playing field, where everyone should be equal and where, if anyone succeeded in rising above normality – whether it be in terms of business success, wealth or even in popularity – it was their job to knock them down. It's a disease, really, which eats away at the fabric of society.

We had been living in Wolsingham for quite a while before my divorce finally came through and I was able to reach a settlement with Karen Brown. It was then that I was able to move back into Witton Hall with my new wife, Susan, but she, quite understandably, did not want to live in a house which had been occupied by my ex-wife. There were too many memories there, a lot of them bitter.

There was only one way around the problem, and that was to completely demolish the old house, which was worth £1 million, and rebuild from scratch. The plot at Witton Hall, one of the most picturesque corners of County Durham, was worth £1 million in itself, without the building, and Susan and I had big plans to build a magnificent mansion, the likes of which had never been seen in the county.

My cousin, the master of all trades, Richie Tennick, master joiner Luke Raine, master of getting the job done, Stevie Molloy, and master safe-blower turned scaffolder Ronnie Heslop, were the core of the team which would work on the house for three years. Susan was adamant that she did not want the house built as some vast country pile mausoleum, all show and no substance; she and I wanted it to be a home we could live in comfortably and one that we would enjoy. We were to bring in some top designers, but most of the ideas for the layout, the colour scheme, the furnishings and the finishing touches came from Susan herself. She had always had a remarkably creative eye: an eye for the aesthetic, that understood texture, colour combinations and the feel of a room.

To me, money was no object in getting the house right, and Susan and I spent many hours flying all over the world to get the furnishings, fittings, objets d'art, floor-coverings, wall-hangings and antiques we desired. One of our trips was to Harrods in London where we spent £1 million in one afternoon.

The fireplaces were to be blue marble, the surfaces for the kitchen were to be imported marble from Brazil and in the dining room there would be a hand-carved fireplace, made by fine craftsman Trevor Dring. Marble floors were to lead to the main reception rooms; the drawing room would be decorated in the most sumptuous cream and black furnishings; every bedroom would be en suite; the Italian-style hall would be dominated by a moulded and galleried staircase, with a hand-forged balustrade, and the pièce de résistance was to be a magnificent dome in the ceiling of the main entrance, hand-painted with scenes of Greek gods.

And amidst all the elegant finishing touches, in the garden, to the side of the house, would be a pillared-archway with an inscription to remind me of my upbringing in Sunderland, the town's motto, *nils desperandum auspice deo*, which, roughly translated, means No Despair – We Trust In God.

The house took three years to complete, and in the end a total of more than £7 million had been spent, but it was worth every penny. It was something that Susan and I, the architects and designers and the lads who worked on it, particularly Richie who oversaw the project from day one, were very proud of. Every room was a masterpiece in itself, the finishing touches exquisite. The house stood in the Durham countryside like a sparkling gem in an ocean of green.

Of course, the £7 million mansion was not the only outward sign of my wealth and success, but I had to dispense with some of the more expensive items, such as the Augusta 109 helicopter, one of the fastest helicopters on the market. *Secret Love*, the £7 million yacht, built to my specification in Amsterdam had to go too. But we still had a nice penthouse in Hampstead, London, where among my neighbours were Baby and Sporty Spice; and a nice apartment in Marbella, where Susan and I spent some lovely holidays soaking up the sun. And there was still the wonderful country house, Overmere, in the Lake District.

The yacht in particular held memories for me. I remembered her maiden voyage from Amsterdam to Palma, Majorca, when I was accompanied by Barry Dunn. It was a hair-raising experience, which even my training in the Merchant Navy could not have prepared me for. We set out in a force-eight gale, the stabilisers came off the boat – making it rock like hell – and we had to moor in the south of France. We set off again, and were again hit by a force-eight gale. I bravely stood on the deck, assembled the crew, put my hands together and said: 'Repeat after me: "Our father, who art in heaven ..."' Some of the crew did not see the funny side.

My hard work had certainly paid off. I had everything I could have wished for, really. Millions of pounds, a beautiful wife, a £7 million mansion in the countryside, property in the capital and in the Mediterranean, and a business with a massive turnover and a loyal and dedicated workforce.

But I craved a new challenge, and opportunity was about to knock on my door again.

CHAPTER 26

A Nice Little Earner

Forty-one million pounds was a nice little earner on which to close the chapter on the kitchen worktops business. It had taken a few years to build the company up to become the biggest manufacturer of kitchen worktops in the world. That had been a challenge, a major challenge, and I had risen to that challenge and met it. I couldn't see any further challenges ahead in the worktops business, so I sold out for £41 million to American laminate specialist and world leader in the field Wilsonart International Ltd, which, with its parent company Premark International Inc, had an annual turnover of about $2.4 billion.

I retained the chipboard plant, and I still had Shildon Cabinetmakers, George Reynolds UK Ltd and other business interests that would keep me busy in the years ahead, and I still had the drive and ambition to succeed. I could have retired to a life of luxury and started to take it easy when I was handed the £41 million cheque. But I was in at work the following morning at 7 o'clock, well ahead of the rest of the team.

My decision to sell up had followed year after year of constant harping, whinging and moaning from local residents about alleged excessive noise and pollution; complaints from the local council – and a number of court cases – about noise levels and even trading standards issues; and complaints from a tiny minority of disgruntled, union-card-holding employees, who wanted nothing more than to take me to a tribunal and win a few thousand quid payout after dragging my name, and that of my company, through the mud. I couldn't have taken them to a tribunal for being lazy, no-mark, good-for-nothing employees, but c'est la vie, that was the way of the tribunal world, heavily stacked against the wicked employer.

It started way back when Arthur Bell, of Staindrop, near Darlington, a worker at Direct Worktops and a card-carrying member of the Transport and General Workers' Union (T&GWU), took me to an industrial tribunal claiming he was unfairly dismissed, after he was selected for redundancy after just two years' service with the company. I accused Mr Bell of bully-boy tactics against a disabled employee and of being a troublemaker. The tribunal panel, in its wisdom, found in favour of Mr Bell.

I was furious at the one-sided and biased arguments put forward at the hearing, and decided I would kick any other union members out of the door. But, after letting off steam, I decided on a cuter way forward. I became a member of the Transport and General Workers' Union myself, and I was appointed shop steward at Direct Worktops. Mr Bell's was the first of several industrial tribunals I would have to attend.

A Leicester company, which installed equipment at the factory, had an employee who suffered serious injuries to his hand. The company was fined £1,500. He later won a £5,000 compensation payout. My company, however, had always done everything it could to ensure the health and safety of its workforce.

Sedgefield District Council launched an investigation into noise levels from the factory, claiming they were over the limit, and I promised to reduce the level of noise by a specified date. The council came back later and threatened legal action if the factory wasn't soundproofed. Because of the council's intransigence, I decided to submit plans for a new factory in the Wear Valley, rather than Sedgefield, with the prospect of up to 200 new engineering jobs. Sedgefield District Council, I always believed, did not want to do business with me, so when an American company announced it was to invest £40 million in the north-east, I personally flew out to the United States and persuaded the company not to locate its factory in Sedgefield. I suggested the Wear Valley would be a better option. It cost the district council much needed work in a job-starved area of the United Kingdom. The business I took to the Wear Valley rather than Sedgefield, Direct Engineering Ltd, produced sophisticated machinery for recycling materials into chipboard.

Sedgefield District Council, Shildon Town Council and then even the minions at the parish pump, Heighington Parish Council, jumped on the moaning-minnie bandwagon, complaining about the colour of the factory silos, as if they had nothing better to concentrate their educated, parish-pump-mentality minds on. I called a meeting and invited six parish councillors along. The silos were coloured blue with yellow tops. I gave all the councillors a piece of paper and asked them to write down what colour they would prefer the silos to be. Half said blue and half said yellow.

'That's what colour they are,' I said.

'Oh yes,' said one, 'but we would really prefer them to be green.'

I told the councillors it would cost £64,000 to have the silos painted green, and I would be willing to do this if they would sign a piece of paper declaring that, if anyone objected to the silos being coloured green, then they would pay for them to be re-painted. The answer was no.

We were getting nowhere fast, so I grabbed a piece of paper and some coloured pencils, and started sketching.

'How about this then?' I asked after completing the sketch and showing it to the parish councillors. They burst into laughter. The sketch showed a cow stencilled on the side of a silo, jumping over a moon. I pointed out that one of their members had painted a door of his house the same colour as the silos – with the same paint. I also told them I was willing to take the matter through the courts, if necessary, and would issue writs against the main three complainants, claiming false and malicious allegations, victimisation, damages and libel. The councillors decided to withdraw their complaints, and even made an unreserved public apology through the parish council clerk, Ann le Druillenec.

I had built up Direct Worktops from nothing in an area of high unemployment, offering many jobs to local people. I always ensured the factories were spotlessly clean, with regular inspections, and used the best hi-tech machinery. I made the product environmentally friendly by using only ten per cent of new wood from forests, 15 per cent residue from sawmills and 75 per cent from recycled timber such as pallets and waste wood packaging to make the chipboard. And for all the business coming into Shildon and all the hundreds of people I employed, there were other spin-off business for local companies, with my workers, delivery drivers and visitors spending their cash in local shops and cafes.

Despite all that, the nit-picking, pen-pushing, faceless bureaucrats at the town hall did nothing but try to put me down, complaining at every juncture, complaining when there was nothing to complain about. The men in suits had taken on George Reynolds many, many times, but they had yet to win a battle, and they certainly never won the war.

During all the highs and lows, the challenges and the battles, the core of my workforce team had stood by me, helped build up the business, worked liked Trojans to rebuild the factory after the fire and remained unstinting in their loyalty. Dave Powles, Ian Robinson, Stevie Molloy, Mike Metcalf, Mark Hayton, Harry Sams and Harry Pincher were, as reported in the local press, the 'magnificent seven'. After selling out to Wilsonart International Ltd for £41 million, I called each of the seven into my office, one by one, and paid off their mortgages, at a cost of £250,000. For my top five men, I had another surprise: I bought them each a new top-of-the-range Mercedes Benz.

The sell-off of Direct Worktops had bumped up my wealth to such an extent that I appeared for the first time in the *Sunday Times* Rich List. I had been placed as the 600th richest man in Britain, but in truth, with a fortune of nearer £230 million, I should have been up nearer the top of the league, alongside the likes of the Queen and Richard Branson.

The news of my inclusion in the list came as Susan and I were reading the newspapers in bed at our mansion in Witton-le-Wear.

Susan said: 'How come you have never been on this list?'

'It takes a long time to get there,' I replied.

Susan read the list in detail and exclaimed: 'Oh, bloody hell. You are in it. Number 600 with £40 million.'

'Then I've been robbed of about £200 million,' I said. 'Shall I call the police?'

I had sold Direct Worktops for £41 million, but still owned the chipboard plant, worth about £150 million, George Reynolds UK was worth an estimated £24 million and I had a £23 million share in a shipping, warehousing and docking plant on the River Tyne.

The directors of Wilsonart International had treated me with respect and courtesy throughout our business dealings. When the deal was coming to its conclusion, they flew me from Teesside Airport to Heathrow and then on to JFK Airport in the United States, booked me into a top hotel in New York, where the model Naomi Campbell was staying at the time, and flew me from a private airport on the outskirts of New York to an airport near Texas. Susan was with me and the company laid on an entourage of six women to look after her every need. The hotel we stayed at was the Inn on the Creek, where, legend had it, Jesse James had spent a few nights. There were towels available at the reception if we wished to swim in the creek. Their hospitality was reciprocated, for when they came to England on a second trip, we put them up at the luxurious Lumley Castle Hotel, near Chester-le-Street in County Durham.

When the deal, or acquisition as the Americans called it, was secured, I gave the local school in Witton-le-Wear a gift of £100,000 to build a new school hall. I knew that my daughter Victoria was in need of a new car, an essential really, rather than an extravagance, so I called into the Sherwood Vauxhall dealership in Darlington, where I met Alistair McConachie, a businessman with links to Darlington Football Club. I didn't buy the car.

'If I can't interest you in buying a car, would you be interested in buying a football club instead?' Mr McConachie said, tongue-in-cheek.

Darlington Football Club was in danger of extinction, lying low in the Nationwide Division Three, and with crippling debts. I had always been interested in football and had an executive box at Sunderland's Stadium of Light. But could I own a football club? I thought, as I made my way home. My only playing days had been in goal at Kirkham Prison in Lancashire, and I was never very good.

I had been an impulsive buyer in the past; once going out for a sandwich and ending up buying a forklift truck. But, could I be the owner of a football club? I thought again. Another thought struck me: Al Fayed owned a football club, and all he did was run a corner shop – albeit quite a big one. If he could do it, why couldn't I?

I talked it over with Susan and with some of my closest friends, and looked at all the possibilities. With so much at stake, this was one decision that could not be rash. It was something that exercised my mind for several days.

Meanwhile, I complained to the *Sunday Times* about my placing. The compiler, Philip Beresford, quipped: 'I am always prepared to eat humble pie when I get it wrong.'

It was nice of the *Sunday Times* to admit they had incorrectly calculated my worth.

CHAPTER 27

The Quakers

Darlington Football Club had, to put it bluntly, had more ups and downs than a tart's knickers during its 116-year history. The club was officially formed in 1883, became professional in 1908 and had taken its hardcore of loyal fans on many emotional rollercoaster journeys, usually fighting for its league survival but, sometimes, tip-toeing on to the touchline of promotional or cup success. I had to think long and hard about throwing it a financial lifeline, and throwing my own considerable energy, enthusiasm and commitment behind it.

The Quakers had always been the minnows in north-east football, only rivalling their closet rivals, Hartlepool, for the trophy as the Cinderella club of the region. But, of course, serving a catchment area of about 100,000 people, it was never going to challenge the might of the Sunderlands, Newcastles or Middlesbroughs of the footballing world.

The financial crisis it faced when I contemplated taking

over the reins was not its first. During World War I, it ran into severe financial difficulties and almost folded, until a local works team, Darlington Albion Forge, paid off its debts. In the early Eighties too, the club teetered on the brink of bankruptcy and, at one stage, if £50,000 could not be found within six weeks, it was destined to fold. But local people showed how much they cared about their local football club and the money came flooding in. That impressed me.

Only 12 years earlier the club had ended bottom of the old Fourth Division and lost its Football League status, but it continued to be full-time professional and returned to Divison Four immediately.

The demolition of the East Stand, erected just after World War I, to make way for a new 3,500-all-seater stand and associated restaurant, executive boxes and bars, was one of the main reasons the club was said to have plunged into such desperate financial straits. It was struggling to pay off debtors and the bailiffs were not far from knocking at the door.

One thing was for certain: there was passion for football in the north-east. Top clubs such as Sunderland had a strong following of loyal fans; I could remember hearing the famous Roker Roar from the streets around Cooper Street and seeing the joy in the face of my uncle Jos Tennick when the team won. Darlington fans, I believed, were just as passionate about their own club.

I thought about the ten golden rules outlined by my old Master Martin at Besford Court School, and wondered if they could shed any light on whether I should go for it or not. Looking after the pennies? Well, there was more than pennies involved here, there was millions of pounds and there was no real prospect of me seeing any return on any investment, at least not in the short term. Never let your heart overrule your head? That had happened to me in the past, but I'd yet to see and hear the passion for the club felt by the Darlington supporters. Business is just a game, it's knowing how to master the game that counts? At the end of the day football was a business, and I had a proven track record in business. Could I apply my business brains to running Darlington Football Club as a business? I couldn't see why not.

After my jokey chat with the chap at the car dealership, I met with directors at the club. Executive director Bernard Lowery had spent many days talking to businessmen in Darlington and further afield, looking for new sponsorship. Speculation in the town, and in the local newspapers, was rife.

I attended a couple of matches at the ground, Feethams, against Brentford – when we were beaten – and then against Chester, when, again, the team were beaten in what was described as the worst home performance of the season. But the Chester game was more than a match for me. When the fans greeted me, giving me a standing ovation, and then the faithful in the stand known as the Tin Shed, sang: 'There's only one Georgie Reynolds,' something clicked. I had bonded with them.

It was my first taste of adulation from fans hungry for survival and hungry for success. After the match, two young fans, who had been waiting patiently for an autograph, approached me. 'Have you made up your mind, Mr Reynolds?' asked one. 'Please will you do it, we just want you to buy the club.'

I was approached by a disabled supporter in a wheelchair. 'I hope you do take over, Mr Reynolds,' he said. 'I love football and I love Darlington. It's all I've got in life, really. I never miss a home match.'

In me the fans had seen a potential saviour and all their hopes and dreams rested on the club being pulled out from the quagmire of its crippling financial crisis, and for it to be injected with new money and fresh hope.

Susan turned to me. 'Listen to those fans,' she said, as the chant went up again. 'There's only one Georgie Reynolds.

'And did you hear those young lads, and that poor young lad in the wheelchair?' she asked. 'You really can't walk away from this, George. You have to do something.'

She was right.

The players began to make their feelings known, too. They said they would stage a player revolt and the management team would leave if my proposed buy-out did not go ahead. The players felt they had been badly let down. There was every reason for them to feel let down; they were still waiting for their monthly pay-cheques. Some of the players had not been paid on time on occasions in the recent past. The team manager, David Hodgson, who had been with the club since 1996, and his assistant, Ian Butterworth, who were both still to sign new contracts, were threatening to walk out of the club after the last game of the season against Scunthorpe.

Another home match at Feethams arrived, and super-striker Marco Gabbiadini, a former Sunderland player, knocked in a hat-trick for a convincing Darlington win over Exeter. And during the match fans again chanted: 'There's only one Georgie Reynolds,' and what was to become a bit of a signature tune: 'Georgie, Georgie, show us your scarf.'

The fans' hero-worship was something I had never experienced before, and I was, of course, flattered by all the attention, but there was still some tough-talking to do in the Darlington boardroom; a real mess to sort out before I could sign on the dotted line. The talks and negotiations were difficult, mainly because the club's true financial difficulties had never been revealed before. The Quakers were not just £1 million in debt, nor were they just over £3 million in debt – another figure that had been bandied around – the true debt was nearer £5.2 million, and that was a lot of debt.

The accounts showed the amount owed to creditors was

£3.6 million by June 1998 – a full £3 million more than was owed only 12 months earlier – and the debts reached £5 million by the end of April 1999. The finances were a complete and utter shambles. Massive amounts had gone on legal, accountancy and other fees but, although there appeared to be signs of financial mismanagement, nothing illegal had gone on. The threat of the club's extinction was still very real, however; the bailiffs were due any day and the club was literally only days away from going into receivership. I had to praise the chief executive Bernard Lowery and vice-chairman Gordon Hodgson, who had put some of their own cash into the club to keep it afloat.

Some were calling for a probe into the club's financial difficulties and the reasons why it had been plunged into such a crisis. But the full answers, as far as I was concerned, would never be known. What I wanted to do was wipe the slate fully clean, put the past behind us and make a fresh start.

After a full day of talks, when the future of Darlington Football Club hung in the balance, I emerged from the club to make an announcement to the waiting media.

'It has been a long and gruelling day,' I said, 'but we got there in the end. The team, supporters and the town can look forward to a new dawn.'

That was it. I had made the commitment, a big financial commitment, and I aimed to pull the club up by the bootstraps and make things happen.

First I paid off the £5.2 million debt, then I announced two other major ambitions I had for the club: one was to build a new 25,000-seater, state-of-the-art stadium; the other was to lead Darlington Football Club, which had never in its 116-year history been out of Division Three, to the Premiership.

I needed to look at the structure of the club, bring in my own business methods and ensure that the foundations we laid those first few, frantic days were solid enough to build my dreams for the future on.

One thing that struck me immediately was that the club was far too highly staffed. There were people walking around with clipboards who appeared to be doing nothing, a little like some joiners in the old Sunderland shipyards who walked about carrying ladders all day, resting them here and there, and never actually climbing them. A total of seventy-eight staff would be disposed of during my first few months at the club.

The players, like those in most football clubs, were grossly overpaid and there were far too many bonus schemes. As well as wages, they wanted appearance money. Players wanting to join the club wanted a signing-on fee. Players also wanted legal fees and other bills paid. It was ludicrous.

There were seven different bonus schemes, including an appearance bonus, a signing-on bonus, a £1000-a-win bonus and a bonus if a player didn't get a bonus. The £1,000-a-win bonus was something never heard of in Third Division football.

I had a problem with the inflated salaries for the players, some getting £2,000 a week for three hours' work on the field and a few hours of preparatory training. A surgeon, who works all the hours that God sends, who has spent years learning his skills and who save lives, could not command a salary like that.

As well as the high wages, the players wanted appearance fees. Well, I can imagine a forklift truck driver coming to George Reynolds UK, agreeing a basic weekly wage, and then saying he wants an additional £400 every day he appears for work. I'd show him the bloody door.

Then there were the players who wanted to come and play for Darlington who would ask for a signing-on fee. That's like me taking on a skilled electrician and saying to him, 'Not only will I pay you a very decent weekly wage, I'll give you £1,000 cash-in-hand just for agreeing to come to work for me!' It was preposterous.

I was on a steep learning curve, but I soon realised that football clubs and footballers were taking the game away from the ordinary working-man football fan by overpricing the game. And it was all down to greed. The average working man, on say £500 a week, has a mortgage to pay, debts to settle and a family to feed. He would not be left with enough from his take-home pay to afford the exorbitant prices some clubs were asking for season tickets or even paying at the turnstiles, if he wanted to take his family to the local match. It was all wrong. What I hoped to be able to do was take the greed out of football and give the beautiful game back to the ordinary working man; the man who paid the club's wages by coming through the turnstiles every week.

I knew from day one at Darlington that there was a hell of a lot of work to be done. I started by bringing in some of my own team of loyal, dedicated and talented workers, who shared my beliefs and my philosopy.

I appointed Luke Raine as a director of the football club, with special responsibility for public relations, dealing with the media, who were showing a great deal of interest in the club, and dealing with the fans, as well as liaison between the club manager and myself as chairman. Luke was an ideal man for the job, because not only had he proven himself to be a grafter, a trusted employee and a man who could deal with people, he also had strong links with football. In fact his family links with the game went back generations. His grandfather had been an official at Witton Park, a local team, his dad was picked to play for England schoolboys and his brother Colin played for both Bishop Auckland and the county team. Luke had also been chairman of Newton Aycliffe in the Wearside League.

My take-over of Darlington Football Club brought it media attention from around the globe. Never had the club had such a high profile. Luke Raine and myself had our work cut out.

CHAPTER 28

The Media Celebrity

The camera flashbulbs popped, several television cameras zoomed in on the faces of myself, Susan and Barry Dunn, and reporters rushed towards us, clutching their pens and notebooks in anticipation. We glided along the red carpet outside the five-star luxury hotel in Amsterdam, our smart clothes revealing our jet-set status, and our expensive jewellery sparkling in the cold night air. One of the television reporters thrust a microphone in front of my face, as the camera lights beamed down on to my brow, and asked: 'Who are you?'

'The name's Bond,' I said in my best plum-in-the-mouth English. 'James Bond.'

The camera crew giggled, and the TV reporter looked slightly embarrassed.

'I'm Miss Moneypenny,' said Susan.

'And I'm P, just P,' said Barry.

The media circus, and the red carpet, outside the hotel where we were staying, was obviously not for us. It was meant for Pierce Brosnan, star of the Bond movies, staying in the same hotel with his entourage and attending the movie première of *Goldeneye*.

That experience, a few years before I took over at Darlington Football Club, was nothing in comparison to the brightness of the media spotlight that shone on myself, Susan and the club, when the media latched on to my safe-blowing past and other criminal exploits and multimillionaire status. The media saw it as the ultimate rags to riches story of a boy born into abject poverty, dragged up the hard way, who had made it to the top, despite the handicap of being labelled backward, illiterate and mentally deficient. Within the media, it appeared, the world, his wife and the family dog wanted to hear our story.

First the local papers were full of it: *The Northern Echo*, *The Darlington and Stockton Times*, *The Sunderland Echo*, *The Journal*, *The Evening Gazette* in Middlesbrough, *The Evening Chronicle* in Newcastle, *The Sunday Sun*; and then the nationals: *The Mirror*, *The Sunday Mirror*, *The Daily Mail*, *The Daily Telegraph*, *The Sun*, *Sport First*, *The Guardian*, *The Express*, *The Financial Times*, *The Times*, *The Sunday People*. We even made a spread in the *Wood Based Panels International Review*. We were contacted by all the local radio stations, and many national ones, including Five Live. Susan appeared in lots of women's magazines.

The television exposure was relentless, with appearances on the BBC locally and nationally, Sky, *The Esther Show*, *Kilroy*, *Tricia*, and we even flew to the United States to appear on *The Oprah Winfrey Show*. Oprah really went a bundle on me, and we drank English tea. North-east regional television station Tyne Tees made a three-part documentary series on my life, *The Boy Done Good*, which won them a Royal Television Society award. Magazines wanted the big story, too. Among them were *Esquire*, *Scene Scania*, *Selective Lifestyle*, *Total Football*, *Match of the Day*, and many others. If the media attention was the gauge of a story people wanted to read, then it appeared their appetite for the story about the rise and rise of George Reynolds was insatiable.

Susan and my celebrity status brought with it meetings with other people in the public eye, many of whom we now consider to be friends. We spent several days with musician and songwriter Paul Weller, of The Jam and then solo fame, who later agreed to write the music for the award-winning documentary series. Television psychic Uri Geller, also chairman of Exeter Football Club, became a good friend and a visitor to our house in Witton-le-Wear, as did Madame Cyn herself, Cynthia Payne, on whom two full-length feature films were based. We also met Ian Paisley, Richard Harris and Bill Roache from *Coronation Street*.

Talented young singer Zoe Birkett, of television's *Pop Idol* fame, who did a great deal of good for Darlington, was a guest at Feethams to watch a match and, during our visits to television stations and on holidays abroad, Susan and I met and chatted to many other celebrities, including Richard Branson, Donald Trump, clothes designers Gucci and Versace, media guru Max Clifford, Peter Stringfellow, Lionel Blair and Cilla Black. We bumped into comedian Roy Walker on a cruise, and he remembered me from the GR Club.

We never met Pierce Brosnan again. Which was just as well, really, as when we met him in Amsterdam and I twice asked for his autograph on a napkin, he told me to stop bothering him.

With every newspaper, radio and television interview, Susan and I became a little more media savvy, understanding how it all works, and never afraid to speak our minds on even the most controversial of subjects. My frankness, which comes from being born into relative poverty and turning to crime at a young age, shocked some interviewers. I think they regarded me as brash, brusque, even offensive. But I wasn't going to water down my personality to suit television producers; they had to take me as I was, the rough edges with the smooth. I have always spoken my mind, no matter who is offended.

With so much media attention, Luke Raine was inundated with requests for interviews. As far as I was concerned, all publicity was good publicity for the football club, and this was borne out when the gates increased. The dawn of a new era at Darlington was headlined as 'The Reynolds Revival' and there was a real buzz about the place. Everyone wanted success on the pitch to follow, and they wanted it quickly.

The club finished the first season with me at the helm on a high note with a win over Scunthorpe. Locally William Hill soon gave Darlington odds of 5–1 to win the Division Three title and they gave odds of 25–1 that The Quakers would be in The Premiership within six years. Ladbrokes were more cautious, with odds of 1000–1 on Darlington reaching the top flight. The club and myself were riding high on a wave of euphoria and there was real hope that things were moving in the right direction.

In my first three months, it was estimated that Darlington Football Club had attracted publicity worth about £11 million; all free and all because of my criminal past. If I had been out of the equation, there's no way the club would have attracted such worldwide attention from the media.

I made my first appearance at the Football League's summer meeting and let fellow football club chairmen know my views on the game in no uncertain terms. I told them the sport was seriously in danger of pricing itself out of the market and what we needed to do was return football to the people.

My vision of a 25,000-seater stadium for the club on a prime site off Neasham Road, not far from the A1, the A66 and only four miles from Teesside Airport, was becoming clearer in my mind. It would have restaurants and conference facilities, a health and fitness centre, a club shop, more than 1,700 car-parking spaces, offices, community offices, a penthouse apartment and a recreation or picnic area with a lake as its centrepiece.

There would be executive boxes like no Third Division or even Second Division Club had seen, and facilities for the disabled which would beat any other stadium in the country, with lifts taking disabled supporters straight on to the terraces and to their own facilities.

I would finish the stadium off with the same standard of fixtures, fittings and trimmings that could be seen in my own £7 million mansion, and fans would be taken to the first floor on escalators. It would be, I believed, one of the finest stadiums in the country.

Not long into my first full season at the club, when it appeared things could not get any better, they did, when number 14 was drawn from a velvet bag containing the names of twenty FA Cup losing teams vying for Manchester United's place in the competition. Manchester United had dropped out, choosing to compete in the World Club Championships in Brazil instead, giving an opportunity to clubs that had lost FA Cup matches already, to win a place through to the next round. Remarkably, Darlington won the place and landed a prestige match against Aston Villa. The town was absolutely buzzing with the news; it was yet another confidence and morale booster for a team that, only months earlier, had stared extinction in the face.

'Not so many people know this,' I told the press, 'but I have a direct line to Him upstairs. He's ex-directory, so it's no good anyone else trying.'

Manager David Hodgson and his assistant Ian Butterworth had signed new three-year deals with the club, promising to deliver. I solved the ongoing problems with the waterlogged pitch at Feethams – which had caused the postponement or switch of nine matches in one season – for about £4,000. My predecessors had spent £200,000 trying to sort out the same problem. I announced I was in negotiations to try and buy the Feethams ground from its owners, Darlington Cricket Club. Everything was on the up; we were heading for great days in the new stadium, with excitement on the pitch and off, possible cup glory and moving up the Third Division league table.

But for all the positive vibes in the club and in the town, I still had the detractors, the whingers, the moaning minnies and all those other people who complain of the heat when the sun is shining. Critics urged caution, telling fans not to get carried away on a wave of media hype and, far from greeting the stadium plan with delight, a group of local people decided they were going to do everything in their power to block it. It was pitiful, indeed, that not everyone wished to savour and enjoy the moment, preferring instead to poison minds with their negativity.

On a personal note, the highs of the Darlington take-over and the first few months of euphoria were tinged with sadness for me. My mother, Doris, one of the most influential people in my life, had died at the age of 89. Her second husband, Jimmy Wilson, a newsagent in Shildon, who was a great man, had passed away seven years earlier.

The negativity from protesters I had heard before. There had been objections to my milk bar in Shildon, the GR Club, my bungalow, my factories, my chipboard plant and just about every other building of any substance for which I needed planning permission.

The detractors were digging in for a fight; and a fight they would get. The Reynolds Revival was in full swing and the dream of a new stadium, which would be my legacy to the fans, was not about to be shattered by the protests of some small-minded, not-in-my-back-yard agitators, whose mentality stretched only as far as their own back doors and the parish pump.

CHAPTER 29

Tomorrow's Fish 'n' Chip Wrappers

The television, the radio and, particularly, the newspapers, of course, relish a good story, and when you're in the media spotlight the old consensus news agenda kicks in and everyone wants to tell the tale. They are all very eager to highlight and praise when you're on the up, but when the fickle finger of fate strikes, and your fortunes are suddenly, for whatever reason, on the slippery slope, the media – in particular newspapers and even more particularly the local sports writers – are even keener to stick the boot in and fan the flames of discontent.

What started the discontent at Darlington, following the halcyon days when everyone was so chuffed that I had paid off the club's £5.2 million debts and had the ambition, and the vision, to plan a spectacular new stadium and promise Premiership football, is hard to pin down, at least in terms of major events or dates.

I suppose it was a gradual thing; a kind of drip, drip, drip process started by the malcontents, expecting success early and painlessly, and latched on to by others easily led and suffering from the north-east disease dictating that the successful must be brought down a peg or two, told to stand in line and accept failure as a consequence of that success.

Billed as the 'lucky losers', we lost the FA Cup third-round tie against Aston Villa, but the team put up a spirited performance and almost pulled off a giant-killing shock. After the exciting match I had a word with Villa's chairman, 'deadly' Doug Ellis, who had a history of sacking managers, and told him why lowly Darlington could have beaten his Premiership side.

'You had more than £40 million worth of players on the pitch and about £8 million worth on the substitute's bench,' I said. 'Either your team is grossly overpaid, or Darlington are exceptionally good.'

The Villa defeat was, of course, a bitter disappointment for myself and the thousands of fans who had travelled to the match, but the team had its time in the spotlight and enjoyed the experience. What we had to concentrate on after that defeat was strengthening the team and pushing for promotion to Division Two.

Nearing the end of my first full season as chairman, Darlington saw off their bitterest rivals Hartlepool United, 3–0 on aggregate, to book a place at the Twin Towers of Wembley in the Third Division play-offs against Peterborough United. Again the town was buzzing and 10,000 of The Quakers' faithful travelled south for the big match, only to come home bitterly disappointed after a 1–0 defeat on the waterlogged, but still hallowed, Wembley turf. The team had played so well we really deserved better, and I felt heartily sorry for the fans.

The summer of 2000 began badly, with the minority of malcontents still hungry for success quickly and critical that the team had lost players. The discontent was started, really, by newspaper sports writers who believed the sports pages of newspapers are there as a type of fanzine for their own views, rather than an objective analysis of the success or otherwise of a team. I do not believe it is conducive to objective and impartial football sports coverage if the man hitting the computer keys is a lifelong fan of the team. For the writer, it just gets personal. If the writer upsets the club chairman and the manager, then he struggles for things to write about, and the only avenue open is to pour out some puerile and fanciful 'fact' that is based on nothing more than rumour, more often than not started by the writer himself.

In the same way, football club managers can put pressure on club chairmen to spend more on players, by having an off-the-record chat with a player and encouraging him to have an off-the-record chat with a sports reporter. The player then gives the writer a publishable 'fact', which neither the player nor the manager would wish to put their names to.

In the summer of 2000 a newspaper published the 'fact' that the chairman of Darlington Football Club – George Reynolds – would not buy any new players because he was 'greedy'. I was absolutely furious and called the manager David Hodgson into my office.

'Who the fuck has said that?' I asked.

'I wouldn't worry about that,' said Hodgson. 'Today's newspaper is tomorrow's fish 'n' chip wrapper.'

I decided, controversially, to publish the players' wages in *The Northern Echo*, and the story was picked up by many national newspapers.

Hodgson stormed into my office, seething with anger. 'What the fuck is all this about?' he shouted.

'I wouldn't worry about that,' I said. 'Today's newspaper is tomorrow's fish 'n' chip wrapper.'

Only ten days before the start of the new campaign, in the summer of 2000, unhappy manager David Hodgson decided to quit, leaving the club in disarray. He did not criticise me personally, at least not publicly, but 'privately' in public – i.e. in the pages of the local newspaper. 'Privately, he has made it known he was not prepared to go on any longer under the Reynolds regime,' stated the article by a sports writer.

I do not wish to make this next statement public, but privately, I stress *privately*, I can say that I thought Hodgson was not the right manager. Just look at the £1,000 bonus he was paying each player for a win; no wonder Darlington had the highest wage bill in the Third Division. A good manager, in my view, can achieve success on the field by getting the most from the talent he has in his squad.

The publication of the players' wages showed the public the extent of the wages bill at Darlington, which, in the season they were published, stood at a hefty £1.4 million, which I considered far too high. The Professional Footballers Association (PFA) criticised the move. The Darlington players accepted a new bonus scheme, in which I offered a good bonus of £10,000 per player if we won promotion.

I sent letters off to the chairmen of the seventy-two clubs in the Nationwide League, urging them to address the spiralling cost of players' wages.

In early 2001 the club, under the management of former Sunderland player Garry Bennett, was yet again facing a potential relegation battle and attendances fell. Fans, instead of shouting 'Georgie, Georgie, show us your scarf', as they had in the early days, were now chanting 'Reynolds, Reynolds, show us your cash'. It was strange how quick fortunes could change. Had it not been for me, the club would not exist.

The fact of the matter is, every football club is run as a business, not a charity, and to get good new players, you have to have the support of the fans coming through the turnstiles. That's why I have always urged the fans to get behind the club. What brings success is the right attitude and the will to win. At every club there is a minority who want to see failure, who want to bring a club down, and they direct their anger when things are not going so smoothly in the direction of the manager and the players. If you whip a horse long enough, you will break its spirit.

Then, when the manager's and the players' spirit is broken, and the team is suitably demoralised, the bile is then directed in the direction of the chairman, who is criticised for not throwing more money at the club. Yet it is the chairman who puts the big money where his mouth is, the man who would remortgage his house to keep a club afloat. It is the chairman who takes the big financial risk, yet, suddenly, everyone knows how to run the club better than he does. (For a detailed analysis of what managers, footballers, the media and fans know about running a football club as a business, see the next chapter.)

By January 2001, the discontented supporters at Feethams were staging a protest in the Tin Shed following a home defeat against Chesterfield, a 3–0 defeat, and I had to leave the ground early, fearing for myself and my family's safety. A group of about fifty supposed fans stayed behind after the match to demonstrate. The small band of fans had, no doubt, had their passions roused by what I considered the style of reporting of one particular football writer, Craig Stoddart, of *The Northern Echo*, who claims to have been a lifelong Darlington supporter.

I visited Mr Stoddart's home, in the Eastbourne area of Darlington, and confronted him on his doorstep, asking why he wrote his reports in the way that he did, as if he was writing for some kind of fanzine rather than a respectable, objective and impartial newspaper. He took offence at my knocking on his door, and the police were called. Mr Stoddart had already been banned from the press box at Feethams for what I considered to be his inflammatory and heavily negative reporting of the club's affairs and matches.

The problems I have had with the media have always been with local sports reporters; news reporters I have always got on incredibly well with, including *The Northern Echo*'s Mike Amos and Marjorie McIntyre. Mike, who has won the North East Journalist of the Year Award many, many times has written numerous stories about me, not all of them complimentary, but we have never fallen out. He scooped the country with an exclusive interview with Vince Landa when he returned from his Mediterranean exile. It was Mike, too, who acted as a witness when old friend Tony Hawkins wanted to hand himself in to police after being on the run. Tony had previously been involved in a job with me and a couple of other lads at a northeastern Co-op Store but the job went badly wrong. He fell from a third-storey window and broke his leg. We rushed him to Bishop Auckland General Hospital, threw him through the admission doors in a wheelchair and then told his wife what had happened. Tony's wife went ballistic and we had to steal Tony from his hospital bed! The theft of a patient from the hospital was reported to police by staff, but detectives never got to the bottom of it.

Majorie McIntyre saw my humorous side, but, more than that, she realised what I was trying to do for the town of Darlington, and this was reflected, accurately, in her reports. She has written scores of reports on the development of the new stadium, and they have all been in a positive light. But even if the reports had been negative, I wouldn't have minded, providing the facts were fair and accurate and not based on one person's opinion.

I have always tried to play local sports writers at their own game. If they take me or the club on at a personal level, then I will take them on at a personal level. It's as simple as that. Once *The Northern Echo* sent a young lad, introduced to me as a trainee reporter down to Feethams to apply for the manager's job. I asked him to run round the pitch twelve times and I'd consider him for the job. He couldn't manage it, so their ploy backfired.

At Feethams I also took on the small band of agitators, one by one, who appeared to thrive on destruction and wanted the club to fail. I can take criticism with the best of them, but I wasn't going to stand for an orchestrated attempt by a small minority of vociferous agitators to undermine Darlington FC. I managed to get the names and addresses of the three ringleaders and I rang each of their parents, asking if they minded if I staged a protest outside their home with 300 supporters and a brazier with a fire to keep them warm. The agitators soon got the message.

I had given my backing to under-fire Garry Bennett, but by October 2001, the pressure on him was mounting and, after a run of five matches without a win, the latter three defeats, and Darlington 20th in the league, Garry decided to call it a day, saying he was leaving for the sake of the club. It was not long before former Leyton Orient manager, Tommy Taylor, was in the hot seat.

With Tommy Taylor's tenure as manager only a few months in, and after more disappointing results on the field, all hell broke lose at a Fans' Forum, which I had called to clear the air and discuss a positive way forward for the club. Susan and I were sick of all the verbal abuse that had been hurled at us by a minority of fans.

Susan took to her feet and, reading from a prepared script, made a statement from the heart about the constant stories in the press that always referred to my safe-cracking days. She was right. I was never 'The Chairman of Darlington Football Club' in any opening story, I was always referred to as 'Millionaire former-safe-cracker', which gets a bit wearing time after time after time. True, I made no secret of my past, and, indeed, used it to attract publicity to the club, wearing a ball and chain at Susan and my wedding reception and at a team pre-season photo shoot, but the constant references to my criminal past did nothing to focus attention on what really mattered, what was going on, on the pitch.

In her statement she said: 'It is not unknown for games to be thrown,' and, before she could finish her sentence, in an unprecedented scene, the whole team got up and walked out. The walk-out, though, had been pre-arranged. We knew at 2.20pm that they were going to stage a walk out.

I stand by what Susan said. If a player does not give 100 per cent on the field, he has thrown the game; if a player is injured and does not tell the manager and goes on to play, again not giving 100 per cent, then he has thrown the game. Throwing the game is a figure of speech. How many times have we heard fans leaving the ground after a disappointing match, saying to each other, 'They threw the game away'? Many, many times.

The statement caused uproar and hit the national newspapers which milked the story for all it was worth. The press commented that my own tenure at Darlington might soon be over and that the team might never play at the new stadium. The club was again in turmoil, said the press. How wrong they were. I have no intention of leaving the club without first fulfilling the third of the three promises I made to fans – taking Darlington to the Premiership.

Susan, who was naturally upset when the fans started booing and jeering, walked out. But she did have an opportunity to have her say shortly afterwards in an interview with *The Northern Echo*'s editor Peter Barron, who could, I think, be a little more objective than his football writer, as he is a Hartlepool United fan.

With tomorrow's fish 'n' chip wrappers dispensed with, it was time to move on and look to the future. Darlington's future looked very promising indeed, with a move to a new 25,000-seater, state-of-the-art stadium. But I had a real war on my hands to get planning permission for the stadium because of a small group of protestors. When the stadium protests first kicked off, I thought, well ... let battle commence.

I had another battle on my hands, too, quite literally, when I was attacked in a London street by muggers after my Rolex watch. What they did not know, however, was that George Reynolds was not a soft target for criminals, because he had been one himself, and a street-fighter to boot.

CHAPTER 30

What Managers, Footballers, the Media and Fans Know about Running a Football Club as a Business

CHAPTER 31

The Rolex Robbers

The evening meal at a top London restaurant was superb, and as Susan and I, and Susan's mother, May, aged 80, walked back to our apartment in Hampstead, we really didn't have a care in the world. The troubles at the football club and the disappointing performances of the team were the last things on my mind. We were just enjoying being away from it all, even if it was just for the weekend.

As we walked along Heath Street I spotted three burly black men, who seemed to be looking at us; I knew from the look in their eyes they were about to pounce.

'Give me the fucking watch!' one of the men demanded, staring into my face and pointing to the £41,000 gold and diamond Rolex on my wrist.

I stared him straight in the eyes and said: 'Fuck off!'

The mugger tried to snatch the watch, though he mustn't

have seen the solitaire diamond ring I was wearing, so I grabbed hold of him. He had a look of real fear in his eyes. This big, big man was frightened of me; a man in my sixties who he thought was a soft touch. With all my strength I wrestled him to the ground, stuck my knees into his back and pressed hard. There was no way I was letting this man have my watch, and no way I was allowing him to get away.

Another of the muggers started raining blows down on to my body: 'Get off the fucking man, man!' he shouted. 'Get off the man!'

One of the muggers confronted Susan and she froze with fear and screamed hysterically. Her mother grabbed hold of the robber hitting me, and tried to pull him off. The big man was struggling, and I could hardly breathe, but I kept him pinned to the pavement.

Out of the corner of my eye, I spotted another man running towards us with what appeared to be a plank of wood in his hand. He was running fast. 'Shit', I thought, 'there's another one.' The man brought the plank down on the back of one of the muggers with such force it almost split in two.

The main man had managed to rip the Rolex from my wrist and the three of them legged it. Seeing their targets, myself, my wife and her elderly mother, they must never have imagined they would be in for such a fight.

The man with the plank turned out to be a London refuse collector who had witnessed what was going on. The have-a-go hero had also memorised part of the registration number on the car the robbers fled in. He was later named Camden Citizen of the Year.

The police caught the attackers following a high-speed chase through London, and when they searched their house they not only found my Rolex watch, but a load of others. The gang was obviously targeting wealthy people.

The main mugger, Tayo Aladesuyi, of West Hampstead,

known as 'killer' to his gangmates – he hardly looked a killer when I took him on – was later jailed for five years at Snaresbrook Crown Court for robbery on me and for attempting to steal from my wife.

The robbery left Susan and myself fairly shaken and, afterwards, we took to wearing fake jewellery when out in public.

After a gap of many years, the robbery, with me as the crime victim, wasn't my only involvement with the criminal justice system during this period. I took the police to court, suing them for wrongful arrest, unlawful imprisonment and malicious prosecution over my arrest almost ten years earlier when it was alleged I had made threats of violence to the family of my ex-wife, Karen Brown.

I was fully prepared for the case, but when I was quoted £60,000 for legal representation, I turned QC for the week – Quietly Confident – conducting my own case.

As it was Cleveland Police who had asked Durham Police to arrest me when the allegation was made, I was suing the Chief Constable of Cleveland, Barry Shaw.

With the packed public gallery at Middlesbrough High Court looking on, and the barristers acting for the police resplendent in their wigs and gowns, and with weighty law books on the desks in front of them, I took to my feet to open the case.

Pacing the courtroom floor slowly and deliberately, I looked towards Judge Michael Taylor: 'I am guilty of one crime,' I said. 'That of being successful.'

I then took the hushed court back 30 years, to the time of Detective Inspector Peter Eddy, when I was charged with thirty-eight offences and spent nine months on remand at Her Majestys's Pleasure in Durham Prison.

'One charge accused me of arson on a factory which Hitler's bombs had blitzed in 1943,' I told the judge. 'I was totally fitted up. Hitler would have been proud of that officer.

'This was an incompetent conspiracy,' I added, and told the court I would be questioning a number of police officers to establish that there had been a miscarriage of justice.

I sauntered towards the public gallery and, with due deference to the court's procedures, nodded and winked to a member of the public. 'What do you think of my performance so far?' I asked.

When it came to me taking the stand, the barrister acting on behalf of Cleveland Police, Aidan Marron, QC, questioned me about what he said was the stormy separation between myself and Karen Brown.

'I can see exactly where you are coming from,' I told the learned counsel. 'In fact, you are like an open book ... *The Beano.*' There was a roar of laughter from the public gallery.

The court heard how I was arrested the day before I was due to appear before a family court fighting for custody of my daughter, Victoria, following the separation between myself and Karen Brown.

'I have been shouting for nine years about one night in a cell because I know there has been a great miscarriage of justice and a police conspiracy,' I told the court.

'Durham Police had been waiting 25 years for the opportunity to get me.'

The police, through Superintendent John Blake, denied waging any kind of vendetta against me and the police barrister accused me of making 'wicked, baseless and groundless assertions'.

Solicitor Gerald Johnson, my brief at the time of the arrest, told the court: 'It seemed an enormous coincidence that the complaint had come at exactly the time of the custody hearing.'

Despite the eloquence of my submissions, and what appeared to be support from the public in the public gallery, I lost the case and the police accused me of using the court as a soapbox to make groundless accusations against police officers. Over the years many groundless accusations had been made against me – more than thirty of them 30 years earlier; the charges on which I was acquitted. I was ordered to pay £50,000 costs but I had had my day in court, and I did think the judge had acted fairly.

The courtroom battles continued, this time away from the pomp and majesty of the high court, to the modern, but still familiar, surroundings of employment tribunals. Since 1984 I had had to fight my corner as an employer about why I had decided to sack people who proved to be lazy or just downright incompetent. One worker who I alleged turned in late for work sixty times and failed to turn up at all forty times took me to a tribunal and claimed unfair dismissal. What's unfair about sacking someone with a track record like that? The tribunal ruled, however, that I had failed to take proper action over her conduct before dismissing her, and ruled in her favour. She won £8,500 compensation in what was my seventh tribunal in 20 years.

Now from courtroom and tribunal battles to the war of words with that small band of protestors intent on blocking Darlington FC's progress by doing whatever was in their power to block the plans for our fantastic new stadium.

One of the main people behind the anti-stadium campaign was Marcus Nimmo, a really vociferous campaigner who took every opportunity he could to whip up opposition to something that he failed to recognize was going to benefit Darlington FC and the whole town.

Mr Nimmo could only see the stadium having an impact in his back yard, complaining about the level of traffic it would generate, the dust and noise from the site, and claiming it would result in devaluing his property. Mr Nimmo could not see the big picture at all.

The Neasham Road Action Group, members of whom lived

near the site, complained about the road layout, so I unveiled plans for new road improvements; they complained about late night noise, and I was cleared by the council; they complained about a park and ride scheme, which wasn't a problem; they complained about me opening a pub, which I wasn't opening; they complained about plans to use the stadium as a concert venue – I had hoped to get the supergroup the Bee Gees for the opening night.

When the action group took to the streets of Darlington to protest and 200 people brought traffic to a standstill, 7,000 people visited the stadium site to see how the development was progressing. There was no traffic congestion there.

When the action group launched a petition, I launched a counter-petition for those in favour of the stadium. I obtained 450 signatures within 20 minutes before a Darlington match, then thousands more.

When the stadium plan was finally given the go-ahead, with strict conditions imposed, protestors vowed to take it to court. I told them I was quite happy for that to happen, provided they put up £100,000 to pay for costs – as I would for security – whatever the outcome. They refused.

When Darlington Council originally backed the scheme, the Secretary of State was happy with it. So away we went, much to the chagrin of Mr Nimmo et al. Building work got under way within weeks.

While the building work was progressing, I went on a £2 million spending spree in London to order the best seating possible, and bought many other items for the stadium which would ensure its finishing touches towered well above those of any other. When the visitor centre opened, it became one of the most popular tourist attractions in the north-east.

At the height of the battle to build the stadium, a cheeky sign had been put up on the site which read: 'Builder 1 –

Reynolds 0'. When the plan got the green light, another sign appeared on the site: 'Reynolds 1 – Nimmo 0'.

Signs, billboards and the words they contained became a big issue for local people. Thousands of motorists passed the site each day to see what the latest 'rumour' was – on a 28-foot-high billboard. None was more perplexed at the wording on the rumour board one day than a certain north-east radio presenter, who, when he heard, almost choked on his cornflakes.

CHAPTER 32

The Charity Man

North-east radio presenter Paul 'Goffy' Gough liked a bit of a joke with his listeners on his morning programme, cracking jokes and winding people up. He and I had a bit of friendly banter over the airwaves, mainly because he is a Hartlepool United supporter, Darlington's arch rivals.

Goffy once teased me about my comb-over hairstyle live on air, so, just to prove I was game for a laugh, I posed for photographs sporting various types of wig. I also ventured into enemy territory with Goffy, a presenter on Century FM, when I helped him open a new hairdressing business in the town.

One of our best on-air wind-ups, however, came after the 5–1 thrashing of Hartlepool in a Third Division semi-final play-off against Blackpool. Hartlepool, it is fair to say, were absolutely annihilated, and I had every reason to call my friendly radio presenter to wind him up, on air or not.

GEORGE REYNOLDS

It started half an hour after the thrashing, when I called Goffy on his mobile phone. There was no answer, so I left a message – every 30 minutes. This went on until about midnight, and I set my alarm for 4am, got up and left many more messages for Goffy between 4am and 8am. He left his mobile on voicemail, and left his landline off the hook to avoid me.

'It was funny for the first 24 hours,' Goffy said. 'He just revelled in it, but it's getting really irritating now. I know I wind people up on my show, but this is past a joke.'

I had been listening to the radio, waiting for the result, hoping they would get beaten, but I never imagined it would have been such a disaster for Hartlepool. Goffy had caught me out in the past live on air when he had someone pretending to be a soccer agent, and I was heard chatting to him – I always said I wouldn't speak to agents – and again when he caught me on tape saying I had never heard of Liverpool player Stan Collymore.

After Hartlepool's defeat, I called him and said: 'Oh dear, oh dear, what a mess, 5–1. At least we are now both bottom of the Third Division; but we have a new stadium.'

Afterwards Goffy said: 'It's a little bit sad, really. You would have thought he would have better things to do.' He threatened to play some of the messages live on air. It was a lot of fun.

Goffy the wind-up merchant was far from laughing, however, when a sign mysteriously appeared on the stadium's rumour board falsely claiming: 'Latest rumour – Goffy is gay. He's come out of the closet at last.' It wasn't true, of course, but it certainly wound him up.

About 14,000 motorists and their thousands of passengers passing the site that day could see the board, and Goffy's radio station was inundated with calls asking him if the rumour was true. Goffy, a married father-of-three, threatened legal action and the police were called. When the media bombarded my office with calls about the sign, I told them the mystery person who erected the sign could easily erect others, revealing more rumours about them. Officials were contemplating ordering me to take the hoarding down, but I told them I could easily replace it, quite legally, with a hoarding on wheels, but this one would be illuminated!

When the rumour mill was operating in the north-east on virtually anything to do with football, I could expect a call from Paul Goffy Gough.

One day he called me about an 18-year-old footballer who was sacked when he failed a random drugs test. The lad had been signed as a trainee. He had been battling to beat his heroin addiction and had hoped to restart his career.

Goffy asked me if I thought the lad should be given a second chance, and I said he should and that I would be willing to give him a trial at Darlington. I'm still waiting to hear from him. It was a charitable gesture, I was told, but, contrary to a Darlington player's assertion that I was greedy, I always did my best for worthwhile charities.

When another of the town's teams, Darlington RA, was in need of transport to make it to a match in Windscale, Cumbria, I gladly loaned the team the Darlington Football Club coach. When I was asked to go to Deerbolt Young Offenders' Institution to give the lads a talk about steering away from crime, I accepted the invitation. When I was asked to help promote Hurworth Grange's Picnic in the Park, I agreed. When two disabled lads asked for sponsorship for a 30-mile wheelchair charity fundraising appeal, I started the appeal for them. When a football-mad young teenager lost a leg to cancer, I gave him a Darlington season ticket. When the Kenyan Quakers football team in Africa were without strips and boots, I kitted them out. When local football teams wanted to play a match to raise cash for the families of the

September 11th victims in America, I allowed them to play the game at Feethams without charge. When a 15-year-old lad with a promising football career ahead of him was badly injured and told he would not walk again, I arranged for him to appear on the pitch before a match at Feethams. When a Darlington woman decided to take part in the Great North Run for a local hospice, I started off the sponsorship. When a couple got married at Feethams, I gave them a £60 wedding gift. Then there was the opening of stores and garden fêtes and the like. All this by a 'greedy' football club chairman. In truth, I had never sought publicity for those or any other of the charitable causes I supported. That's just the way I am. There were others, too, like helping to kick-start a fund that raised £27,000 for a girl with cerebral palsy and donating £5,000 to Shildon Football Club when it ran into difficulties. I could go on, but I won't.

One former crime associate, George 'Blower' Shotton, once stung me for £30,000, but I didn't get it back, I knew he would screw me for it. Shotton and I, and a well-known Newcastle underworld figure and a few other lads who used to meet in a pub in Low Fell once a month to discuss business, decided to fly out to Malta for business-related activities, details of which I cannot divulge. We all ended up in the local nick and I got deported. My visit came back to me years later when I tried to moor the yacht in Malta, and was ordered to go back to the three-mile limit by army gunboats.

Blower Shotton wanted his £30,000 because he had 'rented' a shipyard from a well-known businessman in Newcastle with links to the city's football club, and set about dismantling it, selling off some of the machinery and flogging much more off as scrap. George, who is now dead, came to me begging for the cash to keep what he called the 'Newcastle Mafia' off his back. I gave him a cheque and said: 'There you are, but I know you'll screw me for it.'

He told me he would pay the money back by a certain date and, when I approached him for it on the given date, he said: 'You said you didn't want it back. You said you knew I would screw you for it.' At least, when it came to straight talking, Blower Shotton was straight. I attended his funeral a few years ago, along with hundreds of other people with colourful pasts, and one of the floral tributes was a huge, unopened safe.

Paul 'Goffy' Gough was one of the first in the media to highlight speculation that former England international Paul Gascoigne was interested in a career with Darlington Football Club. It came out during an interview Goffy had with Gazza, but the story first surfaced in a newspaper when I was asked if Darlington would be interested in Gascoigne. I told the reporter that of course we would, but we would never be able to afford him. The story was written as though Darlington were making Gazza an offer.

The club's director of PR, Luke Raine, was quick to try and rubbish the story. He told the newspapers: 'It's absolute nonsense and we can't understand where the stories are emanating from. Darlington is not in a position whereby we can compete with the figures being talked about. We are a Third Division club. Gazza is a great player and of course we would be interested, but not while we are in the Third Division.'

The newspapers reported that Darlington had offered Gazza £1,000 a week, and the player was reported as having said that the figure would only covers his dad's weekly petrol bill. If Gazza, whom I like, had been interested in seeing out the rest of his career with Darlington, I would have gladly paid him up to £7,000 a week.

Gazza's name was linked to Darlington when I had made it known we were on the look-out for a big-hitter, someone high profile whose talent and flair fans would pay to watch and who could maybe act as a catalyst to get Darlington the success the club and the fans so craved.

Gazza went on Paul 'Goffy' Gough's radio show to accuse me of using him in a publicity stunt. I had never intended to use Paul, I like the lad. My comments to a reporter had been misconstrued as offering him £1,000 a week to play for Darlington. That is so unrealistic. We would not have insulted him.

Gazza told Goffy: 'I've trained hard for a month and there have been good offers from all around the world. And then, all of a sudden, George Reynolds embarrasses me by saying he'd give me £1,000 a week and a life.'

Another big-name 'signing' was just around the corner, but the controversial Colombian star, Tino Asprilla, it came to pass, had a hidden agenda.

CHAPTER 33

Tino Does a Runner

The controversial Colombian, Faustino Asprilla, a player of undoubted talent and flair, but somewhat unpredictable behaviour, donned the white, red and black of The Quakers and soaked up the adulation of the Feethams faithful. Never before had I seen Darlington fans so excited at the sight of one player on the once-waterlogged pitch. But excited they were, and so they should have been, for I had pulled off, it appeared, the biggest shock in north-east sporting history; such an audacious bid by a lowly Third Division club for a top-flight international footballer was, to some, unbelievable.

The former Newcastle United striker paraded around the ground before Darlington kicked off against Carlisle United, wearing a broad smile and shaking hands with delighted supporters. This was to be an exciting new dawn for Darlington, and Tino Asprilla would help make it happen by playing dazzling and entertaining football, and inspiring Darlington's regular players in the process. Fans would flood back through the turnstiles, money would come into the club, more top players could be bought and Darlington would be on their way, rocketing up Division Three and proving all the critics wrong.

A crowd of more than 5,100 packed Feethams to catch a glimpse of the star. Whether or not his presence had an impact on the players is hard to determine, but Darlington did win the match 2–0, and it was a very exciting game. The win pushed Darlington to fifth place in the Third Division league table.

Manager Tommy Taylor did not wish to get carried away; he wanted to ensure that Asprilla was fit enough to play before allowing him on to the pitch. Asprilla had not done any pre-season training.

My efforts to sign Asprilla had begun seven weeks earlier when he returned to his old Newcastle club for a pre-season friendly against Barcelona. The early, tentative and delicate negotiations were difficult. Asprilla, however, was open to persuasion.

I put a great deal of effort in during those seven weeks to try to ensure Darlington signed him. As well as the initial approach, there was a great deal of other spadework to do, such as sorting out a work permit, which would involve an appeal to the Home Office, and getting clearance from the Mexican Football Association, the last country in which Asprilla worked. If it came off, it would be the first time a world-class player had played for a Third Division English club.

Asprilla wanted to get back into English football and he was hoping to play in the north-east, as he has friends in the region. Newcastle, Middlesbrough and Sunderland were not interested in him, so if he still intended to play in the north-east that only left Hartlepool and Darlington, both Third Division clubs.

We agreed terms by fax and by telephone, long before he left Colombia. We had offered him a big salary and a percentage of the gate, which would have seen him walking out of Feethams with £7,000 a week. Asprilla was keen on joining us, he said, because he knew Darlington was eventually aiming to get into the Premiership.

Everything needed to be in black and white; the I's dotted, the T's crossed. I had to go along to the Football Association, the Football League, the Professional Footballers' Association and the Home Office to convince them all that everything was above board.

The first signs that everything was not so hunky-dory was during the Carlisle match, when Asprilla appeared disinterested in what was going on on the pitch. He spent 35 minutes on his mobile telephone to his agent during the second half. Before the second half kicked off, he spent an extra 15 or so minutes in the chairman's lounge. That showed a lack of commitment.

We had drawn up a two-year contract for Asprilla on a free transfer and he seemed happy. He had donned The Quakers' strip – the most outward sign that he was a Darlington player – and he told the press: 'I am really happy. It is important for me to be in Darlington. I want to play in the Third Division because Darlington have the intention of getting to the Premier League.'

Newcastle had signed the striker for £7.5 million in 1996 and one of the high spots during his time with the Magpies was a magnificent hat-trick against Barcelona in the Champions League. Asprilla was a colourful character.

He was a man used to living the high life in the fast lane, and during the negotiations I offered to put him up at Witton Hall, and wined and dined him in the manner to which he was accustomed. I spent a small fortune on him and his entourage.

He received his work permit, after I practically got on my knees begging at the Home Office – I almost talked the officials to sleep. Then the time for his medical arrived – and Asprilla failed to show up. The medical was re-arranged, and he turned up late. This time he had a new adviser from Italy in tow, a man I had never seen before.

The deal we had struck with Asprilla would have seen him earning thousands per week. I also offered free accommodation for himself and his girlfriend within Witton Hall, a free flat for his driver, several bonus schemes and a top-of-the-range car, already taxed and insured.

But then came the bombshell. His adviser said Asprilla wanted double what had been offered. I couldn't offer him any more without plunging the club into financial difficulties. It was just not on; the terms had been agreed and Asprilla had given his word. He was, obviously, a man who did not stick to his word.

The following morning, at about 5am, Asprilla did a runner. He was picked up by friends living in Newcastle and taken to the city's airport where he caught a flight to Gatwick, for another flight on to the Middle East. While he had been 'signing on' for Darlington, he had also been in negotiations with a club in the Middle East to play for them.

The biggest football transfer shock in north-east sporting history had crumbled as spectacularly as it had started. And it was all because of a flamboyant and controversial South American world-class footballer who was no gentleman, and who was, basically, greedy. The man had no sense of honour; he had reneged on a deal that had been struck. It was, simply, an act of betrayal.

I know now it was no coincidence that Asprilla's people were the first to leak the news of his 'interest' in playing for

Darlington, after Newcastle and Sunderland had both shown him the door. Asprilla was using Darlington Football Club, and its fans, as a lever to attract interest from a bigger club. When that wasn't forthcoming, he fled to the Middle East where he could attract bigger wages. As far as Asprilla was concerned, the gentleman's agreement we had struck was not worth the genuine handshake that sealed it.

I had reached the lowest point I had known at Darlington Football Club, and that was not because some sports writers were accusing me of naïveté in the extreme, or because I had spent a small fortune trying to secure Asprilla and had put seven weeks' hard work into it. I was gutted, devastated, but it was for the fans whose hopes and dreams had received the biggest boost possible, and had then been shattered in one fell swoop by a greedy footballer, who had no sense of probity and no sense of respect.

It took a couple of days for me to get my head around what had happened. Normally I'm like a coiled spring: push me down and I'll jump back up, raring to go. But the Asprilla débâcle had knocked the stuffing out of me. It took me time to get over it, but get over it I did.

I still needed a big name, a big hitter, to fulfil my dreams of filling the 25,000-seater new stadium and take The Quakers up the Third Division league table and on to better things. I had my eye on three or four players, and I was determined not to give up. Myself, Tommy Taylor, the players and the fans had to realise that we were in this together and that united we stood or divided we fell.

Good housekeeping, going for the best deals and putting the club on a secure financial footing for the future was what was needed. With the collapse of the £315 million ITV Digital TV deal, many were sounding the death knell for Nationwide League clubs, but, personally, I thought it was a blessing in disguise. I would have preferred it if all clubs got nothing to put us all on a level playing field. Clubs which landed themselves with big wage bills were in danger of going to the wall. But I wasn't interested in the mess other clubs had got themselves into. I was only interested in Darlington FC.

Clubs could not rely on hand-outs all their lives. If less money was coming through the turnstiles per week than what was being spent on players' wages, appearance fees, signing-on fees and bonuses, then it was obvious clubs would run into financial difficulties. We just needed to take the greed out of the game. It was as simple as that.

After the sad Asprilla saga, I popped into the stadium on a Sunday morning to look at progress and noticed the generator going. Yet no one was working this Sunday; only a security guard. I drove up to the security cabin.

'Why is the generator on?' I asked the security guard.

'Oh. I was just making myself a cup of tea,' he said.

'Don't you have a flask?' I asked.

'No,' he replied.

'Do you know how much that one cup of tea has cost?' I asked.

'No,' said the security guard.

'That has cost us twenty-eight quid by you firing up the generator,' I said. 'It's probably the most expensive cup of tea you'll ever drink. I hope you enjoy it.'

Obviously, the message I had been spreading about sound financial housekeeping had yet to reach everyone.

With no big new signings announced, a disappointing run of results for the team, and a delay in the opening of the new stadium, the critics started flinging mud in my direction. But I was not prepared to walk away from Darlington FC, and I was certainly not prepared to put up with what some of my fellow chairmen had had to put up with in the past.

I had, during my time as a safe-blower, jailbird and businessman who had been taken to a tribunal several times, seen some grave injustices in my time, but the biggest miscarriage of justice I had ever seen was what happened to an old friend of mine, Michael Knighton, former chairman and owner of Carlisle United.

I had met Michael for the first time about 13 years earlier and, to me, within his tragic story, lay a salutary lesson for any football club chairman. The lesson was: if a band of conspirators with vested interests set out to bring you down, then you must fight them tooth and nail from day one. I was the target of a bit of flack, but I was determined that what happened to Michael Knighton would not happen to me.

CHAPTER 34

A Friend in Need

The telephone was red hot, and the chap on the other end sounded a little intimidated, but he had no answers, and it was only answers that I was seeking.

'Did he take over the club when it was in dire financial straits? Did he or did he not?' I asked.

'Well, yes, he did,' came the reply.

'Did he, or did he not, keep the club afloat for ten years?'

'Well, yes, he did.'

'Did he get Carlisle to Wembley twice and then win them promotion twice?'

'Yes, he did that.'

'Did he, or did he not, sell between £6 million and £7 million worth of players and pump the money straight back into the club?

'Yes.'

'Did he invest in a new stand, which in today's terms would be worth about £6 million?'

'That's true. He did,' came the reply.

'Then, answer me this,' I said. 'What did the man do wrong?'

The voice on the other end of the line hesitated, stammered, then hesitated again. 'Well, er ...'

'Never mind, "Well, er ...",' I said. 'Answer the question. What did the man do wrong?'

'The fans don't like him,' he replied.

'Right, OK,' I said. 'Why do the fans not like him?'

'They just don't like him and they want him out,' the man said.

'Then why do they want him out?' I asked.

'Because they don't like him.'

'All right,' I said. 'You still haven't given me an answer. What did he do wrong?'

Silence.

'Hello, anyone there?'

'Yes.'

'Please tell me, what did he do wrong?'

'Oh, fuck off,' said the man at the other end. 'I don't need to listen to this.' Then he slammed the telephone down.

For me, friendship has always been important and when a friend is in trouble and his back's against the wall, that's when a friendship is truly tested. All my life I have hated injustice, not just injustices to me – and there have been many of them – I hate injustice against anyone. When I heard what was happening to Mike Knighton, I immediately sprang to his defence.

A group of men, including a Carlisle MP, who had claimed to have supported Carlisle United for years, and a tight-knit group of journalists working for the *Carlisle Evening News and Star*, had formed an alliance to oust Michael Knighton and his family from the ownership of Carlisle United. Michael owned more than 93 per cent of the club's shareholding.

Under Michael's leadership, the club had been taken forward through the usual ups and downs of football. During a decade of his stewardship – he owned the club for ten years – a glorious five-year spell between 1992 and 1996 saw him take the club to a Wembley Cup Final twice, in the Autowindscreen Final, achieve a run-away Third Division league championship, a divisional promotion play-off and a second promotion. He also spent £6 million on improving the stadium and broke every record in the club's history. On the up side there was a record number of points, record club profits, record transfer receipts, a record tranfer fee paid and a record number of games unbeaten in a season.

On the down-side, the club had failed to sustain its place in the Second Division each time it had been promoted. In the last three years of Michael's spell, the team had underperformed on the pitch and ended up in the bottom four places of the league, fighting relegation to the Conference (but that's football).

Michael had achieved so much in perhaps the club's most successful decade ever, yet he was the victim of the most vicious and sustained hate campaign known in football. The campaign was organised by a tiny number of people. These people would have remained just the usual bunch of disgruntled fans that every club has when a team performs badly on the pitch, but this group's agenda perfectly suited a group of men who all had positions of power in the city.

These two small groups had the backing of Carlisle MP Eric Martlew, and he played a key role when he lobbied the House of Commons to encourage the Inland Revenue to take action against the club's taxation debt. Nearly every club in the Nationwide League had taxation arrears, and Mr Martlew knew that, but he used Parliamentary privilege to raise the question, nonetheless.

What happened to Mike Knighton was the biggest

miscarriage of justice in English football. He and his family were forced to move out of Carlisle because of threats and assaults, and the man could not even show his face in the city.

There must have been something he had done that sparked the orchestrated and prolonged campaign of vilification in the local newspaper to oust him from his job. I couldn't find anything. Was I missing something? Was this the same Michael Knighton who had gained unbelievable experience as a director of the greatest football club in the world, Manchester United, between 1989 and 1992?

He had taken over Carlisle when it was on the bones of its arse and ploughed many millions of pounds into the club. That was good. He had massively improved the ground. Again, that was good. He took them to Wembley twice. Good. There was so much he had achieved for the club. But where had he gone wrong? What had he done wrong?

I was baffled.

Suddenly, after a few days chewing over the facts, it came to me. What Michael Knighton had done wrong at Carlisle United was that he handled the public relations situation badly. He had been too gentlemanly. Had it been me, I would have been knocking on the doors of every one of the conspirators – much the same as I had done with Craig Stoddart at *The Northern Echo* – and asking them each individually, and directly, what the man had done wrong. And each of them, individually, would not have been able to come up with an answer.

I called Michael Knighton and invited him to our new stadium to have a chat. When I saw him he looked depressed and like he did not have a friend in the world. That was the effect the conspirators had on him; if they could have seen him, they would have been laughing and punching the air with a clenched fist that symbolised victory.

What had happened to Michael could happen to any

football club chairman, or, indeed, come to that, football club manager, and it all boiled down to the power of the local press. Those sports desks occupied by club fans had been expressing biased personal opinions again, and these rumours had grown legs and become facts.

The Carlisle MP stood up in the House of Commons to criticise Mike Knighton. The local newspaper mounted a vigorous campaign to get him out. A group of people wanted the club for nothing. That's like me knocking on someone's front door and saying to them: 'Well, you have a nice £200,000 house here, but I want you out and I want to take over your house for nothing.'

A similar situation happened in Sunderland with the best football manager I had known, Peter Reid. A good manager is the one that can get success on the field and promotion at low cost. Anyone with money can throw money at a team and hope for success; it is the good manager that can bring success without spending too much money. Peter Reid took over Sunderland when they were at Roker Park and languishing near the bottom of Division One, with the very real prospect of relegation to Division Two. If they went down it would have been catastrophic for the club. Peter Reid saved the club from relegation, took them into the Premiership and kept them in the top seven of the Premiership for two seasons. That is a good track record; a success story in anyone's book.

But when more success failed to materialise, and after a series of disappointing results, the press turned on him and, lo and behold, within a few weeks – even days – he was out of the door and Sunderland brought in a manager hardly any of the supporters seemed to want. What the new management team can achieve has yet to be witnessed.

If the worst was to happen and Sunderland AFC were relegated – and I sincerely hope that does not happen – there is only one man who can take the club back to the

Premiership, and that's Peter Reid. I would not be surprised if the club call on Peter's services again.

What the likes of Mike Knighton and Peter Reid needed at the time was some backing. Backing, perhaps, from other club chairmen. With this in mind I intend to be instrumental in setting up a new organisation specifically to look after the interests of football club chairmen and directors. It will be known as the Chairmen and Directors' Association (CDA). The players have the PFA, there's the FA, the Football League, the Managers' Association and the Supporters' Association. But which group looks after the interest of the chairman: the man who puts his hand deep into his pocket and would take all the risks in order to keep the club afloat?

It is not the chairman's or even merely the manager's fault that a team is doing badly. It's down to the players on the pitch. If they're not prepared to give 100 per cent on the pitch in return for their very good salaries, then they should not be in the game.

We – the founder members of the CDA – hope to have offices in Manchester with our own legal team and, when anything is written in the press or broadcast on television or radio which is defamatory, scurrilous or just plainly untrue, we shall fight back with the full might of the law and sing with a united voice. Perhaps then the conspiracy that ousted Michael Knighton, one of the biggest miscarriages of justice in English football, will never be able to happen again.

CHAPTER 35

I Think I've Cracked It!

The young Besford Boys had listened to my story intently and, as the sun shone on that Worcestershire field, I hoped that what I had told them might have some impact on their lives. The same impact, I hoped, that the school they and I had attended had had on me. They had sat quietly throughout, initially almost moved to tears by the horror stories of Sambourne and Besford, but they also, at times, laughed, at times appeared intrigued, and more than once their faces lit up with excitement.

Time was moving on and Ian Robinson and myself had to get back to County Durham for the official opening of the new £25 million Darlington Football Club stadium.

As we boarded the helicopter the young red-headed lad with the freckles approached me.

'That story you told us, was that all true?' he asked.

'All true, son,' I said. 'All true.'

'Does that mean that, one day, I could own a helicopter and a football club and do everything that you've done?' he asked.

'You can do anything you want, son, if you put your mind to it,' I said.

I crouched before the young lad.

'Just remember the ten golden rules,' I said. 'And remember this, you have the power to make things happen. You don't need the best qualifications from the best private school to succeed. You don't even really need to be able to read and write. You've just got to believe in yourself and not let anything or anyone stand in your way.'

'Where are you going now?' the boy asked.

'We're going home, son,' I said. 'Today, we're going to open our brand new football stadium. You'll probably see it on the television news.'

Ian and I boarded the helicopter.

'Goodbye, Mr Reynolds,' said the young lad.

'Goodbye, son,' I said. 'Don't ever forget what I've told you.'

The door to the helicopter closed, the pilot turned over the engine and as we flew off Ian and I looked out of the windows and could see the young Besford Boy and his friends waving.

Within an hour we were hovering over the skies of Sunderland, where we had arranged to pick up some of the old Besford Boys to take them to the official opening of the stadium.

We approached from the coast and, as I looked down, I could see the Bungalow Cafe on the seafront at Roker where as a boy me and my pals had a gang hut. Despite my travels and despite having lived in County Durham for many years, whenever I saw the piers at Roker I knew I was heading home.

Cooper Street and many more of the streets of terraced houses on the Barbary Coast were still there, and looked much like they had sixty years earlier, apart from the streets being covered in tarmac rather than cobbles. But many other homes had been flattened to make way for plush apartments.

The River Wear looked calm. The towering cranes of the shipyards had gone. At the East End of the river stood a small number of fishing cobles. There were no ships being built, no team of master riggers touring the yards; the river was far from the hive of activity it had been all those years ago. I spotted two young lads with fishing rods, casting off from the Folly Bank, and for a moment remembered young Geordie Stephens who had drowned doing much the same.

The helicopter headed for a site near Sunderland's Stadium of Light, and there, waving towards us, were some of the old Besford Boys who I had earlier spoken to by telephone but who I had not seen for more than 50 years. Davey Hopper, Geordie Lavelle, Joe Mather and Jimmy Conley all looked well, and we certainly had a lot to talk about. After the lads boarded the helicopter we headed for Darlington.

At Darlington the helicopter hovered over the 27-acre site, as traffic below headed along the A1 north, the A66 south, east to Teesside and west to Cumbria and the Pennines. Half a mile above Darlington, shoppers in the town centre below looked like ants, scurrying in and out of the shops, going about their daily business, buying the weekly groceries.

To the north I could see the red brick train that symbolised Darlington's rich heritage, steeped in the railways, and on which someone had previously erected a banner outlining the score in the battle for the stadium. Not too far in the distance, planes took off from Teesside Airport for destinations unknown. Directly below traffic was running smoothly along Neasham Road, towards Hurworth or the town centre.

In her full, new, gleaming glory, there she stood; once a blueprint on a drawing board and a vision in the mind of George Reynolds, but now a magnificent, pristine, 25,000-seater football stadium.

It was a proud moment and I'm not frightened to say there were tears in my eyes.

'Would you like to go down now, George?' asked the pilot over the speaker.

'Just give us a moment,' I said. 'There's an awful lot of memories down there, you know.'

'She looks beautiful, doesn't she, George?' said Ian Robinson, as he looked out of the tinted window.

'She does that, Ian,' I said. 'She does that.'

'This really must put the cap on it all for you,' said Geordie Lavelle, sitting in one of the eight seats.

'Do you remember?' he added. 'You still owe me a packet of Spangles.'

I laughed and remembered how Geordie Lavelle looked after me on my first night at Sambourne, and how he had given me his pillow and a packet of sweets.

'There's a few spangles waiting for you down there,' I said.

'Is one of them 25,000 seats for Sylvia?' asked Davey Hopper.

'She'll be in the directors' box,' I said.

Cars streamed into the stadium car park; the chauffer-driven car of the town's mayor and mayoress, one or two Rolls-Royces, a Bentley here, a Jag there, all belonging to the guests invited to witness an important day in the history of Darlington, the history of north-east football and, equally, one of the most important days in the life of George Reynolds.

Around the lake on wooden benches sat local families, with picnic baskets, and on the pitch was the media pack, reporters from local and national television and radio stations, and from many national and local newspapers.

'We can go down now,' I said to the pilot, and he expertly manoeuvred the helicopter, bringing it down to land on a makeshift pad near the car park.

As we alighted, the flashbulbs of the cameras popped, and a few reporters ran towards us. 'There'll be a press conference shortly,' I said.

I was delighted that some of the old Besford Boys had been able to join me. Not because I wanted to prove to them how well I had done; it was simply to give them something back for their friendship.

Inside the stadium, helping themselves to the buffet, were some of my closest friends and many of my loyal workers; the team that had stuck with me through thick and thin: Stevie Molloy, Dave Powles, my cousin Richie Tennick, Harry Pincher, Stuart Johnston, Luke Raine, to name but a few. They all looked as proud as I felt. I didn't have to ask them; I just knew.

It was just a pity that many of the friends I had known and liked, such as Geordie Wallace and Eddie Boddy, from Besford Court, Old Rubber Bones Heslop and others who had passed away, were not there to share the experience.

I walked out on to the pitch and was hit by a wall of noise: 'One Georgie Reynolds; there's only Georgie Reynolds; one Georgie Reynolds, there's only one Georgie Reynolds.' I'd never heard such a roar, an intense wave of sound, since my days living near Roker Park in Sunderland.

The Darlington squad lined up for the photo call, in their new strips, with the mascot vying for a place, all wearing broad smiles.

Telling the entourage of friends, media and guests that I was just popping off to the loo, I went into one of the executive boxes instead, and looked out, alone, on to the magnificent pitch.

As the crowd still chanted, 'There's only one Georgie

Reynolds', it all came back to me. The bombs during the Second World War in Sunderland; the old gang hut under the cafe at Roker; being sent away to Sambourne and Besford schools where bonds were formed out of appalling cruelty. The dark days, and many laughs, inside Durham, Kirkham and Gloucester Prisons; the safe-blowing, the dodgy deals, the street-fighting and the run-ins with the cops and all other forms of authority.

The door to the box slowly opened, and in walked Susan.

'I thought you'd be here,' she said. 'The press conference is about to start any minute.'

'Come here,' I said. 'Look at this.'

Susan walked towards the window, and we both looked out on to the pitch where the team had started a kick-about, looked up to the terraces, where the delighted fans were still chanting, and then we looked at each other.

'You got there in the end, then,' said Susan.

'I did, didn't I?' I said.

'And you deserve every minute of it,' said Susan. 'You've worked bloody hard to get this.'

We turned, linked arms and walked out of the box to the lounge where the press conference was due to start.

We took to the stage, Susan sat by my side, the television camera lights went on, and the reporters scrambled for seats, pulling out their notebooks and pens.

'Do you really believe you will fill this stadium?' asked one.

'Do you honestly believe you can get Darlington to the Premiership?' asked another.

'Can we leave the questions until later?' I said. 'I have a statement to make.

'All my life, things have been stacked up against me,' I said. 'I was born into poverty, sent to an approved school and branded illiterate, backward and mentally deficient.

'I was told I would never do anything with my life; and

with a poor education like that, that I was doomed to fail.

'When I applied to join the Merchant Navy, and they discovered I couldn't read or write, I was told I would fail. At 21, I was the youngest petty officer to sail out of the River Tyne.

'When I turned my back on crime, and started a joinery business, I was told it would fail. It made £2 million profit in the first two years.

'When I collected scrap wood, and sold it off for a few pounds, the bosses looked down their noses at me.

'When I opened a nightclub, I was refused a licence. It was the most popular nightclub in town.

'When I started a kitchen-worktop business and said it would be a world leader, I was laughed at. It became the biggest kitchen-worktop manufacturer in the world.

'When I applied to build the first privately owned British mini power station, people said it couldn't be done. It was, and I sold it off for a hefty profit.

'When I took over Darlington Football Club, I was urged to proceed with caution, as it had huge debts. I paid off the debts, totalling £5.2 million.

'When I applied to build this magnificent new stadium, I was told it couldn't be done, as there were too many objections. Here we are sitting here today.

'All my life,' I said, 'I have been surrounded by critics and doubting Thomases and at every stage, one by one, I have proven those critics wrong.

'I stand here today and I am telling you, in no uncertain terms, that now this stadium is open, Darlington Football Club will be in the Premier League within the next few years.'

I paused.

'Now,' I said. 'Are there any critics or doubting Thomases out there who have any questions?'

The massed ranks of the media, for the first time I had ever known, fell silent.

Then, one by one, the other people in the room stood on their feet and began clapping their hands. The applause was almost deafening.

I grabbed hold of Susan's hand, raised both of our hands in the air, and shouted: 'I think I've cracked it! Next stop ... The Premiership!'